The **politics** and **experience** of **ritual abuse**

Beyond disbelief

Sara Scott

Open University Press
Buckingham · Philadelphia

Open University Press
Celtic Court
22 Ballmoor
Buckingham
MK18 1XW

email: enquiries@openup.co.uk
world wide web: www.openup.co.uk

and
325 Chestnut Street
Philadelphia, PA 19106, USA

First Published 2001

A catalogue record of this book is available from the British Library

ISBN 0 335 20419 8 (pb)   0 335 20420 1 (hb)

Library of Congress Cataloging-in-Publication Data
Scott, Sara, 1962–
    The politics & experience of ritual abuse: beyond disbelief/Sara Scott.
      p. cm.
    Includes bibliographical references and index.
    ISBN 0–335–20420–1 — ISBN 0–335–20419–8 (pbk.)
    1. Adult child sexual abuse victims—Great Britain—Interviews.   2. Ritual abuse
victims—Great Britain—Interviews.   3. Child sexual abuse—Great Britain.   4. Ritual
abuse—Great Britain.   I. Title: Politics and experience of ritual abuse.   II. Title.

HV6570.4.G7 S36 2001
362.76′0941—dc21   00–050173

Typeset by Graphicraft Limited, Hong Kong
Printed in Great Britain by Biddles Limited, Guildford and Kings Lynn

Contents

Acknowledgements

This book would never have been started if it had not been for 'Sinead', whose survival inspired it. It would certainly never have been completed without Kath Dimmelow, whose affection, optimism and sheer tenacity have sustained me through far greater trials than that of book writing. Grateful thanks are due to those who have read and commented on parts and versions of this work at various stages in its gestation: Brenda Roberts, David Morgan, Stevi Jackson, Sue Scott, Chris Creegan, Sophie Laws, Mary Maynard and Jeff Hearne.

The research was financially supported by a studentship from the Economic and Social Research Council and by the Sociological Review Fellowship (1997–8).

Introduction

The terms 'ritual abuse' and 'satanic ritual abuse' were coined in the early 1980s and appeared in print first in North America and then in the Netherlands, Britain, Germany, Sweden and Australia from 1984 onwards. Although the prosecution of day-care workers in the Californian McMartin preschool case was reported internationally, the appearance of the terms in Britain has mostly related to a series of controversial and high-profile child protection cases in Congleton (1988), Nottingham (1989), Rochdale (1990), Manchester (1990), Orkney (1991) and Essex (1991).

The reality of ritual abuse has been highly contested. Any exploration of the experiences of those who claim to have suffered such abuse will inevitably be surrounded by a cacaphony of questions about the veracity of accounts and the motivations of claim-makers. My intention in writing this book has been to 'look both ways': to take seriously the accounts of survivors while simultaneously exploring the politics of the field in which their accounts have emerged. I do not set out to convince readers – on the basis of the evidence I have collected, the impassioned eloquence of the testimony of my interviewees, or the arguments I construct around them – that ritual abuse 'really happens'. My project is both less ambitious and more fundamental; for I am concerned with how validity is accorded to some kinds of life-stories and not others and how some people are constituted as reliable witnesses of their own lives while others are discredited.

In Britain, the trajectory of the term 'ritual abuse' has been from unseen to disappeared over the course of ten years. This is illustrated by the appearance and disappearance of any discussion of such abuse in subsequent editions of *Working Together under the Children Act 1989* – the key government document on child protection (Department of Health 1991). In 1991, the newly recognized possibility of ritual abuse was officially acknowledged as a type or subset of organized abuse:

> 5.26.1 Organized abuse is a generic term which covers abuse which may involve a number of abusers, a number of abused children and young people and often encompasses different forms of abuse . . .

> 5.26.2 A wide range of abusing activity is covered by this term, from small paedophile or pornographic rings, often but not always organized for profit, with most participants knowing one other, to large networks of individual groups or families which may be spread more widely and in which not all participants will be known to each other. Some organized groups may use bizarre or ritualized behaviour, sometimes associated with particular 'belief' systems. This can be a powerful mechanism to frighten the abused children into not telling of their experiences.
> (Department of Health 1991: 38)

In the 1998 *Working Together* consultation document, the equivalent section reads as follows:

> 6.23 Organized or multiple abuse may be defined as abuse involving more than one abuser and a number of related or non-related children and young people. The abusers concerned may be acting in concert to abuse children, or may be using an institutional framework or position of authority to recruit children for abuse.

> 6.24 Organized or multiple abuse occur both as part of a network of abuse across a family or community, and within institutions such as residential homes and schools. Such abuse is profoundly traumatic for the children who become involved.
> (Department of Health 1998: 88)

Following the publication of research commissioned by the Department of Health (La Fontaine 1994), bizarre and ritualized abuse has disappeared to be replaced on the official agenda of concern by institutional abuse. Media attention to cases follows the same pattern, such that a case of multigenerational intra- and extra-familial abuse over a 30-year period and involving bizarre and ritualized features, which reached court in 1998, received almost no national coverage (Davies 1998). By contrast the network of abusers operating in Clwyd children's homes since the 1970s repeatedly achieved headline status throughout the late 1990s.

Although research undertaken by Jean La Fontaine for the Department of Health was officially concerned with the extent and nature of organized and ritual abuse, it is clear from the final report that its main purpose was to clarify whether ritual abuse, in the terms then being reported by adolescents and adults, needed to be taken seriously by those concerned with the protection of children (La Fontaine 1994). In other words, the research task was to discover whether abuse of this kind really happened. Sadly the methods employed were not well designed to address that question rigorously (see Chapter 2 for further discussion of this research) and adult survivors' accounts were simply dismissed as follows:

> It should be recognized . . . that adults who claim to have been ritually abused, usually known as 'survivors', have been very influential. While their stories are said to confirm what children have said, in fact survivors are probably more significant in creating a climate of belief *before* cases involving children are discovered. Most survivors are women, though there is a male survivors' group in London. Some of them are now offering therapy, training or support to workers, often without any further training.[1]
>
> (La Fontaine 1994: 4)

Terminology

In this book I use the term 'ritual abuse' to refer to one dimension of the childhood abuse described by my informants. A widely used definition of what the term 'ritual abuse' refers to has been that provided by David Finkelhor:

> Abuse that occurs in a context linked to some symbols or group activity that have a religious, magical or supernatural connotation, and where the invocation of these symbols or activities, repeated over time, is used to frighten and intimidate the children.
>
> (Finkelhor *et al.* 1988: 59)

Such a definition does not assume that ritual abuse is necessarily coupled to a particular belief system as do the terms 'satanic ritual abuse' or 'satanist abuse'. There are a number of reasons why this might matter. First, it avoids prejudging the issue of what, if anything, those perpetrating ritualized abuses may believe. Second, it remains agnostic about what kinds of symbols or beliefs might support such abuses. I suspect that abuses similar to those described in this book have at one time or another been perpetrated in the name of every world religion. Even minority faiths frequently spawn secretive and corrupt cults which provide for perverse and illegitimate access to pleasure and power. In the course of undertaking the research for this book, I have had contact with individuals who have experienced ritualized abuse in diverse religious contexts: an evangelical church, a 'breakaway' Mormon sect, a Pagan coven, a Roman Catholic convent school and within 'traditional' cults in Southern and West Africa. Their stories are not, however, central to this book, for I have elected to focus on those accounts which have been at the heart of the controversy over the reality of ritual abuse, and

in which the symbols and practices used include those popularly associated with the inversion of Christian beliefs and the worship of Satan. It may seem perverse on my part to reject the term 'satanic ritual abuse' while focusing on the kinds of accounts which have usually been so labelled. This is not, however, merely a politic side-step to avoid a highly charged – and much disparaged – term. My argument is that while those fitting the general 'satanic ritual abuse' profile were by far the majority of my informants (see Appendix), a more thorough examination of the beliefs, symbols and practices they described suggested an eclectic pan-theistic occultism rather than some kind of orthodox satanism (see Chapter 4).

In using the term 'ritual abuse', I am indicating that what is explored between these covers may well turn out to be merely one corner of an ugly global tapestry of organized child abuse which draws strength, security and longevity from the various religious forms with which it is entwined. The acceptance of stories of one sort allows related stories to be told; nowhere has this been more true than in relation to child abuse. The terms we use to discuss the identified problems of the moment help determine whether a field remains open to or closed off from the possibility of different accounts of experience emerging and reshaping knowledge.

A **sociological approach**

The role of sociologists in taking seriously the perspectives of those outwith the places and professions that produce the dominant accounts of how the world is and should be, is a long and honourable one. However, as Howard Becker pointed out in *Sociological Work*:

> We provoke the suspicion that we are biased in favour of . . . subordinate parties when[ever] we tell the story from their point of view . . . when[ever] we assume, for the purposes of our research, that subordinates have as much right to be heard as superordinates, that they are as likely to be telling the truth as they see it as superordinates . . .
>
> [In other words] we provoke the charge of bias, in ourselves and others, by refusing to give credence and deference to an established status order, in which knowledge of truth and the right to be heard are not equally distributed.
>
> (Becker 1970: 126–7)

In any particular instance, things are often more complicated and contested than such a picture – of a binary distinction between those with and those without the power to define the truth – suggests. Controversies over child abuse generally involve multiple hierarchies within and between professions competing for definitional authority; these in turn are crosscut with gendered patterns of power and status. Police officers oppose social work 'sentiment' with a focus on forensic facts; consultant psychiatrists warn nurses against being drawn into patient fantasies. At the same time feminists, children's

rights advocates, the 'falsely accused', service users and parents' groups organize to influence the agenda if not overthrow the entire system. However,
there are still those who rarely get heard amid the clamour, those who are
much discussed but rarely speak, those child victims and adult survivors who
are located as the point of origin of all child abuse discourse but whose
contribution to identifying the problem and its solutions has been quickly
overtaken by a new category of experts speaking on their behalf. Experts
who are in turn interrogated by other experts challenging the truth status of
their testimonies.

Despite the considerable rhetoric about listening to and believing children
who claim to have been abused, professional practices suggest something
quite different. Child sexual abuse professionals list indicators and risk factors, interpret behavioural signs and 'read' the evidence of children's bodies
which other professionals then contest. Parallel practices have converted
adult survivors into patients and plaintiffs. If we trace the emergence of
'sexual abuse' as an acknowledged social problem, we can see the ebbs and
flows of power as different versions of the causes, prevalence and corrective
treatment come to prominence and are superseded. In Ken Plummer's words:
'The power to tell a story, or indeed to not tell a story, under the conditions
of one's own choosing, is part of the political process' (Plummer 1995: 26).

Feminist sociologists, oral historians and activists have often described
their task as that of 'giving a voice' to particular groups of women rendered
mute in patriarchal discourse. The metaphor of 'breaking the silence' has
been frequently employed to describe the emergence of new stories from
previously muted perspectives. Such approaches have sometimes oversimpli-
fied what occurs, assuming that some unitary truth about 'women's experience' could be uncovered by asking women about their lives. More frequently,
however, feminist scholarship has been at the forefront of exploring the
complex ways in which accounts are produced, the interpenetrations of
public and private stories (Jamieson 1998) and the importance of the context
of emergence to the story that gets told.

Dorothy Smith's classic study 'K is mentally ill' (Smith 1990b) of the way
in which a particular account of reality makes itself convincing and the
alternative interpretations of the same 'facts', which could support quite
different conclusions, has provided an inspiration and model for the work
undertaken here. One part of my multi-stranded task is to deconstruct the
(currently) dominant account of ritual abuse which claims that: 'when you
whittle away patients with therapist encouraged multiple personality disorder, patients with therapist encouraged false memories, the deluded, and
those perpetrating a hoax, nothing remains' (Professor Richard Green, letter
to the editor, *Independent*, 12 February 2000). I am concerned to explore the
ways in which this version of reality has come to dominance in the public
sphere, the wider arguments upon which it draws and the constructions of
evidence it employs. In addition, I suggest that alternative readings of survivors' accounts are possible and develop such a reading. Becker has suggested
that it is useful 'to think of every way of representing social reality as perfect
– for something' (Becker 1986a: 125). The politically important questions are
'what and who are various representations good for?'.

My alternative reading of accounts of ritual abuse depends upon paying detailed attention to what those claiming lived experiences of such abuses actually have to say – hence it is based heavily upon the life-history inter-views I conducted with thirteen adult survivors. The carefulness and respect with which I have sought to treat interviewees' words, endeavouring to find a balance between protecting their confidentiality and enabling them to speak openly about their lives, can be summed up as 'taking my interviewees seriously'. The most important aspect of this approach is taking account of people's own accounts of themselves, regarding them as 'persons of serious intent' endeavouring to make sense of their lives:

> This does not mean taking these accounts at face value or as being the last word but at least it means being prepared to use a person's own evaluations as a kind of test against the valuations of others.
>
> (Morgan 1990: 174)

One of the most important ways in which this approach contrasts with the treatment of survivors' life-stories within the discourse of disbelief is in terms of the kind of textual surgery performed upon them. None of the sceptical accounts that I consider in Chapter 2 is based on any direct engagement with first-person testimony. Where survivors' life-stories are referred to, it is as collections of bizarre claims concerning 'human sacrifice', 'cannibalism' and 'satanism'. This decontextualization is a powerful factor in prompting disbelief (see Chapter 2). While the material collected for this book includes the same kinds of 'gruesome stories', my discussion is framed quite dif-ferently. Sceptical accounts disembed such stories from the context of whole lives; by contrast I analyse them in relation to the more mundane details that surround them, maintaining rather than severing their links to other parts of the narrative. My aim has been to apply the same kind of sociolo-gical approach to the life-histories of survivors of ritual abuse as that devel-oped over many years in the work of Ken Plummer (see Plummer 1995). To view them as situated tellings, constructed for a particular audience and particular purposes, but none the less as a crucial route to understanding human experience.

Ultimately we have no special sociological truth test, but must subject all accounts to what Herbert Blumer called the 'everyday tests of practical rea-son: plausibility, illumination and reasonableness':

> This is a matter of judgement, but it isn't wholly an arbitrary matter, because I distinctly feel that one who has an intimate familiarity with the people and the type of experience with which he [sic] is dealing will make propositions which will seem more reasonable than would be true of propositions proposed by someone who lacks such knowledge.
>
> (Blumer 1939: 99)

Or, as Norman Denzin suggested, what counts as evidence, validity and representativeness in assessing life narratives has to be conceived in terms of the adequacy and authenticity of descriptions:

A thick description goes beyond fact to detail, context, emotion, and webs of relationship. In a thick description the voices, feelings, and meanings of persons are heard . . . Verisimilitude derives from authentic, thick descriptions. It is achieved when the author of a document brings the life world alive in the mind of the reader.

(Denzin 1989: 25)

In addition, 'truth status' is tied up with ideas of rigour and clarity and a willingness to be hospitable to facts that could be more comfortably ignored. As Mary Maynard has argued:

At the very least this call for rigour involves being clear about one's theoretical assumptions, the nature of the research process, the criteria against which 'good' knowledge can be judged and the strategies used for interpretation and analysis. In feminist work the suggestion is that all of these things are made available for scrutiny, comment and (re)negotiation, as part of the process through which standards are evaluated and judged.

(Maynard 1994: 24–5)

The difficulty remains, however, that the nature of evidence and the appropriate procedures for verification appear to be very different in different contexts. As the cognitive psychologist Jerome Bruner described it:

A good story and a well-formed argument are different natural kinds. Both can be used as means for convincing another. Yet what they convince of is fundamentally different: arguments convince one of their truth, stories of their lifelikeness. The one verifies by eventual appeal to procedures for establishing formal and empirical proof. The other establishes not truth but verisimilitude.

(Bruner 1986: 11)

One way of describing this book is as stories speaking to arguments – the two will never entirely join up, but we have no choice but to continue to use both. If the stories of ritual abuse survivors are given the opportunity to be considered in terms of their verisimilitude, this may serve to keep the door open to seeking – in particular cases – the corroborative testimony and forensic evidence that will satisfy the 'truth-tests' of courts of law.

I was aware from the outset that researching ritual abuse involved dealing with very specific issues of truth and reality. My interviewees described episodes of mind-bending sensory deprivation, the perceptual distortions caused by alcohol, drugs, dehydration and starvation, and a barrage of tricks, deceptions and deliberate obfuscation as part of their abuse. Some were eager to discuss these complexities, and all were unwilling to give definitive accounts of experiences the reality of which was uncertain. The potent mixture of drugs, dissociation, violence and group 'hysteria' made rituals particularly difficult to recall or describe clearly, and some interviewees made clear that they felt greater confidence in discussing more everyday abuses (see Chapter 3).

These specific distortions of various kinds did not, however, disrupt the story overall; rather they were discussed as being a constitutive part of the experience of ritual abuse, or as one survivor put it:

> They *aimed* to do your head in, you know. If I had said anything
> when I was little it would probably have seemed so unbelievable
> . . . so mixed up. Who'd have listened to the ramblings of a kid who
> probably never seemed to be 'all there' anyway?
>
> (Sophie)

More generally, the construction of their life-stories as a project deliberately and painfully undertaken was part of the active understanding of interviewees. Having 'worked at' making sense of the past and how it had moulded and scarred them, there was a consciousness concerning the ways in which insight and understanding had changed their stories over time. They were aware of the controversial status of 'recovered memories' of abuse and described their own various experiences of 'forgetting', 'repressing' and remembering in relation to this. The five women who were in their late teens or twenties at the time of interview had left their abusive families and dealt with the effects of an abusive childhood at more or less the same time; for them escaping and remembering were intimately entangled. At the opposite end of the spectrum of memory suppression, Elizabeth had hardly any childhood memories until after her parents' deaths when she was in her fifties, and Erik was in his forties when he first remembered having been abused by his uncles and grandfather.

Eight interviewees had seen a range of professionals for counselling (these included psychiatrists, clinical psychologists, psychotherapists and social workers); two more had been supported by foster carers experienced in supporting sexually abused young people. Although everyone I interviewed had previously shared some of their memories with professionals, partners or friends, they were each telling their life-story as a whole for the first time in their interview for this research. Among those interviewees who had no experience of therapeutic support, one woman was particularly articulate about the issues involved in the reflexive project of remembering and narrating her life:

> When I started properly having 'flashbacks' I didn't dare tell anyone
> – this was the 70s remember – I was afraid they'd lock me up and
> take my kids away. I'd got this idea from somewhere that you had
> to remember *everything*, every detail and go through it all. At the
> same time you don't want to think about any of it, so it takes
> forever . . . and I think now that I retraumatized myself picking over
> my memories for years. I wouldn't do it now!
>
> *And do you think they were all true – the memories you recovered?*
>
> Basically I do – but I didn't need that kind of detail to be OK . . . But
> some of the things were so repetitive you know . . . and a lot of the
> times at ceremonies you were so out of it – as a kid you just wanted to
> be anywhere but where you were, and I know I cut just cut off a lot of

the time – so I can't be sure bits from different times didn't get stuck together. It's like you remember one time and it stands in for all the other times doesn't it?

(Lynn)

Of course, Lynn is describing the *normal* process of remembering. 'Flash-backs' may be both vivid and intrusive but they are not CCTV recordings. The images fleetingly seen upon our inward eye must be pursued, recalled and worked up into the narratives we call memories.

My story

I first remember reading the term 'ritual abuse' in newspaper reports of the Nottingham (Broxtowe) case in 1989. Allegations of children being taken to 'witch parties' and being given 'funny drinks' seemed faintly ridiculous. I was annoyed and somewhat dismissive of a case which promised both to distract attention from the ordinary fathers and stepfathers who perpetrated the vast majority of sexual abuse and to make the serious issue of child rape into a pantomime. I had been a counsellor, trainer and activist concerned with issues of sexual violence for some years. I 'knew' what sexual abuse was, who did it and why; I 'knew' it had precious little to do with 'devil worship'. Social workers were still reeling from the 'backlash' of the Cleveland case and I was extremely wary of a case that sounded like a version of Cleveland with horns on.

I still have those 'black magic' moments when I cringe at the Wheatley-esque elements of ritual abuse and have to remind myself that abuse is no less awful because it has such tacky trappings. Indeed, the idea of surround-ing child rape with tawdry occultism may be an additional indignity with which survivors must contend. However, my own relationship to the subject changed irrevocably through becoming personally involved in the case of a 14-year-old girl escaping ritual abuse.

It is rare that the biography of the sociologist is entirely independent of, or irrelevant to, the subject of study. I undertook this research for a number of reasons, not least in order to make sense of my own experience. The epistemological status accorded to proximity of relationship is by no means clear cut. There are situations in which intimate knowledge is privileged above expert knowledge: seasoned general practitioners (GPs) alert junior colleagues that, when it comes to a sick child, mother often does know best. However, emotional entanglement is equally frequently considered to contaminate the perspicacity of professional objectivity. In relation to ritual abuse, my direct involvement with a particular young survivor was doubtless a necessary, but not sufficient, precursor of the perspective I develop in this book.

When I look back towards the early 1990s, it is almost impossible to grasp how much my life was disrupted by coming to know about ritual abuse, or to really remember the fear, anxiety and confusion that enveloped my world. As I write, the young woman who became my foster daughter is embarking on her own professional life, she has friends, interests and qualifications, she is tough and brave and funny and passionate, and I am immensely proud of her. The nightmares and mood swings, terror and dissociation have faded into the past. Her life is now her own.

It is impossible to recapture the 'shock of the new' in listening to her accounts of hypnosis and torture, of killing hens and sheep and babies, of eating maggots and vomit and human flesh, and of child prostitution and pornography. Over the course of five years of caring for Sinead, 'the field' of ritual abuse became my primary location. Discussions of forced abortion and ritual sacrifice began to seem ordinary, while the life-world I had previously shared with friends and colleagues sometimes felt unreal and insignificant. Undertaking the research on which this book is based allowed me to partially reverse this process such that I again defamiliarized that which had become almost taken-for-granted.

The inclusion of my foster daughter as an interviewee was one dimension of this process. When I began the research, I considered that involving Sinead would be ethically 'wrong'. Given our relationship, it would be difficult for her to make a decision based entirely on her own wishes. Given how much I knew about her life, it would be hard for her to edit her story as she might for a stranger, and so decide what would enter the public sphere and what remain private. In addition, I was anxious that combining the personal with the academic would cast doubt upon the credibility of my work. However, as the fieldwork progressed it became apparent that there was no clean line between Sinead being involved in the research and being excluded from it. Her life-story was so much part of my knowledge of ritual abuse, that it was always with me as a point of comparison and contrast with each new account I collected. I was struggling with how I could acknowledge this knowledge without bringing in Sinead's story by the back door, when she asked me if I would interview her as part of the research. In many ways my PhD was a 'family project', Sinead and I had become students at the same time, and she was well aware that I might still be working in broadcasting if she had not arrived in my life. Her analysis of the problem was straightforward: 'If you don't interview me, I'll be in there anyway as a voice without a name. I'd rather be included as myself'.

Our two-day interview was a tremendous experience. On a personal level, it allowed Sinead to talk 'as an adult' of experiences she had last whispered of in terror in the aftermath of nightmares. It was an opportunity for both of us to discover how far we had travelled in the course of five years.

The **chapters**

The Politics and Experience of Ritual Abuse mobilizes the life-stories of survivors in response to the discourse of disbelief that has discounted them as 'false memories' produced by a 'moral panic'. However, it begins by exploring first the historical antecedents that have enabled such life-stories to be told, and second, the reaction that has endeavoured to silence them once again. Chapter 1 'Child sexual abuse: the shaping of a social problem' provides a brief history of the development of knowledge about child sexual abuse in order to describe the nature of the 'field' into which the accounts of survivors of ritual abuse emerged.

The sexual abuse of children was considered both rare and relatively harmless for most of the twentieth century. Feminists challenged this with evidence that sexual abuse was widespread and categorized it as one outcome of power relations within the patriarchal family. The chapter describes the challenges that ritual abuse survivors' accounts posed to what by the mid-1980s had become a feminist-informed orthodoxy on child sexual abuse. These challenges included the fact that in survivors' accounts of ritual abuse, women were *routinely* described as sexual abusers, and the apparent intergenerational transmission of ritual abuse which suggested the necessity of understanding how abuse may sometimes provide an apprenticeship in perpetration.

If a feminist-influenced discourse on child sexual abuse is the context within which ritual abuse has found a voice, a powerful backlash has been endeavouring to silence it since the mid-1980s. Chapter 2 'Unreliable witnesses: memories and moral panic' explores the discourse of disbelief and its twin claims that ritual abuse accounts are a product of moral panic and/or of false memories. The task of this chapter is to deconstruct the discourse of disbelief, exploring in detail the textual strategies mobilized to 'make doubt stick' and thereby to fracture the certainty of claims that the life histories of ritual abuse survivors are either fantasy or fraud.

In Chapter 3 'The nature of the beast: pornography, prostitution and everyday life', I turn for the first time to the life-history interviews themselves. I put aside the 'ritual' in accounts from survivors of ritual abuse in order to explore the 'ordinary' domestic and organized forms of sexual abuse and exploitation that dominated my interviewees' childhoods. I focus in this chapter on the abuse that interviewees described as taking place within the extended family, abuse in the form of prostitution and involved in the production of pornography. In doing so, I consider how far their accounts support or contradict what little is known about these 'other' forms of abuse more generally. At the same time, I am concerned to show that there is no easy way of filleting the 'ritual abuse' out of these narratives in order to transform them into some more readily digestible form of organized abuse.

Each of the four chapters that follow focus in turn on the least believable and most frequently dismissed aspects of accounts of ritual abuse. In Chapter 4 'The flesh and the word: beliefs and believing in ritual abuse', I explore survivors' claims concerning the importance of an occult belief system to those involved in ritual abuse – as the issue of whether any abusers who use ritual *believe* in their performances or merely dress up to frighten the children has been one of the issues central to the discourse of disbelief. Overly simplistic understandings of 'belief' may have contributed to scepticism about the possibility of contemporary ritual abuse. I show that in the experience of ritual abuse, the 'occult trappings' cannot easily be stripped away to expose the 'raw' abuse beneath but must be understood as an integral part of the suffering of victims and the satisfactions of perpetrators.

The women I interviewed did not analyse their experiences in feminist terms; on the contrary they often emphasized the 'equality' of men and women among their abusers. None the less they gave strongly gender-differentiated descriptions of abusers, and described the domestic and cult divisions of labour which I discuss in Chapter 5 'The gender of horror'. In this chapter I also discuss the three interviews I conducted with male survivors in the USA and how these both supported and contrasted with women's accounts. I argue that the gender differences and dynamics described in relation to ritual abuse are grotesquely plausible; women who sadistically sexually abuse their own children and grandchildren do not cease to be believable as women.

In Chapter 6 'Making death meaningful', I turn to the claims in ritual abuse survivors' accounts which have probably attracted the most disbelief as being incredible and implausible: the reports of witnessing and participating in murder. I show how these accounts make sense within the life-histories of interviewees, cast light on their survival, and on the gendered nature of ritual abuse.

The reality of Multiple Personality Disorder has been almost as contested as that of ritual abuse – with which it is associated. In the final chapter 'Composing the self', I turn to the subject of identity, and explore the ways in which the survivors I interviewed explained the development of both loving and recalcitrant selves in the context of overwhelming abuse. I examine how the phenomenological experience of parental inconsistency, torture and dissociation help make sense of how a divided or multiple construction of self might map on to a remembered childhood, as well as providing a metaphor for the simultaneous acceptance and denial of unbearably painful memories. I argue that an understanding of life-stories and the identities which emerge from them as 'purely' discursive productions fails to account for the ability of survivors to act back on the schema set up to help, explain or discredit them.

Note

1 As far as I can ascertain, no group specifically for survivors of ritual abuse, male or female, existed in London at this time. Only one adult survivor was publicly active in training or support in the UK in the early 1990s.

1 | Child sexual abuse: the shaping of a social problem

From the mid-1980s, sexual abuse rose so high on public agendas of concern about children that it all but eclipsed deprivation, neglect, cruelty and physical assault. It is therefore unsurprising that when ritual abuse emerged as an issue in child protection, it was located primarily as an extreme – or an unbelievable – type of sexual abuse. However, while the available discourse clearly made possible the emergence of ritual abuse accounts, these also contained potential challenges to what had become established knowledge about child abuse. Survivors' stories raised questions about the relationship between gender and generation in sexual abuse and between different kinds of child abuse; questions concerning the motivations and satisfactions of abusers, and the nature of the social groups within which children and young people might be sexually exploited and abused. For many people they also raised questions about the general reliability of children's testimony or adults' memories concerning sexual abuse.

My purpose in this chapter is to describe briefly the development of modern knowledge about child sexual abuse as it is constituted in theory, research, activism and professional practice in Britain and North America. (I consider more closely, in Chapter 2, local inflections as these have impacted on emerging accounts of ritual abuse.) Overviews of the issue of child abuse frequently lay out a palette of perspectives without indicating how developments in ideas are closely linked to historical change or how approaches interact with each other over time. I shall try by contrast to portray something of the knowledge/power struggles that have marked the field, at the same time as exploring which of the analytical tools these conflicts have honed and made available might be usefully articulated with the problem of ritual abuse. The very limited knowledge base concerning any kind of organized abuse available at the time ritual abuse allegations first emerged will be of particular interest.

I shall argue that the second-wave feminist challenge to a patriarchal inheritance which minimized and legitimized at least some kinds of child sexual abuse has been extraordinarily successful in amending mainstream perspectives. Conflicts in the field have often involved different kinds of knowledge developed from different kinds of evidence being set up to explain child sexual abuse in general. I shall therefore examine the strengths and limitations of attempts at synthesizing approaches, and suggest that the task of producing a fully integrated understanding of the relations between gender and different forms of sexual abuse remains unfinished.

Child abuse discourse

There is no reliable consensus about what constitutes abusing a child – or even who counts as 'a child' or what counts as 'abuse'. People may be more or less condemning of particular treatment of children, more or less 'liberal' about variations in 'parenting styles' or in relation to adult–child sexual contact. What counts as the acceptable exercise of 'parental authority', or as 'openness about sex and nudity', and what is regarded as physical or sexual abuse, are by no means subjects of ready agreement; some of those most concerned about 'premature sexual experiences' would strongly defend the rights of parents to administer 'physical punishment' (see Greven 1992). The very category of 'child abuse', with its subcategories of sexual, physical and emotional abuse or neglect, is of recent advent (see Gordon 1989), and there are numerous ways of characterizing such abuses from a variety of perspectives – medical, legal, religious, feminist. Explanations of their causes can be strung along a continuum from 'psychological' to 'sociological', or they can be divided according to their emphasis on social exclusion, patriarchal gender relations, the family system or the perpetrating individual.

Struggles for hegemony between different definitions and perspectives have characterized the child abuse field as it has developed since the late 1940s. However, contemporary discourses concerning child abuse have nineteenth-century roots. Middle-class Victorians can be described as having expanded childhood, idealizing and universalizing their vision of childhood as a period of life which ought to be characterized by adult protection and dependency. Psycho-historian Lloyd de Mause has described the entire history of childhood as a history of child *abuse*, claiming that:

> The further back in history one goes, the lower the level of childcare, and the more likely children are to be killed, abandoned, beaten, terrorized, and sexually abused.
>
> (de Mause 1976: 1)

From this perspective, the nineteenth and twentieth centuries saw a great awakening to the suffering and needs of children. 'Child abuse' can be regarded as a 'residual category' of a long history of western violence towards children – much of which was framed as legitimate discipline, first by the Christian churches and later by the medical profession. Two things have occurred with the rise of the concept of child abuse: first, much previously public violence has been outlawed, and second, philanthropic and later state intervention into the 'private business' of families has dramatically increased.

More influential with sociologists has been the work of Philippe Ariès (1972), who claimed that 'childhood' as a category of social existence was invented in the early modern period as part of a hierarchical concept of the family, and the privatization, or enclosure, of children within it. He argued that it was only with the emergence of a description of childhood as a distinct phase of life, that serious emotional and material investment in children began. Ariès emphasized the twin tracks along which increasing concern over children ran with both the care *and* control of children gradually increasing, at some times in tandem, and at others in contradiction.

The way in which concern over children can be made up of anxiety for their welfare, and fear of the adults they might become, was at its most explicit in Britain in the second half of the nineteenth century, with increasing concern for the health of the nation, the introduction of universal primary education from the 1890s, the provision of domestic education for girls, the emerging specialism of paediatrics and the birth of the clinic. The foundation of the children's charities, to provide institutional care for orphaned and abandoned children, was followed in 1889 by the first legislation to protect children from parental cruelty, and the introduction by the National Society for the Prevention of Cruelty to Children (NSPCC) of 'cruelty men' provided a further institutional context for the articulation of the problem of child abuse. There was also mass political concern on the subject, and for the first two decades of the twentieth century a vigorous women's movement fought a number of campaigns on behalf of children.

However, with the general improvement in the material conditions of children's lives between the First and Second World Wars, with lower birth rates, better health and housing and lower mortality, child abuse was generally considered to have been reduced. From then until the 1970s, the issue of child protection was seen almost entirely in terms of neglect, rather than abuse, and therefore as a problem of 'bad mothers'. There was little funding of preventive or family support work – as opposed to provision of care – until the Children and Young Persons Act 1963 made possible the range of interventions in family life that we now think of as constituting the practice of child protection work.

Social work began to professionalize, and by the 1970s social services departments in their modern form had a nationwide remit for ensuring the protection of children from abuse and neglect. Changing ideas about what was best for children, combined with financial pressures to reduce the population of children in care, brought issues of child protection to the fore. Paediatricians renewed their interest in 'battered babies' at the end of the 1960s, and the Department of Health issued guidance a number of times on dealing with cases of non-accidental injury. The Women's Liberation Movement was on the rise, and together with the factors just mentioned provided a fertile context for the (re)discovery of child sexual abuse.

The **patriarchal inheritance**

In broad terms, the patriarchal inheritance in relation to child sexual abuse minimized its frequency, impact and effects, asserted children's complicity or seductiveness, and blamed mothers for colluding with the incestuous abuse of their children. Such views can be seen as an example of the general patriarchal imperative that women 'manage' male sexuality in relation to themselves and their children (see Jackson and Scott 1997). Over 50 years after Freud's rejection of 'real' incest (Masson 1984),[1] Alfred Kinsey and colleagues interviewed 4000 young, middle-class women, 28 per cent of whom reported that they had had a sexual 'encounter' with an adult before the age of 13 (Gagnon 1965), and 5 per cent reported that the adult involved had been a family member. Although the Kinsey report provoked much debate about previously taboo topics such as homosexuality and masturbation, these 'encounters' with adults experienced by over a quarter of the women surveyed were subject to little discussion and were certainly not framed as 'sexual abuse'. Kinsey himself minimized its significance:

> It is difficult to understand why a child, except for its cultural conditioning, should be disturbed at having its genitals touched or disturbed at seeing the genitalia of other persons, or disturbed at even more specific contacts.
> . . . the [sexual] experiences were repeated because the children had become interested in the sexual activity and had more or less actively sought repetitions of their experience.
> (Kinsey *et al.* 1953: 121)

Most of the literature on incest and sexual abuse published after Kinsey and throughout the 1960s and 1970s had two main strands. First, it tended to minimize the impact of 'sexual molestation' on children, and second, it laid responsibility for much adult–child sexual contact on the children involved or on their mothers. The focus of the 'sex researchers' of the time was on sex as pleasure, not sex as power.

Kempe and Kempe (1978) did take incestuous abuse more seriously than most, but like Masters and Johnson (1976) before them, they reserved their most serious concern for one of the most rare forms of incest – that between mother and son – believing that: 'Incest may be overcome – with or without help – by many girls, but it is ruinous for boys' (Kempe and Kempe 1978). The sexual abuse of girls was clearly regarded as less damaging because it was closer to the norm of adult heterosexuality: older, more powerful males interacting sexually with younger, submissive 'women'. Even those authors who were concerned about the emotional impacts of abuse tended to suggest that children were at least acquiescent in the abuse, or might be bought off with small favours (Rogers and Weiss 1953; Peters 1976). What is entirely absent is any analysis of power between adults and children, and their different abilities to control or define the nature of any interaction.

One result of the patriarchal inheritance in minimizing the effect of child sexual abuse is a disinclination in the literature to advocate legal interventions. Unusually, this was a position that criminologist Donald West was still maintaining in the mid-1980s:

> The minimal damage attributable to most sexual encounters does not justify extreme reactions on the part of the child's parents or guardians. In particular, police questioning, appearances in court, family dissension, and eventually perhaps the imprisonment of a parent, friend or relative to whom the child was strongly attached, are likely to be far more traumatic than the sexual incidents themselves.
>
> (West 1984: 10)

The **family** as a **social system**

Much of the literature of the 1960s and 1970s focuses on the family system within which incest occurs and frequently holds wives responsible in large part for their husbands' actions. Garrett and Wright (1975) claim that the wives of rapists and incest offenders tend to have more years of schooling than their husbands, and deliberately chose husbands to whom they could feel superior. Their husbands were then 'driven' to their crimes by their feelings of inferiority. More commonly, wives are blamed for being uninterested in sex, and for pushing a daughter towards her father as a substitute partner (Schechter and Roberge 1976). Such accounts rely on an unquestioned assumption that wives ought to provide sexual services for husbands who have – equally unquestioned – sexual needs. Men deprived of such services may even be described as 'saving' or 'stabilizing' the family unit by raping their daughters (Lustig *et al.* 1966). Less extreme versions argue that mothers often force an eldest daughter to assume domestic responsibilities, which then leads to role confusion, and sexual abuse follows (Summit and Kryso 1978). This perspective dominated discussions of sexual abuse in Britain for many years – due in large part to the family therapy pioneered by a team at Great Ormond Street Hospital led by Arnon Ben-Tovim (Ben-Tovim *et al.* 1988). As Sheila Jeffreys has commented: 'The implication is that the husband gets confused because he is used to imposing his sexual demands on whoever does the housework and he does not really notice who it is' (Jeffreys 1982: 63).

Mothers have been widely believed to 'collude' in the sexual abuse of their children within the family. Indeed, Kempe and Kempe (1978) go so far as to claim that they never came across an 'innocent' mother in a case of long-standing incest. Although the family system was seen as central, it went largely unanalysed: women and children's relative economic dependency and their loss of status and security with the break up of a family were never discussed.

Despite the commitment of a family systems approach to understanding relationships, rather than pathologizing individuals, the literature tends to place greatest responsibility for incest in the laps of mothers (Furniss 1984) and to minimize the power differences within the family such that each family member – irrespective of differences of gender or generation – is accorded a slice of responsibility for the 'incestuous situation'. In addition, there is the assumption that families in which incest occurs are entirely different from 'normal, healthy families'. An important part of the feminist critique was to problematize the whole idea of the 'normal' family, and to ask for which members they might be considered 'healthy'? A strong critique of the 'mother blaming' of the patriarchal orthodoxy on child abuse has been provided by Hooper (1992).

However, a family systems approach does not have to ignore inequalities or be unsympathetic to women and children as it can be uncoupled from the patriarchal family plot and take on board egalitarian, child-centred views of what constitutes a 'healthy family' (Barrat *et al.* 1990). Its strength is in recognizing that sexual abuse takes place within a social context, either the family, the family within a wider network, or another institutional or group context. It can therefore help us to focus on the social nature of child abuse by locating both victim and perpetrator within social relationships. The family systems model moves the focus of analysis away from the internal pathology of an abuser and towards the network of relationships within which abuse occurs. As David Morgan (1996) has pointed out, a focus on the family may occlude gender but the inverse is also true, and paying attention to the systems within which different forms of abuse occur may facilitate the insertion of more complex accounts of gender into explanations of child abuse.

The **individual perpetrator**

Prevalence studies suggest that sexual abuse within families rarely comes to the attention of outside agencies. When it does do so, an emphasis on solutions aimed at the family system combined with the difficulties of prosecution, and perhaps also with what Dingwall *et al.* (1983) labelled 'the rule of optimism' among social workers, results in extremely low numbers of convictions. One effect of this is that 'incest offenders' have not been readily available as research subjects. Claims to knowledge about perpetrators of sexual abuse are therefore based almost entirely on studies of convicted sex offenders. As David Finkelhor has pointed out:

> Caught and convicted sex offenders are those who are the most compulsive, repetitive, blatant, and extreme in their offending, and thus also those whose behavior stems from the most deviant developmental experiences.
>
> (Finkelhor 1984: 35)

Throughout the 1960s and 1970s, numerous studies of this population focused on explaining their 'deviant psychopathology' by reference to developmental experiences including a background of chaotic family life, emotional deprivation and sexual abuse in between 30 per cent and 60 per cent of cases (Weiner 1964; Groth 1979; Groth and Burgess 1979; Meiselman 1978). This work took place before the feminist rediscovery of how widespread sexual abuse actually was and the authors assume an adult, heterosexual, masculine identity as a benign developmental norm which in rare cases may be blocked or thwarted. As the 'rejecting wife' haunts the family systems literature from this period, so the 'castrating mother' hovers behind the 'inadequate' paedophile's 'sexually anxious' inability to relate to adult women.

It is tempting to speculate that family systems theorists and researchers focused on individual pathology are actually talking about two entirely separate groups of child abuser: 'incest perpetrators' and 'career paedophiles'. Groth (1979) suggested something along these lines when he distinguished between two types of perpetrators, the 'fixated' and the 'regressive'. (The former is described as having been sexually attracted mainly to children (usually boys) since his adolescence, the latter as having an adult heterosexual orientation, but commits incest in response to stress related feelings of 'phallic inadequacy'.) Certainly the profiles of the 275 perpetrators discussed by Ben-Tovim et al. (1988) – only five of whom had been sexually abused themselves – suggest very different types of men from those studied by Groth and Burgess (1979). One problem with this is that it may create a false dichotomy between what happens in families and the sexual abuse of children perpetrated by non-family members (Russell 1983a). Survivors' accounts certainly suggest that family-based abusers may abuse a number of related children and there is increasing awareness that 'career paedophiles' sometimes marry into families in order to gain access to children.

From studies of convicted offenders came the idea of 'intergenerational transmission' whereby those previously victimized might attempt to overcome the trauma they had suffered by victimizing others. From this developed an extraordinarily simplistic, single-factor 'theory' of the 'cycle of abuse' which was enormously popular with many professionals and in the mass media throughout the 1980s. In the UK it was frequently used both to explain child abusers in general and to support intervention in the lives of victims and thereby 'break the cycle'. The logical flaw in this theory – that girls are far more likely to be sexually abused than boys, but women are far less likely to be abusers – did nothing to stem its popularity. Interestingly it inspired little further research on offenders but a further wave of interest in the 'incest mother', which tended to conclude that women whose children are sexually abused are more likely than other mothers to have been abused themselves (Goodwin et al. 1981; Faller 1987). The inference from such research is often that such women are implicated in their children's abuse. The obverse hypotheses, that as the research subjects have all been involved in cases where abuse has come to official notice these mothers may have been more vigilant, or their children more likely to disclose abuse, have rarely been explored.[2]

At first sight, work that focuses on the histories and proclivities of individual abusers provides a welcome relief from some of the victim and mother blaming which occurred within the family systems model. However, the focus on individual pathology was often at the expense of both wider social factors, and the immediate relations of power and influence with which the abuser interacts. Although obviously focused on male offenders, such a perspective has rarely been enriched by any consideration of the relationship between masculinity, violence and sexuality (Hearn 1990).

The **impact** of **feminism**

The majority of recent books and articles on child sexual abuse from a range of perspectives acknowledge a debt to the Women's Liberation Movement (WLM) of the 1970s for having brought the topic of child sexual abuse to public attention (see Finkelhor 1984; Glaser and Frosh 1988; Elliott 1993). The feminist authors most frequently referred to as having opened up the issue of child sexual abuse are Florence Rush (1977, 1980) and Judith Herman (1981), albeit often with little reference to the analysis of the patriarchal family of which their work was part. Groundbreaking though their particular work was, it is important to place it (as they do) within the wider context of feminist work on male violence.

The British WLM of the 1970s, like the radical feminist movement in the USA, was founded by women active in Left politics who, despite their supposed 'sexual liberation', found that they shared experiences of sexual objectification, manipulation and threat. When some of those women began to speak out about rape they analysed their experiences not as individual misfortunes but as 'lessons' in female subordination directed at the whole class of women and intended to teach that their situation was ultimately natural and unalterable. In Susan Brownmiller's memorable phrase, rape was *the* archetypal act 'by which *all men* keep *all women* in a state of fear' (Brownmiller 1976: 15, original emphasis).

Rape began to be seen as one feature of the patriarchal control of women through sexuality which included compulsory heterosexuality (Rich 1980) and prostitution and pornography (Barry 1979). Adrienne Rich writes about Kathleen Barry's characterization of this system as one of 'female sexual slavery'

> which includes wife-battery; incest; marital rape; the Muslim code of 'honour' regarding female chastity; marriage through seclusion, arrangement and bride-price; genital mutilation; and enforced prostitution, of which pornography is the ideology.
>
> (Rich 1980: 24)

'Incest' appears here in a list of practices linked by the theory that male control over women's sexuality is central to patriarchal societies. However, it is noteworthy that a number of these practices happen primarily to *young* women, or in some instances to girl children, and that some are perpetrated or enforced by adult women.

Practical strategies

Feminists designed practical responses to male violence, and refuges and rape crisis centres were set up all over Britain and North America throughout

agencies, unless they are much better resourced and given a broader remit, will inevitably continue to focus on intra-familial abuse.

(Corby 1993: 63)

In his highly influential model, Finkelhor incorporates the feminist analysis as a set of 'social preconditions' to child sexual abuse. He then goes on to review the research evidence for a variety of explanations for why individual abusers abuse. Grouping hypotheses under four headings – 'emotional congruence', 'sexual arousal', 'blockage' and 'disinhibition' – he suggests some findings such as the use of alcohol as a disinhibitor to abuse to be fairly robust, while others such as 'poor impulse control' are unsupported. There are three linked problems with Finkelhor's attempt to synthesize theories about child sexual abuse. The first is that he fails to bring to the fore the assumptions about the 'nature of the beast' under dissection that inform different kinds of theory and research. Second, although he criticizes the methodology, and thereby raises questions about the reliability, of much of the research on why abusers abuse, he does not question the presumption of psychopathology which structures such work. Third, feminist analysis is incorporated only in the form of a kind of sociological set dressing, a patriarchal backdrop to the main action of individual players. The attempt to incorporate different kinds of theories as a set of factors that operate at different 'levels' is ultimately unsuccessful. However, it does highlight the fact that while feminist theory helps explain the prevalence and gender patterning of sexual abuse, there has been far less attention given to exploring how some men rather than others come to abuse children (or how a small number of women come to do likewise).

There is a small amount of research with perpetrators of sexual violence which has taken feminist theory, rather than models of individual pathology, as its starting point. This includes Diana Scully's (1990) interviews with 114 convicted rapists in which they describe the 'excitement', 'adventure' and enjoyment of power that rape gave them and the aggrandizement of their masculinity it provided. Conte *et al.* (1989) developed an innovative method of data collection in asking convicted child sex offenders to 'write a manual on how to sexually abuse a child'. The result was considerable information about the deliberate, conscious process involved in grooming children for abuse, and the pleasures of power and control:

They report targeting children for victimization, systematically conditioning them to accept increasing sexual physical contact and exploiting the child's needs in order to maintain them as available victims.

(Berliner and Conte 1990: 35)

There has also been work, such as that undertaken by Deborah Cameron and Elizabeth Frazer, that explores the historical and cultural specificity of particular sexual violences and unpicks the knot of discourses surrounding them:

nineteenth and twentieth-century 'scientific' discourses, and lay understandings and experience of sexuality in this culture, carry traces of this complex link between individual freedom, domination, transgression, the erotic, and the beautiful . . . It means that men in our culture have the option (which some of them take up) of taking the sex murderer role.

(Cameron and Frazer 1994: 161)

However, once having described the discourses that facilitate this particular configuration of abuse, Cameron and Frazer along with most feminist theorists seem to suggest that it is merely a matter of 'lifestyle choice' whether any particular man takes up the abuser role or not.

What is interesting, if not explicit, in this work is that we can begin to glimpse the possibility of linking the discourses of gender identified by feminism as causes of child sexual abuse with the ways in which particular men represent themselves and their actions to themselves. Rather than the analytic separation between 'society' and 'the individual' which limits Finkelhor's attempt to synthesize different kinds of knowledge about child abuse, we can instead explore how people are made up (and make themselves up) out of the various roles made available to them within different discourses. Such an approach avoids the determinism of theories like the 'cycle of abuse', allowing us to explore how people can make quite different lives out of apparently similar materials. However, it can instead appear overly voluntaristic. What is absent is any attention to the fact that rapists and child abusers develop their investment in particular behaviours and identities over time, and have differential access to different discourses of gender and sexuality. As past 'ways of being' tend to overdetermine present ones (interrupted occasionally by instances of 'conversion', 'rebirth', 'cure' and suchlike) biography, and the meanings attached to experiences, are far from irrelevant in understanding how some men come to abuse children.

We need to tease out the different levels of analysis that are necessary in answering the different questions which need to be asked about both the social conditions that make possible the sexual abuse of children and why particular individuals abuse. Given that the majority of such individuals are men, theoretical work on the plurality of masculinities and the ways in which intra-gender differences are hierarchical – with 'lesser' masculinities often being feminized – needs to inform future research with a range of abusers (Morgan 1992; Moore 1994).

Women abusers

It has often been suggested that we know so little about child sexual abuse perpetrated by women because the topic has been caught in a pincer movement of denial. From one side there has been a strong cultural investment in images of women as maternal, nurturing, non-violent and sexually unassertive. From the other has come the reluctance of feminists to explore the possibility that child sexual abuse is not always, or only, an issue of male power.

It is certainly true that the discovery of sexual abuse by women was used to attack the view of child sexual abuse as being an issue of sexual politics. It was sometimes suggested that 'in the end', women's abuse of children would be found to be just as extensive as men's, and some professionals in the field claimed that 'people were the problem' and questions about 'why men do it' should be dropped forthwith (Hanks *et al.* 1989). Feminists saw such debates as an extension of the backlash against a gendered analysis of child sexual abuse dating from the mid-1980s (see Chapter 2) and responded accordingly:

> Powerful establishment forces merely went into brief retreat under the weight of feminist evidence. Today's stress on female sex offenders is part of the fight-back on behalf of 'gender-free' theory and practice . . . It safeguards a professional elite's right to treat and cure, offering an unthreatening, individualistic answer to a major social problem.
>
> (Nelson 1992)

Although at the same time there were calls from feminists to tackle the issues raised by women abusers (Scott and Kelly 1989; Kelly 1991) there has been little development of feminist informed research.

The first collection of essays and personal accounts on the subject to be published in Britain, *Female Sexual Abuse of Children: The Ultimate Taboo* (Elliott 1993), exemplified many of the problems in the field. Significant among these is the small numbers of 'cases' upon which discussions are based – a problem that facilitates different contributors making contradictory claims based on limited data. So, for example, Jane Matthews (1993), an American clinician who worked with thirty-six female abusers over a six-year period, argues that women use force, violence and threats far less often than do male abusers of children. Cianne Longdon (1993), a counsellor and survivor, sets out to 'challenge the myth' that female abusers are 'gentle and loving' in their abuse and emphasizes the violence and sadism which have been described to her.

There is general agreement that women sexually abuse children far less commonly than men – making up between 5 per cent and 10 per cent of abusers reported in a wide range of studies (Finkelhor 1984; Russell 1984). It is often argued that a range of inhibiting factors in the socialization of girls, and the dominant discourses of female sexuality and maternity dramatically reduce the likelihood of women sexually abusing children. However, the hypotheses that women abusers are socialized differently, have failed to invest in the discourses of maternity or have developed identities based on marginal femininities, have not been explored through research.

Taken together, research and clinical studies (Goodwin and DiVasto 1979; Faller 1987; Speltz *et al.* 1989; Allen 1991; Matthews *et al.* 1991) agree on a limited number of characteristics of women (convicted or in treatment) who sexually abuse children. These include low self-esteem, abusive and problematic childhoods, frequently unsatisfactory and abusive adult relationships with men, and the likelihood of their being drug or alcohol dependent (Faller 1987; Speltz *et al.* 1989; Allen 1991; Matthews *et al.* 1991). These features appear not entirely dissimilar to those identified in between 25 per cent and 50 per cent of convicted male offenders in some of the studies already discussed (Panton 1978; Groth and Burgess 1979; Morgan 1982). However, they tell us as little about women who abuse as they ever told us about men, as well as giving a gloss of similarity which may well be unfounded given that each of the features they refer to are in themselves gendered (for example, self-esteem is often related to successful fulfilment of gender roles and expectations, while 'involvement in abusive relationships' is more likely to involve the perpetration of violence among men and the receipt of it among women).

Based on their clinical work in a female sex offender treatment programme, Speltz et al. (1989) distinguished between three types of women abusers: 'male-coerced abusers', 'teacher-lovers', who had abused adolescents, and 'generationally predisposed abusers', who tend to begin abusing much younger children. This typology was largely adopted by Jacqui Saradjian (1996) in her study of fifty women who had sexually abused children in Britain.

Saradjian emphasizes that all the women in her study, including those who were initially coerced into abusing by men, had experienced *profound* abuse and isolation in their own childhood. By adolescence, they had developed extremely negative images of themselves and their continued isolation deprived them of contexts and relationships in which these might be challenged. Saradjian's work provides a useful description of the abuse experienced and perpetrated by women who have sexually abused children, their views of themselves and their victims. In addition, she is able to demonstrate an extremely close relationship between the extent, duration and proximity of relationships within which the women were themselves abused and the nature of the abuse they later perpetrated.

Organized and ritual abuse

Prior to the 1990s, discussions of organized sexual abuse of children had been quite separate from work on sexual abuse in general. For feminists, a focus on abuse within the family made political sense just as it made practical sense for those working in the field of child protection. Up until the 1980s, organized abuse rings were generally assumed to consist of male paedophiles recruiting pubescent boys for sex. In Britain the campaigning activities of Paedophile Information Exchange (PIE) in the 1970s left a lasting image of the inadequate and homosexual child molester. The public profile of the incest offender might have been redrawn as a 'respectable' paterfamilias and pillar of the community, but he was rarely thought to be related to 'Uncle Ernie' or his dirty pictures. Pornography and prostitution were assumed to involve adult women, and to be linked to child sexual abuse largely in terms of the numbers of adult survivors working in the sex industry. Despite feminist theorists' insistence on the interconnectedness of all forms of sexual violence, different groups of professionals, activists and researchers tended to focus on particular forms of abuse.

A number of factors began to change perceptions of sexual abuse in the late 1980s and early 1990s, so that the field simultaneously expanded and fragmented. Adult male survivors' accounts of abuse in children's homes, by priests and sports coaches, suggested that paternal authority in the family was not the only social structure that could support abuse. Such accounts and the court cases sometimes built upon them made clear the skill, determination and sadism of many abusers. In addition, the emphasis on 'working together' in the child protection field brought a police focus on prostitution, 'obscene publications' and 'career' paedophiles more into the purview of social workers mostly concerned with abuse within families. Therapeutic work with offenders increased awareness of the way abusers networked and organized in and out of prison, exchanged pornography and passed on victims (Wyre 1996). Finally, a focus on international 'trafficking' and sexual exploitation of children led by children's charities such as UNICEF and Save the Children provided a new global lens through which to examine the issue of child abuse.

In 1993, I reviewed the available literature on 'organized abuse' for a special issue of *Child Abuse Review* (Scott and Kelly 1993). Part of the problem and project of literature reviews is deciding what counts as 'the relevant literature'. Literature reviews are one of the scholarly practices of knowledge production. They help to define new fields and in doing so discipline diverse work into a 'body' for particular purposes. The term 'organized abuse' had emerged out of controversies over cases apparently involving numerous perpetrators and victims in sadistic and perverse abuse, some of which involved group rituals (Rochdale in 1990, Nottingham in 1989 and Orkney in 1991). 'Organized abuse' or 'sadistic organized abuse' was sometimes used as a more acceptable euphemism for 'ritual abuse', but quickly became established as an umbrella category within which abuse involving 'rituals' might prove to be a particularly perverse variant. Throughout the 1980s those working with perpetrators (Berliner and Stevens 1982; Wyre 1987) had emphasized that sexual abusers were not 'overcome by lust', but well planned and inclined to 'groom' their victims with considerable skill. The term 'organized abuse' brought together a range of experiences of being sexually abused in which the abuse appeared to be organized in ways that lent individual abusers additional power and legitimacy, and thereby affected the experience of being abused. The first widely circulated definition appeared in the second edition of *Working Together* as quoted on page 2.

La Fontaine has provided a more limited definition of organized abuse as:

Abuse by multiple perpetrators, some or all of whom are outside the immediate household of the victim(s), and who act together to abuse the child(ren).

(La Fontaine 1993: 226)

This definition has been criticized for focusing on the number and proximity of those involved rather than the processes of organization involved (Bibby 1994). It excludes many of the most widely recognized types of 'sex rings', where one perpetrator abuses numerous victims and familial abuse within a single household, no matter how many of those resident are perpetrators or victims. It also excludes cases of institution-based abuse, or abuse supported by rituals or religion where only a single perpetrator is involved.

The literature review (Scott and Kelly 1993) suggested developing a much wider concept of organized abuse of children to include 'normalized' organized abuse, such as corporal punishment regimes and 'Pindown' (Levy and Kahan 1991), child labour and slavery; child pornography and prostitution, both domestically (Sereny 1984; Tate 1990) and globally (Ennew 1986; Ireland 1993); paedophile and other networks, including sex rings (Burgess 1984) and day-care abuse (Finkelhor *et al.* 1988); and ritual abuse. Very little of the literature on any form of organized abuse reported on academic research. However, as we wrote, two linked research projects seeking to explore the nature and extent of organized abuse in Britain were underway (La Fontaine 1994; Gallagher *et al.* 1996).

The **role** of **research**

Two rare pieces of research from the mid-1980s dealing with some form of what we now call organized abuse stand out. The first is a study by Ann Burgess of 60 children abused in sex rings. Burgess defines a 'ring' as 'a situation in which at least one abuser is simultaneously involved with several victims, all of whom are aware of each other's participation' (Burgess *et al.* 1981: 111). The men involved were mostly middle class and middle aged, abusing children outside their own families, often, but not exclusively, sexually orientated to boys, and who used older victims to recruit other children. Some groups were 'syndicated' and these tended to involve higher levels of sadomasochism, more often exchanged children between groups, and used video as well as stills cameras to produce pornography.

Only once in *Child Pornography and Sex Rings* (Burgess 1984) is a possible connection suggested between familial abuse and children's use in pornography and prostitution. Burgess describes a hand-written manuscript in the possession of a child abuser dealing with the sexual training of infants:

> The self-stated purpose of this manuscript was to serve as a 'good guideline for developers who want to facilitate desirable responsiveness in those new-borns and infants that are to be made available for a wide variety of sexual use'. Parents were referred to as 'developers' whose desire was to 'guide the new-born child to be a satisfying sexual object'. The infants were developed for the 'customers'' sexual pleasure. The manuscript discussed taking advantage of the child's reflexes and interest in play. It stated that infants should learn basic commands, such as 'lie down' and 'turn over', because it enhanced their desirability and demand.
>
> (Burgess 1984: 91–2)

The manuscript constituted a detailed training manual for the period from birth to 15 months intended to 'produce' an infant capable 'of handling one or two customers a night'. Although, as Burgess points out, the manuscript may only reflect fantasy, I have made reference to it here as a rare point at which the literature on sex rings clearly overlaps with recent accounts from survivors of ritual abuse.

The second study from this period provides a description of 32 child sex rings involving over 300 children discovered over a two-year period in Leeds

(Wild and Wynne 1986). The ratio of girls to boys involved was ten-to-one and almost one-third of the groups involving only girls were interconnected with many of the girls being in care. Three rings involved parents and children and five prostituted children to men outside the group.

There was almost no other research into any form of organized abuse until after the appearance of controversial cases of ritual abuse in US preschools. A rush of studies focused on these cases were undertaken from the late 1980s. Finkelhor *et al.*'s (1988) study of 270 cases of abuse in US day-care programmes (nurseries) between 1983 and 1985 revealed that 1639 children were believed to have been abused. Almost three-quarters of the abusers were staff members. In 83 per cent of cases they were male perpetrators acting alone. However, 17 per cent of cases involved multiple perpetrators (including women) and these accounted for 66 per cent of the children abused. Of these 46 multi-perpetrator cases, 36 were classified as involving forms of ritual abuse. Other studies (Kelley 1989; Faller 1994; Waterman *et al.* 1993) emphasize reports of the use of threats and fear in controlling children and preventing disclosure, the apparent use/production of pornography, and the high levels of emotional disturbance among the children in these most controversial cases.

While there have been cases in the UK involving prosecutions of nursery staff for the sexual abuse of children in their care, there have been no accusations of ritual abuse in this context. The controversial cases involving allegations of ritual abuse in the UK have involved family and neighbourhood networks, and the research response to them has been to map the pattern of all known cases of organized abuse. Research at the University of Manchester (Gallagher *et al.* 1996) involved two stages of data collection. The first involved the distribution of questionnaires to all police forces, social services departments and NSPCC teams in England and Wales. This stage produced some of the data on which Jean La Fontaine based her 1994 report on organized and ritual abuse (see Chapter 2). Concern that the postal survey had produced under-reporting – particularly of smaller scale cases – led to a second stage involving a search of 20,000 police and social services child protection records in eight local authority areas. This exercise suggested that the survey results had underestimated the number of cases by a factor of more than nine.

This research defines organized abuse in terms of more than one abuser acting together, but ritual and institutional abuse as possibly involving a single abuser. A total of 149 cases of organized abuse and 62 cases of ritual abuse were identified as having been reported between 1988 and 1991. The survey requested that respondents classify the cases they reported according to a set of categories based on the literature, for example a paedophile ring, commercial prostitution, a cult. One of the most interesting findings of the research was that 44 per cent of respondents found none of the categories appropriate or did not know how to classify the cases. This finding makes it clear that knowledge about organized abuse was in its infancy and that research such as this was as much about 'discovering' a field as defining one.

Gallagher *et al.*'s (1996) work, like most of the reviews of preschool cases in the USA, avoids entanglement in the controversy over ritual abuse by simply counting what is reported. It was left to Jean La Fontaine to use their findings, examine the cases involved more closely and conclude that, while there was evidence in 3 cases of a perpetrator having invented rituals and abused children in them, there was no such evidence of organized ritual abuse in any of the other 81 cases. These cases resembled the other large cases of family-based abuse in the survey, and La Fontaine concludes that while equivalent kinds of abuse may well have occurred, the ritual type allegations were 'grafted on' by foster parents and social workers who had been influenced by stories of ritual and satanic abuse in American day-care cases. In Chapter 2 I shall consider La Fontaine's arguments in the context of the widespread construction of ritual abuse as a moral panic.

Conclusion

A view of the history of childhood being one of the slow progress of kindness, penetrating finally to the secret of incestuous abuse is not one supported by this chapter. I have described the (re)discovery by feminists of the banality of incest and their success in disseminating a definition and analysis of the issue of child sexual abuse based on this perspective. The fit between feminist theory, evidence of the prevalence of abuse, and the social work focus on problems in families, meant that in the early and mid-1980s a feminist paradigm of child sexual abuse was in the ascendant. For a few years it partially eclipsed previous models of the psychopathology of paedophiles, the culpability of victims, or the collusion of mothers. However, as the 1980s progressed, the paradigm was increasingly challenged by the emergence of diverse forms of abuse which did not fit the model. Research and therapeutic interventions largely engaged with extrafamilial and women abusers from the unreconstructed perspective of individual pathology. Fearing the erosion of the understanding of the relationship between sexual abuse and male power within the family, and feeling the first sting of a backlash against such a perspective (see Chapter 2), feminists failed to develop analyses to deal with diverse forms of abuse.

Accounts of ritual abuse did not therefore emerge into a well-developed field of 'organized abuse' informed by research and staffed by experts. Indeed, I have suggested that the notion of such a 'field' was at least partly developed in response to the controversy over ritual abuse cases. The abuse-saturated lives that the women and children described did not fit the sparse knowledge of 'sex-rings' or of 'ordinary' domestic abuse. In Britain at least many such accounts were first encountered by feminists and social workers in the course of everyday practice in women's refuges, child protection teams and on telephone helplines. Not only did they fail to fit readily into the dominant paradigms of child sexual abuse framing practice in those contexts, but also they embodied a number of challenges to the paradigm. However, adults and children generally told their stories to people predisposed to believe accounts of abuse in general. Adult survivors additionally gave experiential accounts of forms of abuse including those of child pornography and prostitution which feminists had always connected theoretically with more domestic forms of male violence but rarely encountered directly through survivors.

Accounts of ritual abuse promoted attention to the variety of contexts in which child sexual abuse could occur. While challenging some aspects of the feminist paradigm they affirmed others. The involvement of numerous members of the same family – both men and women – suggested the need to re-examine the importance of some family systems in facilitating abuse and the roles allocated to mothers in such systems. Multigenerational involvement indicated a need to look again at ideas of 'intergenerational transmission' and to explore the possible differences between 'opportunistic incest' and a life-long commitment to multiple abuse. Ritual abuse affirmed the centrality of power and control in the experience of both victims and perpetrators, but suggested that this did not always involve a binary divide between men and women or adults and children.

Ritual abuse emerged in the context of routine work focused on child sexual abuse, but accounts are of profound emotional and physical abuse, torture, forced abortion and even murder, raising questions about the ready categorization of the experiences described. Most controversially of all, adult survivors claim some aspects of their abuse to have been legitimized and justified by an occult belief system and to have taken place in the context of group rituals. The next chapter examines the responses of social commentators and professionals who are convinced that such abuse does not occur.

Notes

1 Freud (1896) first accepted his female patients' reports of sexual abuse, reporting his views in *The Aetiology of Hysteria*, and then repudiated them in response to considerable criticism. This was first documented by Florence Rush (1977) and is thoroughly discussed in a collection of essays: *In Dora's Case: Freud-Hysteria-Feminism* (Bernheimer and Kahane 1985).
2 An exception is a Canadian qualitative study *Recollecting Our Lives* (Women's Research Centre 1989).

2 | Unreliable witnesses: memories and **moral panic**

Satanism appears to have been imported from the Bible Belt of America. The signs of satanism and its connection with child abuse were first reported in the US by people who had an interest in the existence of Satan. Satanism gives their religion a sort of ghostbusters glamour. Fundamentalists have always had a taste for the apocalyptic.

(Sunday Correspondent, 23 September 1990)

The mythical beast known as satanic sex abuse was born in America, where it has all the hallmarks of a panic craze fed by films, television and books, nurtured by fantasy, maintained by a plethora of accusations and bolstered by the credulity of psychotherapists and the public . . . America, and now the rest of the world, wants to believe in this many-headed monster. It is, perhaps, the way society excretes its darkest fears and fantasies: a beast that refuses to die.

(The Times, 3 June 1994)

These views expressed in British broadsheet newspapers are representative of what I shall describe as a 'discourse of disbelief' which developed in response to allegations of ritual abuse in Britain, the Netherlands, North America and Australia from the mid-1980s. This discourse described ritual abuse as a 'moral panic' stirred up among a credulous public by a coalition of Christians, feminists, therapists and social workers. This portrayal of the issue of ritual abuse developed at the same time as the concept of a 'false memory syndrome' in relation to sexual abuse, and the establishment of a False Memory Syndrome Foundation (FMSF) to contest the accounts of individuals who had 'recovered memories' of abuse in childhood.

The purpose of this chapter is to deconstruct the discourse of disbelief around ritual abuse, to examine it as a set of situated claims, to scrutinize the discursive strategies utilized in making doubt stick, and to suggest the kinds of interests with which disbelief may be associated. This is a table-turning enterprise, for the discourse of disbelief itself incorporates a deconstructionist exercise. Characterizing ritual abuse stories as 'moral panics' and 'false memories' involves mobilizing social constructionist explanations of public anxiety or of the making of memory, and assumes complex, mediated relationships between 'what happens' and discursive presentations of 'what happens'. My interest here is in the construction of these particular social constructionist accounts and in locating them within wider controversies over child abuse, the position of women, the status of the family, the rise of fundamentalism and the 'decline of rationalism'.

Such accounts are not purely 'academic' any more than are the proselytizing books and pamphlets of campaigners against child abuse; they are 'active texts' – active in courtrooms, therapists' consulting rooms, professional organizations and families. The discourse of disbelief helps organize courses of concerted social action such as parental opposition to the investigation of certain child protection cases, or the public maintenance of wronged respectability by alleged abusers. It also provided part of the backdrop against which each of my interviewees had to speak. I have therefore been concerned to understand how the claims which dismiss ritual abuse as a product of moral panic or false memory make themselves convincing. Many would suggest that they are much aided by having 'common sense' on their side, but common sense is socially produced through the very discourses that appeal to it. In other words it is formed within debates about the truth and nature of things and cannot be appealed to as an external arbiter.

In her classic paper, 'K is mentally ill', Dorothy Smith wrote that: 'An account which is immediately convincing is one which forces that classification and makes any other difficult' (Smith 1990b: 16). In this chapter I use some of Smith's ideas about precisely how texts impose on their readers a particular version of their subject matter (Smith 1990a). The ideals and prejudices they appeal to, the ways in which they assimilate the previously unknown to the familiar, order the evidence in terms of a particular explanatory framework, and categorize certain informants as unreliable witnesses. This task of deconstruction is made possible by the fact that: '[t]he text enters the laboratory, so to speak, carrying the threads and shreds of the relations it is organized by and organizes' (Smith 1990b: 4). However, such tasks are generally undertaken only by those who have an interest in them. I 'read' the discourse of disbelief about ritual abuse as a feminist active around issues of sexual violence for almost two decades. My critique is a specifically situated one, aimed at questioning the adequacy of moral panic or false memory explanations.

I am not suggesting that disbelief has comprised the totality of responses to allegations and investigations of ritual abuse. The discourse of disbelief has developed in reaction to claims which themselves have been made in the public sphere. Initial news reports of child protection cases involving allegations of ritual abuse have usually been shocked or neutral rather than sceptical in tone. Television documentaries maintaining that ritual abuse really happens, as well as those 'debunking the myth', have been aired in both the USA and Britain (*Geraldo Rivera Special* 1988; *Dispatches* 1991; *Dispatches* 1992).[1] However, in both sympathetic and sceptical responses the discourse of disbelief quickly came to hold centre stage.

The **context** of the **debate**

Scepticism concerning the veracity of women's claims about sexual abuse has a history as long as the claims themselves (Brownmiller 1976; Clark 1987). The issue of disbelief preoccupied feminist services for survivors from their establishment in the 1970s. Rape crisis helplines specifically advertised that: 'You can speak to another woman in confidence – we will believe you'. For a couple of years in the mid-1980s I gave a regular talk at a police training college on a course entitled Advanced Sexual Offences. My task was to introduce what was always referred to as 'the victim's perspective', and without exception the first question after my introductory presentation was: 'But what about false allegation?' It seemed that, from the perspective of senior police officers, the problem with rape was that it was an allegation women could make in order to get men into trouble – or themselves out of it. As one chief constable had put it in a speech he gave in 1982: 'It is quite extraordinary the extent to which complaints are made which prove to be wholly unfounded' (James Anderton, quoted in *Rochdale Observer*, 10 February 1982).

I remember the atmosphere in those talks, the sarcastic smiles and raised eyebrows. Many of the officers made it clear that they were insulted by my presence. After all they already knew 'the truth' about rape and the sort of women who reported rape. At the time it seemed clear to me that such attitudes were out of step with a wider society in which ideas about gender, sex and male violence appeared to have changed irrevocably, and where the idea of generally 'believing' women and children who claimed they had been sexually assaulted seemed to have found wide acceptance. However, any idea that this was part of an inevitable forward march of feminism would have been a little premature.

Susan Faludi (1991) has used the concept of 'backlash' to make sense of the double messages about women's equality which she found in the US media in the late 1980s. The double message was that on the one hand, feminism had succeeded and women were now liberated, and on the other, that it had failed entirely to improve women's lot:

> In the last decade, publications from the *New York Times* to *Vanity Fair* to the *Nation* . . . hold the campaign for women's equality responsible for nearly every woe besetting women, from mental depression to meagre savings accounts, from teenage suicides to eating disorders to bad complexions.
>
> (Faludi 1991: xi)

Faludi barely mentions violence against women and children as a feminist theme which has attracted reaction, but a number of similar dynamics can be seen to be at work. In the most acrimonious battles over child abuse, it is feminists, not child abusers, who have been accused of 'breaking up families'. Bea Campbell's (1988) account of the Cleveland child abuse case describes the demonization of two feminist professionals by the police and the media. Sue Richardson and Dr Marietta Higgs became the focus of a dramatic backlash over child *sexual* abuse in Britain. Of course media attacks on social work in general have regularly swung between calls for less interference in families and condemnation of its failure to protect vulnerable children. None the less, the impact of feminist theory and research I described in Chapter 1 had not been confined to childcare professionals, and concern over the prevalence and 'ordinariness' of sexual abuse in the family was widespread. In the years immediately prior to 'Cleveland', media sympathies seemed to be entirely with Esther Rantzen, and publicity was heaped upon the infant ChildLine.[2]

In his account of the 'backlash' against child sexual abuse in the USA, David Hechler (1988) traces a straight line from feminist protest against the iniquities of rape trials in the 1970s to the child advocacy movement of the 1980s. He describes a slowly mounting backlash against feminism which reached its height in the late 1980s and focused its discontents on the issue of child sexual abuse within the family.[3] Accusations of child sexual abuse may well terminate the involvement of a particular man in a particular family, while discussion of such abuse inevitably raises questions about the relationship between men, women and children more generally. Some of the first 'defensive' responses came from men who feared that their everyday involvement in childcare (such as changing nappies and bathing their children) might lead to unwarranted suspicions of sexual abuse. However, it is the popular support which feminists had won over child abuse (rape and battering of adult women have always been more ambiguous issues in the public sphere) which Hechler (1988) believes made this particular issue a focus of reaction.

If such a description of the gendered battles around child sexual abuse in general is accurate, one might not be surprised to find similar issues beneath the surface of the discourse of disbelief about ritual abuse. As we have seen, ritual abuse emerged into the field of child sexual abuse often into the laps of the same workers who were already under attack for exaggerating such problems in general. What complicated the situation in the case of ritual abuse was both the alleged and actual involvement of evangelical Christians. Child sexual abuse has been a tricky subject for the Christian churches – reliant as they are on promoting the godliness of the family and church community. Especially challenging are the accusations that priests and ministers have abused young people in their congregations. For those of a fundamentalist persuasion, child sexual abuse committed by outsiders in league with Satan might seem far less problematic.

The rise of Christian fundamentalism in the USA has been well documented and in some ways feminism and fundamentalism had grown up at loggerheads with each other. Their mutual hostility has found its most public expression over abortion. (The name 'Operation Rescue' itself suggests the kind of 'holy war' which fundamentalists identify as their mode of engagement with the world.)[4] Despite this the association of feminism with the Christian Right is not a new critical strategy. Opposition to pornography in Britain led to the reclassification of feminists from practitioners of 'free love' to allies of the Festival of Light by the industry and its supporters.

The linking of ritual abuse with its 'discovery' by evangelical Christians has had a profound effect on the overall debate about the status of ritual abuse as truth or myth: pulling the strings of suspicion in secular, liberal audiences. However, this is only one strand in the portrayal of ritual abuse as a moral panic or contemporary myth. Other strands include a perceived crisis within American society focusing on the family, and the characterization of ritual abuse as the pinnacle of a much larger moral panic about male violence in general. Much of the literature discussed here on 'the satanic panic' is a subsection of a wider literature on 'the child abuse panic' often invoked by the same authors (Best 1989, 1990; Jenkins 1992; Best 1994).

That evangelical Christians are concerned about satanism and ritual abuse is hardly surprising and is evident from the number of books on the subject written from this perspective (Sanders 1975; Logan 1988; Scott Peck 1988; Raschke 1990; Wagner and Pennoyer 1990). The association within the evangelical literature between believing in Satan and believing in ritual abuse has caused many believers of a more secular persuasion to reframe the problem of ritual abuse, so as to minimize the importance of any belief system. Most of the disbelief literature is consistent in its use of the term 'satanic ritual abuse'. Through this usage the taint of evangelicalism is always present. 'Believers' have responded to the issue of naming in various ways. In response some have selected terms such as 'organized' and 'severe sadistic'. Others have continued to use the label 'satanic' because they believe this best reflects survivors' descriptions of the context of their abuse. Valerie Sinason (1994) coined the term 'satanist abuse' in order to emphasize the people active as perpetrators rather than the belief system *per se*. Some writers use the term 'ritual abuse' in order to suggest that a range of religious ideologies may be used to support such abuse, others may do so to avoid being dismissed as religious fanatics.

The difficulty over terminology is not just one of 'believers' responding to the discourse of disbelief, but of deciding 'the nature of the beast' in any particular instance: are we talking about a 'dysfunctional family' or something like 'The Children of God' with horns? Is this primarily an instance of sexual or religious 'perversion'? How does an evangelical concern with an international conspiracy of satanists planning to establish His kingdom on earth relate to the experiences of abuse described by survivors? Without evidence beyond the testimony of children documented for child protection purposes, these remain unanswerable questions.

A **satanic panic**

The discourse of disbelief uses a number of strategies in order to dismiss ritual abuse reports as features of a social scare or moral panic. These include the consistent coupling of 'satanism' and ritual abuse, the claim that a complicit media have promoted a unified scare-mongering 'line', the homogenizing of 'believers' so that differences between such diverse interests as those of feminists and fundamentalists are obscured, the trivializing of claims, hystericizing of claim-makers, and slipping between a view of claims as socially constructed and as individually invented.

As the quotations which open this chapter suggest, journalists have largely focused on dismissing ritual abuse as a Christian conspiracy, but some sociologists have developed more sophisticated analyses of a 'moral panic'. Since the coining of the term by Stan Cohen (1972) to describe the media amplification of mods and rockers' Bank Holiday sprees, the term 'moral panic' has been used to imply over-reactions of respectable/reactionary sections of society to hippies, drug users, teenage pregnancies, 'the AIDS scare', and so on. It has also been used in historical work to explain phenomena such as the witch burnings of medieval Europe (Cohn 1975). It has been suggested that the term 'has become a form of sociological shorthand, or insult to throw at societal reactions to everything from soccer hooligans to welfare scroungers' (Thompson 1990).

Cohen (1972) maintained that moral panics asserted the dominance of established values against external threats – such as mods and rockers – who were constituted as 'folk devils'. This 'demonizing' was primarily a media production, but the stories so produced then influenced the activities of police, holidaymakers and 'wannabe' mods and rockers. I would suggest that the term 'moral panic' is more descriptive than explanatory, and in Cohen's usage it describes a specific, short-lived 'emotional spasm' to which societies are occasionally prone, brought on by certain journalistic strategies within a practice of news-making that is partially defined by the deviant, bizarre and sensational. This 'news' is then responded to according to the positions, interests and values of those who consume it. It was Howard Becker's ([1967] 1990) suggestion that processes of this sort are consciously exploited by those he calls 'moral entrepreneurs' to aid them in their attempts to win public support.

My concern here is to show how ritual abuse has been frequently *constructed* as a moral panic *and nothing else* (for things can be both fodder for 'moral panic' and real events in real lives) and to evaluate the persuasiveness of the arguments. The writers considered here aim to show the ideological underpinnings of believers' claims, but their accounts are in turn limited in a number of ways. They may indeed explain how aspects of the claims about ritual abuse operate, but they can explain such claims *away* only if the life-stories of survivors are in some way fabricated. In other words they depend ultimately on the arguments over 'false allegations' and the existence of a 'False Memory Syndrome' which I go on to discuss.

The notion of a 'moral panic' belongs within a social constructionist approach to social life which emphasizes the 'creation' of social phenomena rather than their 'discovery'. The focus of interest is in how and why issues become defined as social problems at particular historical and geographical junctures, rather than why particular social problems occur, increase or are exposed to public view. Some post-structuralist versions of constructionism bracket off questions about the 'real' nature and extent of a social problem and veer towards a view of 'reality' as being the most loudly voiced or widely accepted definition thereof. However, the analyses of ritual abuse that I am concerned with here fall short of such a strong postmodern claim. Indeed they frequently claim at the same time that the problem with ritual abuse claims is that there is no hard (scientific) evidence for them, and claim a constructivist approach to 'social problem' phenomena. Other people are the 'claim-makers', while the sociologists engaged in deconstructing such claims and exposing the interests of those involved appear to be above the process they describe, exempt from criticism as disinterested social scientists.

The categorization of a phenomenon as resulting from a moral panic frequently masks underlying social relations. The claim of a moral panic over AIDS can be seen as both homophobic in itself and as serving to mask the reality of homophobia in policies and practices (Watney 1987). In addition it can be seen to collapse together 'the panic' and 'the problem'. For instance, a critique of the 'New Right' panic over the incidence of teenage pregnancies does not mean that these might not be problematized from other perspectives, including those of feminism. Concerned parties are often collapsed together, as Chris Attmore points out in her discussion of moral panic arguments around child abuse:

> Despite constructionists' general insistence on distinctions among different claims-makers interests, there is no consideration that claims-makers can and do *compete* for the meaning of child sexual abuse, and that the demonized molester, still an extremely common cultural typification of abusers, is a figure promoted by the right but *criticized* by feminists.
> (Attmore 1995: 24, original emphasis)

Jenkins and Maier-Katkin (1992) claimed authority for their categorization of satanic ritual abuse as a moral panic, on the grounds that there are a small number of 'self-styled experts' on satanism (who they claim are 'not-very-bright policemen' or Christian fundamentalists, or both). These 'experts' make 'unsubstantiated' claims, propose right-wing solutions to the problems they describe (such as a return to 'traditional family values') and advocate the outlawing of a wide range of New Age or occult practices. In addition, they claim that the police have spent a lot of time and resources on 'wild goose chases' in relation to alleged satanic crimes and found very little evidence. In addition, Jenkins and Maier-Katkin (1992) claim that contemporary satanism, as proclaimed by Anton LaVey, leader of the entirely unsecretive Church of Satan (LaVey 1969), takes its beliefs and practices from the novels of Denis Wheatley and Stephen King. Therefore as an 'invented' religion of the twentieth century, satanism cannot be taken seriously as the progenitor of widespread secret criminality. It is not made clear why the modernity or syncretism of American satanism is taken as evidence of the implausibility of ritual abuse; after all the Ku-Klux-Klan is not exactly steeped in ancient liturgy.

It is interesting that the *role* of the media is barely considered in this or other accounts of ritual abuse as a moral panic. Newspapers and television appear as neutral conduits for the beliefs of believers. As Chris Attmore puts it: 'The media is implicitly viewed as transmitting a univocal message to an equally helpful audience who overwhelmingly want to and do believe in "it"' (Attmore 1995: 13).

Stories about ritual abuse are described as having spread uncontested from evangelicals to feminists, and from the USA to a credulous Britain and beyond. Such a notion of porous receptivity to messages through the infectious quality of hysteria is an element in most moral panic explanations of ritual abuse.

In order to construe ritual abuse as a moral panic, it has been necessary to highlight the interests of a group of moral entrepreneurs. Jenkins and Maier-Katkin (1992) suggest that these are evangelical Christians who believe that scaring the public with stories of satanism will serve to push them into seeking the safety of the Church. While this may be true, it cannot account for the diverse group of therapists, social workers, priests and feminists who teach, write and counsel around the subject.

Jenkins and Maier-Katkin (1992) are concerned with the American situation and the authors appeal to their readers' snobbery regarding the intelligence of policemen, Bible-belters and American culture in general:

> American Satanism appears to be overwhelmingly a game for teenage dabblers and mentally unstable adults . . . (British magicians are a much more substantial and intellectually credible group).
>
> (Jenkins and Maier-Katkin 1992: 71)

In his book *Intimate Enemies: Moral Panics in Contemporary Great Britain*, Philip Jenkins (1992) takes a somewhat different approach to explaining the ritual abuse 'panic' in the UK. He places the phenomenon firmly within the context of a series of 'panics' about male sexual violence generated largely by feminists:

> There have since the late 1970s been repeated scandals and public panics focusing on different types of sexual predators, who targeted women and especially children. The image of the male predator had several facets – the rapist, the serial killer, the child molester, the ritual or satanic child abuser, and the child murderer but as the 1980s progressed, the different stereotypes became increasingly intertwined.
>
> (Jenkins 1992: 9)

In the British context, a different group of moral entrepreneurs has to be emphasized, as Christian fundamentalism is much less visible in Britain. The problem that remains is the inability to adequately explain the transfer of the panic from US fundamentalists to British feminists. There is ample evidence that concern over child sexual abuse built up during the 1980s, and that feminists were influential in this. However, the dismissal of this as a moral panic suggests a less than rigorous attention to research on the incidence and prevalence of child sexual assault.

Jenkins (1992) identifies a set of interest groups behind this 'moral panic', but the picture is far more complex than he suggests. Feminists and the moral Right, Christians and organizations like ChildLine and the NSPCC are sometime enemies with territory in common. It is only from a sexual-libertarian perspective that they can be portrayed so unproblematically as allies. The characterization of all those involved in this debate as 'interest groups' discourages the differentiation between different types of 'groups', whose concerns range from radical political change to professional protection. This conceptual conflation can disguise both inequalities of power and status between groups, and wider social changes around sexual violence and gender relations which cannot be reduced to the machinations of interest groups.

Jenkins' argument is that having had such success in railroading the Left, social services and law enforcement into treating male violence as a serious social problem, feminists then had no choice but to believe ritual abuse stories when they came along. To disbelieve the children would have cast doubt on a generation of assertions about child sexual abuse and lose for feminists a major weapon against the nuclear family.

Exactly the opposite can and has been argued (Scott and Kelly 1991). For many feminists ritual abuse has appeared as an unwelcome contradiction of feminist analysis:

> what had been fairly clearly established – that child sexual abuse happens mainly at home, and is overwhelmingly perpetrated by men – is now being obscured in the public consciousness by the idea that it is carried out by some god hating weirdo devil worshippers who do it at the behest of their satanic master.
> (Letter to *Community Care*, 7 March 1991)

It is largely those feminists directly involved with child or adult survivors who have overcome their initial disbelief:

> I didn't want to believe it, I still don't want to believe it, because it's horrible. I don't want it to be in my nightmares, in my knowledge. I don't want it to be on the same planet as me. The fact is that I think we have to appreciate the real difficulty – the imperative to resist the information that is coming from people . . . by anyone who is going to have to hear it, because who would *want* to hear it?
> (Bea Campbell, *After Dark*, Channel 4, 9 March 1991)

Jenkins (1992) refers only briefly to why he believes British society was generally receptive to moral panics about male violence and child abuse. He suggests that increasing numbers of women living alone had led to increased fear of rape, and therefore made them more anxious about the role of pornography. Working mothers feel guilty about leaving their children and therefore fears about abuse are just waiting to be fanned. These are bizarre arguments, given that feminists have focused almost entirely on the threat of violence from *known* men rather than strangers or female child-minders. However, similar explanations are a central theme in Jeffrey Victor's (1993) book *Satanic Panic: The Creation of a Contemporary Legend*.

Victor argues that the best way to understand ritual abuse is as a 'rumour panic' or 'contemporary legend'. His book begins with a discussion of a rumour panic in a small town in New York State, where Victor and some of his students were able to conduct some contemporaneous interviews. In early 1988, concerns about the activities of a group of punk teenagers culminated in a rumour that satanists were planning to kidnap a blonde, blue-eyed virgin for a ritual sacrifice on Friday, 13 May. Victor claims that the rumour was widely 'half-believed' and some people kept their daughters home from school on that Friday. His analysis is that those most affected were 'economically stressed and inadequately educated'. This seems to be in contradiction to the therapists and feminists whom Victor and Jenkins hold responsible for the wider ritual abuse panic, although perhaps the implication is that 'the poor and ignorant' are most vulnerable to believing the claims of moral entrepreneurs.

This discussion sets the scene for an analysis of the 'satanic panic' as displaced aggression on the part of small town, blue-collar America. This section of the community suffering the effects of rapidly changing women's roles and economic insecurity has found a convenient fantasy scapegoat. The argument is a less pretentiously expressed version of that made by David Bromley in *The Satanism Scare* (Richardson *et al.* 1991).

> Its cultural plausibility derives from contractual-covenantal tensions that have recently been exacerbated by expansion of the contractual sphere and increased vulnerability of the family. Satanism constitutes a metaphorical construction of a widely experienced sense of vulnerability and danger by American families.
>
> (Bromley 1991: 199)

Victor regards 'the symbol of Satan as a perfect metaphor for the widespread belief that American society is in moral decline' (Victor 1993: 226). Even so, the switch in the unit of analysis from a particular neighbourhood rumour to a nationwide moral panic involves an extraordinary conceptual leap.

Victor (1993) criticizes the vagueness of the 'satanic cult' label which has been applied to serial murderers, teenage gangs responsible for heavy metal graffiti, child abusers and the relatively respectable Church of Satan. It is an important criticism; however, he then exploits exactly the same imprecision and sets up the small town 'virgin sacrifice' rumour as the lens through which to view all accounts of ritual abuse.

In Victor's account, 'survivors' are dismissed as 'mostly' multiple, and therefore fantasy prone and manipulative (see Chapter 7).[5] Therapists attend workshops which neutralize dissent and encourage 'groupthink'; they are already Christians or feminists or child advocates and therefore predisposed to believe. There is apparently no place for individuals with different perspectives struggling to make sense of accounts and dealing with doubt.

Dungeons and discourse

The same problems exist in *The Satanism Scare* (Richardson *et al.* 1991), a collection of eighteen essays examining various aspects of the presentation of a satanic threat in contemporary USA. The editors claim that taken together, such presentations of satanism as lurking in heavy metal lyrics, fantasy games such as *Dungeons and Dragons*, the minds of mass murderers and the motivations of child abusers have decisively influenced public opinion.

Some of the chapters are informative and carefully argued and the two that examine police perspectives on ritual abuse in terms of the interplay between seminars, experience and existing beliefs and prejudices are particularly interesting. It is the specific nature of the influences and interests described and the contextualizing of a model of satanic crime within the police organizational environment which renders these pieces so convincing. The case for a moral panic analysis of the beliefs of 'cult cops' (Crouch and Damphouse 1991) and the evangelical bent of US police training seminars on the occult (Hicks 1991) is this analysis at its strongest. Such a reading fits with my discussion (below) of the need to reconceptualize the notion of 'moral panic'.

If the 'satanism' narrative is constituted of many strands, as most of the writers considered here agree it is, then detailed examination of differences in content and orientation would seem to be in order. In addition, attention to ritual abuse at the level of public discourse – while important – is only one possible avenue for sociological analysis. The view that this discourse is all that exists rests on the prior assumption that accounts of child and adult survivors bear no relationship to their lived experience. It seems a premature assumption given the state of knowledge. The possibility that there may be *both* unwarranted panic about 'satanism' or ritual abuse in specific contexts *and* real experiences of ritual abuse (or even satanic ritual abuse) seems not to have been considered.

The **research record**

This possibility was, however, considered by Jean La Fontaine in her research on organized and ritual abuse in Britain.[6] Her report endorsed a moral panic type explanation of how particular cases had come to be erroneously defined as satanic ritual abuse:

> The study of cases in detail showed that the Evangelical Christian campaign against new religious movements has been a powerful influence encouraging the identification of satanic abuse . . . Equally important in spreading the idea of satanic abuse in Britain are the professional 'specialists', American and British. Their claims or qualifications are rarely checked. Much of their information, particularly about cases in the United States, is unreliable.
>
> (La Fontaine 1994: 31)

However, La Fontaine also claimed that:

> Three substantiated cases of ritual, not satanic, abuse were found. These are cases in which self-proclaimed mystical/magical powers were used to entrap children and impress them (and also adults) with a reason for the sexual abuse, keeping the victims compliant and ensuring their silence.

In these cases the ritual was secondary to the sexual abuse which
clearly formed the primary objective of the perpetrators.

(La Fontaine 1994: 30; emphasis in original)

La Fontaine considers ritual abuse allegations to have taken the form of an
'epidemic' comparable to the witch-hunts of early modern Europe rather
than simply a 'moral panic'.[7] In part this is because moral panics are conceived of as an over-reaction to a real, but probably insignificant, phenomenon, while La Fontaine believes that *satanic* ritual abuse is a myth. The
mythical horror of baby-killing satanist conspirators is clearly differentiated
from the actual occurrence of ritual/ritualized abuse in a few isolated cases
involving one or two abusers 'dressing up to scare the children'.

The importance of clarity of terminology to differentiate these rumoured
and real forms of abuse is emphasized by La Fontaine, who believes that a
lack of such has tended to add credence to the most extreme versions of ritual
abuse by grouping them under a large umbrella (although it is equally possible
that this could have served to discredit 'moderate' allegations by tarring
them with the ritual abuse brush). However, La Fontaine's own definitions
have developed and changed over time. In her original research findings
report (La Fontaine 1994), the term 'ritual abuse' is used throughout as she
believes that satanic abuse implies 'a ritual directed to worship of the devil',
a specific which might not have been indicated in the data. She is careful,
however, to reiterate that the three ritual abuse cases she considers to have
been substantiated are definitely not *satanic* abuse. In a paper published two
years later discussing the same findings, her definitions are as follows:

'Satanic abuse' [refers to] . . . allegations of sexual abuse that took place
in rites directed to a religious objective and including human sacrifice,
cannibalism, sadism and other extremes of sexual and other behaviour.
    'Ritual abuse' refers to the sexual abuse of children in rituals without
the other acts, where the ritual was secondary to the sexual abuse which
was the main objective of the perpetrator(s).

(La Fontaine 1996: 206)

In 1998, a book based largely on the same research was published in which
the terms are described a little differently. La Fontaine claims that the original
study used the term 'ritual abuse' in order to encourage the reporting of cases:

Subsequently it became clear that the bulk of cases involved allegations
that were unsubstantiated; these I relabelled satanic abuse cases, by ana-
logy with the accusations in the early witch-hunts, in which the witches
were perceived as followers of Satan . . . The term is chosen to reflect the
connotations of extreme evil that most believers give to it.

(La Fontaine 1998: 11)

In this system of classification, satanic ritual abuse cases are by definition
'unsubstantiated'.

La Fontaine has some criticisms of the moral panic explanations of ritual abuse in that they fail to analyse the meaning or cultural significance of such allegations. However, her own explanations share a great deal in common with those already discussed (Jenkins 1992; Victor 1993). La Fontaine describes the development of an 'anti-satanist' movement in Britain originating with a couple of evangelical campaigners getting the subject aired by an initially sympathetic media. Once in the public sphere, it became available to foster mothers attempting to explain particularly 'damaged' and 'difficult' children in their care, and to post-Cleveland social workers, who were anxious and undertrained for dealing with child sexual abuse. Feminists 'joined the movement' because particular cases were presented as a gender struggle between disbelieving police and beleaguered social workers. Such 'recruits' distanced themselves from the evangelicals but remained tainted by the underlying beliefs: 'all the members of the anti-satanist movement appear to adopt the concepts of good and evil presented in Christian discourse' (La Fontaine 1998: 172).

'The movement' developed in a late-modern era which La Fontaine considers to be characterized by the rise of anti-rationalism and the development of an individualistic 'therapy culture'. In a period of rapid social change, there has been considerable anxiety over gender roles and the nature of 'the family'. Out of this arose what she describes as a contemporary western 'witch-craze' – comparable to the outbreaks of concern over witchcraft and sorcery in various cultures documented by anthropologists, or to the witch-hunts of early modern Europe. La Fontaine believes that the attractiveness of a story concerning the existence of a 'secret and wicked conspiracy to destroy society' in 1990s Britain overwhelmed the lack of material evidence that abusive rituals had taken place in specific cases: 'It is this belief in unverified and unverifiable mystical evil that, par excellence, classes belief in satanic abuse with belief in witchcraft' (La Fontaine 1998: 185).

Textual strategies

The importance of empirically grounded work such as that of La Fontaine is that potentially it takes discussions about ritual abuse a little closer to experiential accounts. However, it is important to examine exactly how such data are used within the overall argument. The following lists are provided by La Fontaine as one of two examples which are purported to show 'the discrepancies in accounts that allegedly concern rituals of the same cult or even rituals performed on the same occasions' (La Fontaine 1998: 152). The lists of 'features' are extracted from records of interviews with two sisters. As readers we are told that the girls had been placed with the same foster mother and took long walks together while in care but had been separated 'before the final interviews when they described the rituals analyzed here' (La Fontaine 1998: 152). We are told that therefore 'collusion was not ruled out'. Their descriptions are of 'what was said to be the same occasion', but we are not told by whom this was said, nor whether witnessing an infant sacrifice was supposed to be something the girls had experienced just once in their lives. A Catch-22 reading is set up whereby similarities are evidence of collusion while discrepancies are evidence of invention.

Comparison of girls' descriptions of baby sacrifice
(similar features emboldened)

First Girl	*Second Girl*
Child naked	Child clothed
Child awake, injected, went to sleep	
Curtains drawn	
Candles	**Candles**
Lord's Prayer backwards	No mention of Lord's Prayer
Written on black crosses	Crosses upside down – no mention of writing on them or colour of them
Sweetish sickly smell	No mention of smell
Mother wore black dress	
Others normal dress	No mention of special dress
	Decorations: earth stars moon
High pitched **chanting**	**Chanting** to Satan
Child on silver dish, in alcove	Child on table
Mother kneeling	A mother of young children stood
	She poured hot water
Knife white handle, with three black dots and silver blade	Knife black handle
Hands on knife: second girl's, then mother's	Baby marked with satanic symbols, blood drawn, baby beaten; salt rubbed in eyes and wounds of baby
Cut made in stomach near navel	Throat cut, baby slashed with knives,
Saw and felt warm blood	blood saved, put into chalice, flesh cut
Saw no more	from baby (account stops no clear
Woke when it was all over	end)

Source: La Fontaine 1998: 152 (emphasis in original)

The lists are headed with the note that similar features appearing in both have been highlighted although in fact only 'candles' and 'chanting' are emboldened, while 'crosses', 'blood' and 'knife' (with significantly, albeit differently, coloured handles) are ignored. The lists themselves begin with a bald contradiction – 'child naked'/'child clothed' – setting up the apparent impossibility that the sisters really witnessed what they claim. However, even within the fragments made available, it is possible to find contradictory evidence. For example, at the end of the list drawn from the second girl's interview, it is apparent that the child who was clothed at the start of the ritual was most certainly naked later on for his body is 'marked with satanic symbols', blood is drawn, and salt is rubbed into his wounds.

In the 'second girl' list a number of features referred to by 'first girl' are referred to as 'not mentioned', including the Lord's Prayer, a sweet, sickly smell and clothes worn by the participants. This serves to suggest that features not being mentioned by both sisters is in itself suspicious. The reader of course has no access to the questions asked of either girl in these or previous interviews which could have influenced the descriptions given, nor have we any idea of the ease or difficulty, the affect or lack of such with which these stories were told. However, it is significant that even on the basis of these out-of-context fragments, we can surmise that the foci of the sisters' narratives were probably quite different. The first girl apparently gave a far more detailed account of the early stages of a ritual but 'blacked out' when the baby was first cut. By contrast the second girl has little to say about what she heard, saw or smelt *until* the baby was first cut with a knife when the details become plentiful. (A discussion of recall of core/peripheral elements in traumatic memories can be found in Berliner and Briere 1999.)

Reconceptualizing moral panic

Much of the literature describing ritual abuse as a moral panic itself reads like moral panic. Grand narratives are a constructed warning of mass hysteria at the millennium. The lurking danger of brainwashed believers, and the lumping together of feminists and fundamentalists, is not dissimilar to evangelical assumptions that heavy metal fans, New Age hippies and crusading paedophiles are all members of the same satanic club. Recognizing elements of moral panic within the very discourse of disbelief engaged in labelling others as moral panic promoters leads me to consider that the very concept of moral panic is in need of reconsideration.

Perhaps the zenith of moral panic explanation has been reached by Elaine Showalter (1997) in *Hystories: Hysterical Epidemics and Modern Culture*. Showalter describes late-modern individuals adopting a variety of off-the-shelf fictions to explain their failure or unhappiness. In what is in part a defence of Freudian psychotherapy, Showalter argues that contemporary 'hysterical patients' blame external factors for their psychic problems from which develop 'psychological plagues' such as 'Gulf War' or 'Chronic Fatigue' syndromes, recovered memories of sexual abuse or ritual abuse. For Showalter hysteria is 'a cultural symptom of anxiety and stress' historically associated primarily with women and interpreted by feminist historians – herself included (Showalter 1987) – as a form of inarticulate protest against patriarchal control. However, in relation to contemporary hysterics such as ritual abuse survivors, Showalter believes that any acceptance of 'symptoms' being a consequence of lived experience is deplorable credulity. 'Gulf War Syndrome' and 'recovered memory' are categorized with accounts of 'alien abduction'. The questions which her analysis raises concerning the cultural meaning and appeal of exotic and paranoid fantasies, or the nature of the needs women are seeking to meet through telling such stories, are acknowledged but not answered.

In Showalter's account, hysteria is the interiorization of moral panic phenomena. It is a long way from Stan Cohen's formulation of 'moral panic' or his interest in the relationship between such panics and the operations of power:

> More fundamentally, a theory of moral panics, moral enterprise, moral crusades or moral indignation needs to relate such reactions to conflicts

of interests – at community and societal levels – and the presence of power differentials which leave some groups vulnerable to such attacks. The manipulation of appropriate symbols – the process which sustains moral campaigns, panics and crusades – is made much easier when the object of the attack is both highly visible and structurally weak.

(Cohen 1972: 198)

In his concern with responses to youth culture, Cohen renders morality a property of a middle-aged and middle-class status quo. By contrast, in the indignant crusade against 'the ritual abuse moral panic', one can observe a particular Left-libertarian morality at work. While the 'folk devils' of this counter-moral panic are evangelicals, therapists and feminists: 'visible reminders of what we should not be' (Cohen 1972: 1). Public concern is generated through a 'symbolic crusade' against 'over-zealous social workers', feminists out to destroy family life, and Christians out to protect it. It matters little that the 'folk devils' have their pitchforks aimed at each other, for 'the creation of a new fragment of the moral constitution of society' (Becker 1963: 145) arises equally well out of the moral panic – panic of the discourse of disbelief.

McRobbie and Thornton (1995) have suggested that theories about the operations of moral panics need updating to cope with changing times. In particular, they argue that the mass media have become a complex and multifaceted series of spaces within which social issues are repeatedly fought over and redefined. The term 'moral panic' is one of the tools which the media use in their definitional work, rather than just being a label applied by sociologists to censorious media campaigns. It is a term used freely to describe, or to 'put down', a plethora of issues and concerns from a range of perspectives. Cohen's (1972) analysis was based on the idea of a conservative media feeding middle-aged, middle-class anxieties about 'working-class youth', and thereby increasing demands for greater social control. McRobbie and Thornton (1995) suggest that moral panics have become more complicated, and folk devils 'not only find themselves vociferously and articulately supported in the same mass media that castigates them, but their interests are also defended by their own niche and micro-media' (McRobbie and Thornton 1995: 559). They suggest that what is needed is a much more specific and localized conception of moral panics, an understanding that these can be 'stirred up' by a variety of interested parties, and a grasp on the ways that modern 'folk devils' fight back.

I suspect that part of the power of the moral panic argument in relation to ritual abuse in Britain may have been its surprise element, for moral panics have been traditionally seen as operating straightforwardly in the interests of the established order. Concepts and categories of analysis have a history, so that the application of the label 'moral panic' ties those concerned about ritual abuse/child abuse to the forces of reaction. Feminists, despite occasional accusations of 'getting into bed with the Right' in relation to pornography, are traditionally allied with the Left. However, the divisions between radical and reactionary are by no means simple in relation to issues of sexuality. From a sexual libertarian perspective, for example, feminist concerns over child abuse can be regarded as sexually conservative, being supportive of increased state intervention and control.

Moral panics are brought into discursive existence both through the activities of 'moral entrepreneurs' stirring up concern, and through the labelling activities of moral panic hunters. Ritual abuse has been claimed by US folklorists as part of the late-modern landscape of urban myths where the tendency is to see 'everyday folk' as dupes of media-inspired nonsense. However, the designation of ritual abuse in terms of moral panic is also linked to anxieties of previous decades concerning various religious cults, whose existence was not disputed, but which were redescribed by sociologists as far less harmful or controlling than flutters of panic about 'brainwashed Moonies' suggested (Barker 1989). Within a discourse of disbelief, commentators tend to be sympathetic towards the 'harmless' activities of teenage dabblers in satanism or paid up members of the official Church of Satan.

What becomes apparent in reading numerous accounts of ritual abuse as a moral panic is the imprecision of the term and its polemical nature. The distinction is between what is conceived as intolerant, status quo discourse which stirs people into a state of 'moral panic', and 'alternative' discourses which produce only ripples of rationality: '**your** worries are evidence of "panic", **mine** are legitimate concerns' (Waddington 1986: 247, original emphasis). Ritual abuse accounts may or may not describe lived experiences, but the concept of 'moral panic' does little to explain them. It seems we know very little about how various people respond to media amplified anxieties or their rebuttals as moral panics.

False memories

What moral panic is to the social, False Memory Syndrome is to the individual. What moral panic is for the sociological element of the discourse of disbelief, false memory is to its psychological component. The concept of 'false memories' developed in relation to recovered memories of childhood sexual abuse – although the more extreme claims of ritual abuse are often used as exemplars, as they lend credibility to the idea that false memories *must* exist, for the outrageousness of such memories is evidence enough for their falsity.

Moral panic theories have been developed to explain two separate, if linked, moral panics. One is a generalized panic about child sexual abuse, or even male violence in general, in which feminists are regarded as the moral entrepreneurs; the other is concerned with (satanic) ritual abuse for which evangelical Christians are held largely responsible. Both moral panics about abuse are seen to have 'infected' therapists, who, believing that child abuse happens frequently and can be forgotten/denied/repressed, 'implant' false memories of abuse in their clients as the obvious explanation for the inexplicable distress that has brought them to seek therapy.

My intention in the second half of this chapter is to examine the arguments of False Memory Syndrome promoters and explore the political underbelly of their claims. My aim is not to prove that 'false memories' do not exist, but to show that claims about such phenomena are being used in particular ways, to particular effects, and that their ideological content is crucial to making sense of them. Although I am discussing the work of individuals, and will point up differences as well as similarities between them, my interest is in the overall nature and impact of the false memory case (see also Brown 1996). Other critics have taken a different tack: exposing the links between individuals involved in promoting the problem of false memories and pae- dophile publications (see discussion in Pope 1996), analysing the distortions and inaccuracies of supposed expert testimony given in courts (Salter 1991; Conte 1999), or conducting research on the relationship between individuals' attitudes to gender equality and their belief in the existence of a False Memory Syndrome (Kristiansen *et al*. 1996). Such approaches are also important in making sense of the False Memory Syndrome debate.

At their simplest, accusations about false memories focus not upon the therapeutic client but upon the unprofessional therapist:

'We have a large number of poorly trained, inept therapists who are propagating a cottage industry of discovering child abuse in their patients', warns New York psychiatrist Herbert Spiegal.

(*Newsweek*, 14 March 1994)

It sounds reasonable; some therapists are very good and some people have been abused, while other therapists are incompetent or on the make, and some of their clients are easily influenced. Everyone knows there are dentists who fill non-existent cavities, so of course there must be therapists who are more interested in profit than problems. However, the importance of ther- apeutic influence and excess is only one part of the 'false memory' debate. The particular memories that stand accused of falsehood are memories of childhood sexual abuse within the family, and the sexual politics of the debate lies not far beneath the surface. Psychiatrists, such as Herbert Spiegal (quoted above) – overwhelmingly men – are unlikely, almost by definition, to be 'inept' or 'poorly trained'. While the home-workers in the 'cottage industry' – overwhelmingly women – may have no more than a couple of years' training as a counsellor.

The claims around false memories operate on two levels: on the first the accusation is of political and moral corruption on the part of therapists, on the second the claims are about the scientific authenticity of memories. My counter-claim is that both levels are inevitably constructed within a political praxis.

The **pendulum swings**

The False Memory Syndrome Foundation was set up in the USA in March 1992, in Britain Adult Children Accusing Parents (ACAP), now renamed the British False Memory Society (BFMS), in 1993.[8] Why did the process of remembering sexual abuse and seeking therapy suddenly become such a public contro- versy? The answer may lie in the move into the public spheres of litigation and legislation in mid-1980s USA. In some states, statutes of limitations have been extended to allow civil and criminal prosecutions to take place as long as 30 years after the alleged crime.[9] Judith Herman described the shift thus:

> Sexual abuse of children was once the perfect crime. As a perpetrator, you were fairly guaranteed never to be caught or held accountable for your crime. Women, for the first time have begun using the courts to hold perpetrators accountable, and we see them fighting back.
>
> (Herman 1993: 6)

The move into the public sphere involves a crossover from therapeutic into legal discourse, and the nature of what counts as truth and evidence is different in each. In order to be successful as an advocacy group for parents (mostly fathers) who were being sued for sexual abuse by adult children (almost exclusively daughters), these organizations had to construct an alternative hypothesis to explain the accusations. False Memory Syndrome allows the 'victims' to stay 'victims', not of incestuous fathers, but of unscrupulous therapists. It is the truth claims of therapeutic discourse that are most directly under attack. The FMSF parents consistently describe their daughters as high achievers, and their family life as close and loving. Some psychiatrists take a different line and tend to make generalized diagnoses of borderline personality disorder (Guze 1993), characterizing 'alleged' survivors as lying, inconsistent, unstable and antisocial. The difficulty is that while child abuse is said to have identifiable psychological effects, those same 'symptoms' can be used as grounds for scepticism about people's stories of how they got that way.

From the outset, press reports were generally sympathetic to the FMS position. They tended to highlight the 'new victims': respectable, middle-class parents whose lives had been torn apart by the accusations of an adult daughter (Gerrie 1993; Grant 1993; Hoggart 1994; Purves 1994). Feminism was frequently scapegoated as the originator of the problem:

> In the past decade, new attention to abuse was fuelled by some feminists who worked hard to demonstrate that incest is more prevalent than previously supposed and that assisted memory recall is an essential tool in exposing perpetrators.
>
> (*Newsweek*, 14 March 1994)

> Among the problems generated by the proliferation of new 'therapists' in America is the question of how to address the often solicited and mistakenly elicited revelation of child sexual abuse with the concomitant destruction of the nuclear family.
>
> (Harold Lief, *Psychiatric News*, 21 August 1992)

Founding members of the FMSF established a journal, *Issues in Child Abuse Accusations*.[10] In this the underlying sexual politics are more explicitly expressed. For example, the psychiatrist, Richard Gardner, has argued that false accusations are rooted in women's anger with men in general and the fact that women therapists were often abused themselves (Gardner 1992).

That some therapists treat some patients for free is here given as evidence of their fanaticism (by contrast with the accusation that the 'child abuse industry' exploits 'survivors' for profit), as is the fact that many therapists believe that all sex between adults and children is 'unhealthy': 'no matter how short, no matter how tender, loving and non-painful'. These texts set up feminists as popular scapegoats by appealing to existing stereotypes of vengeful, lying and castrating women. In her book on 'the abuse industry', Goodyear-Smith (1993: 32) suggests that the women's movement can be seen as: 'groups of self-defined victims obsessed with codes of political correctness and focused on blame'. 'Survivors' are characterized as bored, inadequate and spoilt, seeking to evade responsibility for their own failures and disappointments:

> For those plagued by anything from serious mental disorders that cannot presently be effectively treated to those haunted by the simple feeling that their lives are not as fulfilling as those of the people around them, the message that they are controlled by subterranean forces carries a type of absolution: the patient is forgiven the sins she appears to have committed against herself.
>
> (Ofshe and Watters 1994: 48)

False Memory Syndrome is the adult version of the 'manipulated child responding to leading questions':

> To the growing number of children trained to say and believe things which never happened is now added a growing number of adults, usually women, being trained to say and believe that they have 'unblocked' memories of childhood sexual abuse.
>
> (Coleman 1992: 12)

The difference, of course, is the matter of memory.

The way in which claims to science as the rebuttal of feminism are entwined with the construction of (feminist) therapists as folk devils is clearly illustrated by the best known of the recent 'false memory' books, Richard Ofshe and Ethan Watters (1994) *Making Monsters: False Memories, Psychotherapy and Sexual Hysteria*:

> Recovering memories of abuse has proved a powerful metaphor for the larger goal of exposing the unfairness of patriarchal family structures and of a male-dominated society ... As recovered memory therapy became a metaphor for feminism, defense of the therapy became synonymous with defense of the women's movement.
>
> ... [not] brave healers but professionals who have built a pseudoscience out of an unfounded consensus about how the mind reacts to sexual trauma. In the process they have slipped the ties that bind their professions to scientific method and sound research. Free from any burden of proof, these therapists have created an Alice-in-Wonderland world in which opinion, metaphor, and ideological preference substitute for

objective evidence. While claiming to uncover the truth of their clients' past, these therapists have pursued a treatment regime that persuades clients to accept hypnotically generated images, gut feelings, dreams and imaginings as valid memories.

(Ofshe and Watters 1994: 5–11)

An **analytic alternative**

Other FMS defenders place more of the responsibility on to the clients of therapy. George Ganaway is a psychiatrist who specializes in treating dissociative disorders, and a leading clinical advocate of the unreliability of memory. He has promoted a number of different hypotheses to account for untrue allegations. At the first national False Memory Syndrome Foundation Conference in 1993, Ganaway explained false accusation by an adult daughter as a delayed adolescent rebellion. He describes such women as unhealthily close to their families and unconsciously angry at their parents for not letting them go. Lacking self-confidence, such a woman

> displaces her dependency onto the therapist. He or she becomes the ideal substitute mother figure, who will be all-accepting, all-believing, all-approving, who will offer the patient a mechanism by which she can finally separate from her parents . . . the belief that her parents committed such heinous crimes that her previously unacceptable and troubling anger towards them is now explained and is totally justifiable.
>
> (Ganaway 1993: 5)

In two earlier papers, he emphasized the part that might be played by 'screen memories' in accounts of satanic ritual abuse where an intolerable memory, perhaps of incest, might be 'screened' by a more terrifying, but paradoxically, more tolerable tale of witnessing a satanic sacrifice (Ganaway 1990, 1991). The difficulty with this is that few ritual abuse survivors claim *any* tolerable aspects to their childhood, and therefore have nothing to 'screen'.

There is a strong whiff of paternalism in these accounts. Women in therapy are described as weak, childlike and therefore unreliable. The truth of their lives is not in what they say, which is 'false consciousness', but lies buried in the unconscious. In Ganaway's accounts of false memory, the well-trained therapist is the interpreter of truth. Mind and memory are so treacherous and deceptive that lay people should not approach them unaccompanied. This is the position of what Ernest Gellner (1985) has called 'shaft-watching psychoanalysts'. It sits somewhat uncomfortably alongside the powerful FMS claims to the territory of common sense.

A **science** of **memory**

Elizabeth Loftus is an experimental psychologist who takes a less extreme position in support of a False Memory Syndrome, and makes this a feature of the reasonableness of her case. In the introduction to her book on the subject (Loftus and Ketchum 1994) Loftus writes of the shock at being labelled the 'Evil Paedophile Psychologist from Hell' in a highly political and acrimonious debate. Her stated aim is to side-step the politics and place the debate firmly in the realm of 'value-free science'. Her argument concerns the lack of proof that 'repression' exists against what she believes to be compelling evidence of the constructed nature of memory. Loftus insists that the false memory debate is a debate about *memory*, not about ideology, sexual abuse or 'the hard won gains of the women's movement'.

In the light of this, it is interesting that the book itself is written in an anecdotal, journalistic style, with each chapter unfolding the story of a case known to the author (often one in which she appeared as an expert witness for the defence). However, it is 'the other side' and its concepts that Loftus berates as unscientific; indeed, in her characterization 'repression' becomes a mytho-poetic concept:

> 'Repression' . . . The word whispers of dark secrets and buried treasures, of rooms filled with cobwebs and dust, with a strange unearthly rustling in the corners. Repression is the most haunting and romantic of concepts in the psychology of memory: *Something happens*, something so shocking and frightful that the mind short-circuits and the normal workings of memory go seriously awry. An entire memory, or perhaps a jagged piece of memory, is split off and hidden away. Where? No-one knows, but we can imagine the crackle of electricity and the blue sparks of neurons firing as memory is pushed underground, into the furthest and most inaccessible corners of consciousness. There it stays for years, decades, perhaps forever, isolated and protected in a near-dead, dormant state. Removed from the fever of consciousness, it sleeps.
>
> Time passes. And then *something happens*. Sunlight slices through trees. A black leather belt lies curled up, snakelike, on the floor. A word or phrase is dropped, or a strange but familiar silence falls. And suddenly the memory rises from the deep, a perfectly preserved entity drifting up from the still waters of a once frozen pond.
>
> (Loftus and Ketchum 1994: 49, italicization in original)

It is a great cinematic portrait, with a touch of both sci-fi and horror genres. It sets up the otherness of the opposition: dramatic, romantic, literary, in opposition to the everyday, straightforward, science-plus-common-sense image of Loftus's own position. It is not that there is no real issue about the meaning and implications of a term like 'repression', but at the same time as pointing to this, Loftus constructs a very particular reading of the problem. It is interesting that later in the book Loftus provides a facsimile of a conversation with Ellen Bass – one of the authors of *The Courage to Heal*: (Bass and Davies 1988) a book which has been a key focus of the false memory controversy – in which Bass suggests that they drop the term 're-pression' as a red herring and talk instead about forgetting and remembering. Loftus replies:

but that's simple forgetting and remembering, it's not this magic homunculus in the unconscious mind that periodically ventures out into the light of day, grabs hold of a memory, scurries underground, and stores it away in a dark corner of the insensible self, waiting a few decades before digging it up and tossing it back out again.

(Loftus and Ketchum 1994: 214)

I have considerable sympathy with these concerns about the concept of repression as an almost magical 'trick of the mind' and I am equally doubtful about the concretization of other metaphors for mental life (see Chapter 7 for further discussion). However, Loftus does not allow that an understanding of 'repression' as a far more social, intentional, deliberate or motivated form of forgetting, such as that she imputes to her reading of Freud (Strachey 1957), might be equally effective in keeping certain knowledge 'out of mind',[11] or that it is with a broad, 'everyday' understanding of 'the repressed' that Bass and many other therapists actually work:

as I listen to patients talking about their experience of forgetting and remembering traumatic childhood events, what is striking is that the amnesia often does seem to be based on a partially conscious attempt not to think about something awful, or upon a wish to deny that something happened . . . The phenomenology of remembering and forgetting is not of some mysterious process completely beyond consciousness.

(Mollon 1996: 84)

Elizabeth Loftus is important as the memory expert whose work is most frequently quoted in support of the FMS position. In an article in *American Psychologist* (Loftus 1993) she lays out her doubts concerning repression and the accuracy of memory. Unlike some of the FMS psychiatrists who are sceptical that memories of repeated sexual abuse can ever be repressed, here, Loftus questions only its *frequency* in relation to child abuse, and the reliability of memories that are reported to have been once repressed. This is a quantitatively different position from that which she takes in her book.

In questioning the frequency of claims to repressed child abuse memories, Loftus refers to three studies. In a study of 100 women substance abusers in a New York hospital programme (Loftus *et al.* 1994), 50 were survivors of child sexual abuse, of these 18 per cent claimed to have repressed memories of their abuse at some point. A study of adult clinical clients claimed repression in 59 per cent of cases. The difference suggests to Loftus that repression could have been 'suggested by therapists' in some of these cases. The difference could of course have numerous explanations. For example, if repression of memories and substance abuse are both strategies to block out distress that some survivors use, it could equally well be that successful 'repressers' do not need to use drugs or alcohol on top, and are therefore less numerous in the substance abusers sample, or that forgetting or repressing is a strategy more often adopted by the same women who are likely to seek psychotherapy (primarily white and middle class) than heavy drug or alcohol use.

Loftus also refers to a longitudinal study by Linda Williams (1994), which followed up 100 women known to have been abused 17 years previously. Of these, 38 per cent were amnesic or chose not to speak of the abuse when interviewed, and another 10 per cent reported having forgotten the abuse at some time in the past. (Loftus fails to mention the very high levels of correspondence with the original records of the memories of those women who did recall their abuse on follow-up.) This study supports the view that repression is most common when abuse began in early childhood or was of a violent and sadistic nature. This is significant in that much of the FMS claim to common sense rests upon the idea that if something *really bad* happens to you, you do not forget it.

In this text, research is claimed as supporting evidence for the false memory position; indeed it is the starting place for the author's claims. This 'works' in spite of the somewhat weak support the research actually lends, by virtue of the way it interlocks with the case from 'common sense'.

Comparing like with like

The claim to 'common sense', in arguments about repression of memories, generally fails to compare like with like, and shows little familiarity with the child abuse literature:

> It is common to see analogies drawn between Vietnam war veterans and the incest survivors ... do they share in common the use of 'massive repression' as a mechanism for coping? If so, how do we explain findings obtained with children who witness parental murder and other atrocities? In one study (Malmquist 1986), not a single child aged 5 to 10 years who had witnessed the murder of a parent repressed the memory. Rather, they were continually flooded with pangs of emotion about the murder and preoccupation with it.
>
> (Loftus 1993: 520)

It is not difficult to explain the findings by looking at the likely differences between the two experiences. The child who has witnessed a parent's murder is not likely to face much denial of his experience. There will be no school, and a number of police officers and journalists. Everyone will listen to his story with belief. Nightmares and tantrums will be regarded sympathetically and appointments to see the priest or therapist arranged. The murder will be a family and community 'event' and the child will be part of a larger experience. The funeral will probably be followed by a trial and the child may testify. With luck there will be the resolution of a conviction, followed by a period of mourning and recovery.

We can compare such an experience with that of a child raped by her grandad every time he baby-sits for nearly four years. She never tells anyone. Everybody likes grandad. He says it is her fault he does these things, and if anyone finds out she will be sent away to a children's home. He buys her presents and calls her his 'special girl'. She has no words to describe what he does to her, even to herself.

In Loftus' argument the strategy of collapsing together the experience of child abuse and that of witnessing a murder serves a secondary purpose. The connection serves to suggest that abuse, like murder, is a rare incident of extraordinary terror – the sort of thing no one is likely to forget but which is also unlikely to be happening as often as is claimed.

The FMS claim concerning the ease with which entirely fictitious memories can be implanted frequently returns to the evidence of an 'experiment' in which 24 subjects, all friends and relatives, were led by the reports of an older family member to believe that they had been lost in a shopping mall at the age of 5 (Loftus 1994a; Loftus and Pickrell 1995). A total of 25 per cent of subjects claimed to remember, fully or partially, the false event. When told at a debriefing that one of the four events their relatives had prompted them to remember may have been false, 79 per cent correctly chose the 'lost in the mall' event as the false one. Loftus claims that these cases provide proof that it is possible to create false memories. However, the experimental circumstances are very different from 'remembering' sexual abuse: the case was made by a trusted relative who claimed to have been present at the time; the scenario is an everyday one and there is little emotional significance to the event. Loftus' claim is to the 'proofs' of science as opposed to the anecdotes of therapy. It is therefore interesting that testifying in a court case the same year, Loftus admitted that she had thrown out the first part of her 'lost in the mall' study when the student she was supervising left the project and its paperwork in disarray (Loftus 1994b).

Conclusion

Despite its much-vaunted desire for 'truth' and 'science' to combat the irrational emotionalism of the 'child abuse lobby', the FMSF has found itself with postmodern allies. It is, after all, one of the defining tenets of postmodernism that all stories are contested and that memory-making is a narrative process. More generally, sociologists 'know' that audience and context, later experience and ideological commitment, have powerful effects on the nature of memories. We 'know' that therapists are both authority figures and role models, and that both inequality and idealization affect therapeutic outcomes. What we do not know is *how much* these influences and reworkings distance our current accounts from our past experiences. I believe that this is an empirical rather than an epistemological question and one on which future research is vital.

While they accuse the 'survivor industry' of being a money-making racket, the false memory 'experts' discussed in this chapter appear regularly as expert witnesses in the defence of those accused of child abuse. In 1997, fees were as high as $350 per hour. Such facts are crucial in making sense of the politics and economics of a supposedly neutral 'scientific' debate.

Throughout my own research, I have been aware of the impact of the discourse of belief on survivors of ritual abuse and their supporters:

> Our close friends, neighbours and relatives, even my GP and employer, are bombarded with FMS literature which has done considerable damage

with letters saying I am mentally sick. This means I am constantly having to defend myself against the abuse for which I should have no guilt.
(Letter to *Accuracy about Abuse*, 10 March 1996)

Books and papers can be weapons that hurt and abuse. The materiality of
their effects cannot be separated from the contents which I have unpicked in
this chapter. Cases are reported in the press and impact on survivors and
therapists:

> Knowledge of cases like Ramona would put clients on notice that abus-
> ive parents could sue their therapists and possibly gain access to confi-
> dential information. No client could feel completely safe sharing private
> thoughts under these circumstances.
> (Bowman and Meertz 1996: 638)

'Moral panic' and 'false memory' are two faces of the discourse of disbelief.
From different directions they accuse people of having imagined childhoods
involving rape, lies, cruelty, and terror, when nothing of the sort occurred.
While I have raised some doubts about both conceptualizations of the 'un-
truth' of ritual abuse, the attitudes towards a whole range of women (feminists, survivors, foster mothers and social workers) which they embody, and
the textual strategies they employ, this does not mean that I dismiss their
concerns out of hand. Accounts of organized involvement in ritual abuse
arrived in Britain before the first complex child protection cases involving
abusers within and beyond an extended family came to public attention.
It seems to me feasible on the basis of the talk and behaviour of young
children that one *could* be mistaken for the other. Nor do I doubt that
entirely fictitious 'memories' can emerge in a therapist's office whether as
the product of an elaborate 'folie à deux', highly suggestive or bullying
'therapy', or out of a client's desperate desire for attention and meaning.
On the merits of the evidence and after detailed attention had been paid to
the accounts of all of those involved, I would be happy to concede cases to
such causes. My argument is with moral panic and false memory as blanket
explanations for all accounts of ritual abuse without any attempt to pay
serious attention to what those who identify themselves as survivors have to
say for themselves.

In this chapter, I have suggested that the discourse of disbelief has much
in common with the 'moral panic' discourse it opposes, and that the same
kinds of questions it asks of those who believe in the reality or possibility of
(satanic) ritual abuse can be asked of its promoters also. It is my contention that
the 'discourse of disbelief' serves a motivated course of social action, supports
the interests of particular actors and the silencing of others. I have been
concerned to expose for scrutiny the textual strategies of those engaged in
constructing a sceptical reading of ritual abuse and thereby to open up the
possibility of other readings.[12] When Dorothy Smith (1990b) showed how the
'K is mentally ill' narrative made itself plausible, the incisions made in the course
of her dissection 'bled' the alternative story that 'K' was the scapegoat in the
triad of flatmates. In my operations upon the discourse of disbelief I trust that

an equivalent alternative reading has become possible. At the same time, I recognize that even in the harried and dissected form in which it appears here, the discourse of disbelief will sound a powerful note of cynicism throughout this book – a questioning counterpoint to my analysis of my interviewees' life-stories.

Notes

1 *Geraldo Rivera Special*, transmitted 25 October 1988, CBS; *Dispatches*, 'Listen to the Children', transmitted 3 October 1990, Channel 4; *Dispatches*, 'Beyond Disbelief', transmitted 19 February 1992, Channel 4.
2 *ChildLine* is a national, confidential helpline for children in trouble or danger, founded in 1986 after a BBC television series *Childwatch* presented by Esther Rantzen attracted thousands of calls.
3 David Hechler locates the 'start-date' of the backlash in the USA as 1994, and its location as Jordon. A complex case prosecuted by a woman attorney with a high profile in 'going after' child abusers involved over twenty people allegedly involved in two overlapping 'sex rings'. There were numerous ritualistic accusations in Jordon which were absent in the Cleveland case, the 'anal dilation test' relied upon by Cleveland paediatricians had no role in Jordon, and cooperation between police and social services did not break down in the latter as it did in the former. What the cases have in common is that they took place in small communities, were led by 'crusading' women, were criticized for their investigatory practice in relation to children, and are remembered as witch-hunts against the innocent, rather than flawed investigations which failed to protect abused children.
4 Operation Rescue is a national organization campaigning against abortion and abortion clinics. Many of these have led to criminal harassment charges. Other campaigns, committed by supporters of Operation Rescue but not condoned by it, have led to the murder of doctors who conduct abortions.
5 Victor (1993) cites Spanos *et al.* (1985).
6 The distinction implicit in the work of La Fontaine is between child abuse that is *ritualized*, either for the purposes of frightening the children or for the pleasure of the adults, and the performance of religious/magical (specifically satanic) rituals which involve the abuse of children. This is a sophisticated distinction that does not appear in most of the disbelief literature.
7 La Fontaine draws on the work of Trevor-Roper ([1967] 1990), Thomas (1971) and Macfarlane (1970) which is resolutely agnostic about the existence of actual witches in the period of the European witch-hunts and dismisses Carlo Ginzburg's (1990) challenges to this orthodoxy. The perspective was inspired by Evans-Pritchard's view that witchcraft accusations among the Azande provided ways of channelling social tensions. La Fontaine ignores Evans-Pritchard's equally interesting writing on magical performance and power: here he described witch doctors being trained to fake supernatural events such as psychic surgery for example (Evans-Pritchard 1937). However, recent 'microhistories' written from different perspectives have reopened the case for examining the folk beliefs and magical practices of some of those accused of witchcraft (see Behringer 1998).
8 A shorter version of this section has been published in *Feminism and Psychology* (Scott 1997a).
9 Statutes of limitations define the amount of time that may elapse between a crime being committed and a prosecution occurring.

10 The editors of *Issues in Child Abuse Accusations*, Ralph Underwager and Hollida Wakefield, have been subject to a detailed critique by Anna Salter (1991), which questions the honesty and accuracy of their expert testimony in child abuse cases.

11 For a review of the research on the forgetting/repression of sexual abuse see Williams and Banyard (1997). Recent research in Britain also suggests the variety of ways that survivors may 'block out' memories of abuse (Andrews *et al.* 2000).

12 I am not alone in adopting such an approach. Detailed analysis of the 'expert' testimony of two founders of the FMSF has been undertaken by Salter (1991); Conte (1999) has dissected the expert testimony of Elizabeth Loftus in a New Hampshire sexual abuse trial and numerous reviewers (see Butler 1995) have exposed the omissions and deceptions in the case studies of Ofshe and Watters (1994).

3 | The **nature** of the **beast**: **pornography**, **prostitution** and **everyday life**

Attempts to define ritual abuse have focused on those elements that are presumed to differentiate it from other forms of familial or organized child abuse: the use of religious/magical practices and symbols, the occult beliefs of abusers, and the sadistic ceremonies performed by cult members. Attempts to discredit survivors' accounts have focused on similar features. The stories of survivors are more complex than definitions of ritual abuse suggest and include descriptions of abuse across a range of familial, commercial and ritual contexts. Those women whose life-histories provide the basis of this book described childhood neglect, cruelty, sexual exploitation and perverse abuse. They described how as children they had regarded sexual abuse – and a measure of everyday violence – as perfectly normal. (Indeed, two interviewees emphasized this point by telling me that a day without abuse had made them extremely anxious – certain that something particularly awful must be just around the corner.) However, they also described experiences that were outside the everyday: experiences of abuse which had been especially terrifying and traumatic and for which they had later adopted the label 'ritual abuse'. Despite their identification as survivors of ritual abuse, only a small part of the life-histories they recounted to me concerned rituals, and each woman emphasized that as far as she was concerned, it was the *abuse* with which her childhood had been saturated that really mattered; the fact that some of this had occurred in the context of sadistic, occult rituals was of secondary importance.[1] Following this lead, I focus in this chapter on the abuse that interviewees described as taking place within the extended family, abuse in the form of prostitution and involved in the production of pornography. In doing so, I consider how far their accounts support or contradict what little is known about these 'other' forms of abuse more generally.

Difficulties of definition

A serendipitous finding, reported by Gallagher *et al.* (1996) in their survey of cases of organized abuse dealt with by police and social services, was that 44 per cent of respondents found that none of the predefined questionnaire categories fitted the case they had dealt with, or they were uncertain how best to classify it. The largest single category of cases was of family-based abuse which, although 'based' in a family, might involve abuse by non-family members. (This, however, became clear only after researchers undertook their own file searches in a number of regions, suggesting that such cases were not readily considered as cases of 'organized abuse' by police and social workers.) In other complex cases, definitions associated with discrete contexts such as a 'paedophile ring' or 'commercial prostitution' were rejected, although the descriptions then might include elements associated with either of these. Recent discussions under the newly adopted umbrella term of 'organized abuse' have been heavily focused on problems of definition (see Bibby 1996). They have attempted to define a key factor that would permit a clear distinction between 'organized' and 'non-organized' abuse: a factor such as the number of victims or perpetrators, the involvement of non-family members, the amount of planning involved, or the context in which abuse takes place. Such debates are probably fairly unproductive given our current state of knowledge; issues of definition may be usefully resolved only through the detailed analysis of experiential accounts. The problem with imposing definitions prematurely is the impact they may have in terms of limiting the field to be investigated or the nature of interventions into complex cases.

A slightly different problem of classification exists in relation to the accounts discussed in this chapter. To refer to the survivors in this study as survivors of ritual abuse distorts their experience by focusing on only one strand of their reports of abuse. Doing so may magnify the import of the most bizarre of their remembrances – it may also discredit their life-stories *in toto*. It is therefore important to undertake two tasks: to explore the similarities and differences between these accounts and what little is known about various forms of organized abuse, and to examine the accounts in terms of their internal separation/integration of different strands.

Research on organized abuse

With the exception of the survey by Gallagher *et al.* (1996), all of the extant studies of organized abuse have focused on a previously defined form: sex rings (Burgess 1984; Wild and Wynne 1986), child prostitution (Silbert and Pines 1981; Sereny 1984), poly-incestuous families (Faller 1991) and child pornography (Tate 1990; Svedin and Back 1996). However, what these studies have in common is the evidence that emerges – often unsolicited – of the interlinked nature of different forms of abuse within the experience of child victims. At the very least, incestuous abuse increases children's vulnerability to other forms of sexual exploitation. At the most extreme, it provides a structured training for children in performing for clients or cameras. Pornography is made and used to coerce and condition children to further abuse, as a record of abuse for 'collectors' and as a commercial enterprise – in some cases the same tapes or photographs could serve all these ends. Indeed, Campagna and Poffenberger (1988) conceptualize child pornography as being a by-product of abuse and prostitution. These studies show that while some abusers are relatively isolated individuals, recruiting children into a 'solo ring' and making pornography for their own consumption, others are well connected and that higher levels of networking correlate with more severe abuse of their victims. Wild and Wynne (1986) reported that five of the thirty-two rings they studied prostituted children to men outside the group, including to group 'parties' where the children would suffer multiple rape. Burgess (1984) found that the production of pornography was a core activity of most sex rings but that 'syndicated' groups used video as well as stills cameras, 'exchanged' children more, and tended to involve higher levels of sado-masochism. Bagley (1997), reporting on Canadian research, also identified a strong relationship between sex rings involving prostitution to strangers, sado-masochistic practices and the use of hard drugs. They also reported that, in rings involving very young children, teenage girls frequently acted as 'chief lieutenants', while the appearance of an older girl 'leading' younger children is common in child pornography.

Studies agree on the lack of disclosure by children involved in organized abuse, with different authors emphasizing their 'loyalty' to their abusers or the silencing effects of their terror and shame. Svedin and Back (1996) describe the absence of spontaneous revelations by children exploited in pornography such that only occasional police identification from photographs and films exposes particular victims.

Most research on organized abuse has been concerned to develop a typology – in order to classify cases according to certain features. The difficulty is that the typology has been based largely on cases that have become known to the police, the majority of which involve perpetrators 'recruiting' older children. The alternative of beginning with the experience of victims of various forms of organized abuse has rarely been explored. The accounts of my interviewees fill in something of the phenomenological experience of the most organized and severe forms of abuse identified in studies of sex rings, child prostitution and pornography, particularly where these involve very young children.

Limitations of the research

The research on organized abuse is 'thin' in two respects. First, there is very little of it, and second, very little of what there is provides the kind of 'thick description' that helps us grasp the nature of the experiences, or the meanings and relationships of those involved. Few researchers in the field have been concerned to allow either victims or perpetrators to tell their own stories. One exception is Catherine Itzin (1996), whose work on pornography makes considerable use of survivors' accounts. The immediate effect is to query the categories into which 'types' of sexual abuse are often divided:

> My first conscious memories are from when my sister was born when I was two-and-a-half; I was sent to my grandparents and stayed with them. My abuse started there. I have a memory then of my grandfather holding me, putting his fingers into me . . . I was abused by my mother's younger brothers – my uncles – when they were baby-sitting, and also by the older aunt. They told me that they'd been taught by their father, my grandfather . . . The physical abuse [in addition to the sexual abuse by her uncles] included needles put under my toenails and fingernails, being tied up, being frightened . . .
> In my early childhood, in addition to what was going on at home – the incest as I later learned it was – I'd be taken to places for group sex, group pornography and group prostitution . . . They go together, and I was prostituted to make the pornography. But also I was just prostituted, sold for sex. Sometimes, there was a combination of prostitution and filming. Whereas the pornography was set up for pornography, prostitution was set up so you could be sold for sex, but sometimes filmed. This film wasn't necessarily sold, it was for the individuals that were there, as distinct from the pornography which was to make pornography for sale.
>
> ('Alice' quoted in Itzin 1996: 175–80)

In many respects, 53-year-old Alice's account of a multigenerational abusive family involved in commercial prostitution and pornography is extremely similar indeed to those of the women over 40 years of age interviewed for this book. In her account, as in those of most of my interviewees, the family is the key site from which other forms of abuse are organized, and children are prepared within the family for commercial exploitation.

Weaving ritual in

Unlike Alice, the women I interviewed did not stop at describing how intra-familial and commercial forms of abuse were interwoven in their childhood. Rather they tried to describe the multiple forms that their abuse had taken and the way in which these were variously enmeshed with or semi-detached from the occult beliefs and ritual practices of their primary abusers. In analysing their accounts, I have been mindful of a hypothesis suggested by the research of La Fontaine (1994) and Weir and Wheatcroft (1995) into child protection cases where ritual abuse had been alleged. They suggested that in many such cases *sexual abuse* had probably occurred within an extended family based network, but that allegations of *ritual abuse* were sometimes the result of leading questions and misinterpretation by social workers and others caught up in the 'moral panic'. Although similar research has not been conducted with adult survivors, it has been suggested that a similar dynamic might occur in cases wherein extremely vulnerable and highly dissociative people encounter stories of *ritual abuse* through the media, or from discussion with therapists, and incorporate 'occult embellishments' into their narratives of abuse. Analysis of survivors' life-stories can neither demonstrate nor disprove when or if this may be the case. It can, however, illuminate the connections which appear to hold together 'a life' as well as those that suggest similarities between lives. Taking survivors' accounts seriously can help us decide whether lives such as they describe could conceivably have been lived.

Domestic abuse

The collective picture that emerges from the life-history interviews I conducted is of family lives suffused with violence, cruelty and sexual abuse (the exception to this being Beth, who I discuss below). Intergenerational and lateral sexual abuse as described in Faller's (1991) research into 'poly-incestuous families' was routine and involved parents, grandparents, siblings, aunts and uncles. Some interviewees described abusive relationships over three or four generations, involving those who had married into the family as well as blood relations:

> *You said that there was also abuse by your uncle at this time?*
>
> Yes, that's my dad's brother-in-law. He . . . because especially once I was at boarding school he used to have to pick us up from the airport and stay over night and going back to school and things like that; he used to abuse me then a fair bit . . . My uncle, in many ways, was like my dad. He'd come across as a very nice bloke, good laugh and a joke. They managed to do what my parents had done, build up an image of everything's fine, nothing's wrong . . . 'we're the perfect family'. My uncle has a daughter and four grandchildren – at least one I know that's been abused. I'm almost certain he's abused his own daughter, he abused my sister, he abused my dad . . . very much into abusing people.
>
> *He abused your dad when he was young?*
>
> Yeah, from what I can gather from what my sister's told me, from when he was fairly young until his teens. Quite badly abused my dad. Because of the 18 years [between them].
>
> (Kate)

In the case of middle-class families such as Kate's, relatives might be geographically distant. Despite this, contact tended to be maintained and new abusing relationships established just as these seem to be among sexually abusive extended families living in a deprived neighbourhood (see Cleaver and Freeman 1996).

Interviewees emphasized the 'ordinary', routine nature of sexual abuse within their families. Such abuse was so 'everyday' as to be barely worth mentioning:

> Yeah, I can remember what I call 'normal' abuse . . . which basically didn't have any sort of cult meaning, it was just my father. That was pretty much a regular occurrence as much as eating my meals actually. I can't really distinguish particularly . . . It would happen at home or he used to take me for walks in the park. He used to say we're going shopping and in the car park . . . anywhere really . . . I don't think it really bothered him at all.
>
> (Kate)

Interviewees assumed that abuse had begun in infancy: 'before I could re-member', and most had memories of routine abuse before they started school:

> What used to happen was I used to get a bath every morning, well the first time . . . it could be the afternoon . . . As soon as I saw my mum each day I would get a bath. And my mum used to pay particular attention to my private parts. She would wash me quite roughly and she would insert her fingers inside me. Sometimes my dad would help, and he would do the same thing. That must have gone on since I was born really. I do remember my dad would quite often insert things inside me, his hand was a favourite. It got to be normal, I used to just relax and it didn't hurt as much. It was so ordinary, I didn't think: 'O, my God, what are they doing?' That went on till I went to school.
>
> (Sinead)

> my sister and I used to be bathed on a Sunday night, and Mum would keep her in the bathroom and Dad would disappear off with me. That's the first clear memories that I have.
>
> *Where would he take you?*
>
> The living room. So I remember sexual abuse from being 3. And I suppose it started gradually and just . . . got worse.
>
> *Do you mind me asking you what he did to you when you were that small?*
>
> No, [*sigh*] Oh, various things. Well I suppose his speciality was that . . . we had a coal fire, and he used to take the poker out of the companion set and use that, or his fingers, or anything that was lying around basically. I also remember him putting his penis in my mouth, that's the earliest time I can ever remember him doing that. That's all there was to that . . . at that stage.
>
> (Kathleen)

For most interviewees, routine sexual abuse was combined with physical 'punishment' and degradation:

Sometimes . . . I can remember being put into baths of really hot water and really being quite badly burned. And . . . being pulled up the stairs by my hair, that was quite a frequent one. Burns, they don't smoke but they used to buy cigarettes . . . I suppose it was rare that it would start and stop with the physical assault, it would usually lead onto a sexual assault after. Or it would be sparked off by Mum and Dad having an argument, then they would come and get me. That was a quite well established pattern.

And how often . . .

It would be at least two nights in the week that would just involve Mum and Dad. It could be on occasions, nightly, but it wasn't always like that.

. . .

There was always violence of some description. It usually started with a beating and ended up with a sexual assault, but after that you would be confined to the room, tied to the bed, not allowed [?], not allowed food, not allowed anything to drink, not allowed to go to the toilet . . . or . . . I mean . . . one of . . . my dad quite often . . . when I was not allowed out of my room . . . his favourite was to come and urinate on me. I think that just about covers it.

(Kathleen)

He also used to do nice things to me like pissing on me when I was in the bath, and putting my head down the toilet and putting faeces in my mouth. Nice, you know, nice stuff like that. . . . I hate him . . . And um, in that room I can remember him and my uncle when one of them would be at one end and, holding my shoulders down while the other was . . . One time he put a pencil inside me. They put the pencil into my navel as well. Sometimes I can't even bear clothing touching my stomach. There are times when I can't wear a skirt because I can't abide the feeling of anything in the vicinity of my navel because it's one of the things they did to torture me. They had these yellow pencils that Dad got from his work.

(Gillean)

Such abuses were combined with emotional deprivation and neglect. Interviewees from both impoverished and affluent homes described being frequently left alone, as very young children they were often tied to their beds for long periods of time and suffered from cold and hunger:

That house was freezing cold, always. But I just got used to that, and in the end I was just completely unable to differentiate between hot and cold, because my bedroom at home as well . . . I was the only one . . . I didn't have any blankets on my bed at all. And you could get . . . do you remember when you had bottles of sterilized milk? You could get a bottle of sterilized milk and the top would be that thick, so it would come off, and that's how cold it was. Frost on the windows, thick frost. And I'd be sent to school in a pair of 50p plastic sandals from Woolworth's, even in the snow. And sent out with short sleeves on, things like that, so you just got used to the cold, you just didn't feel it. But my brothers on the other hand had blankets in their bedrooms. They were treated differently by both my parents and my grandparents, they used to always get fed properly as well.

(Sophie)

Sophie was one of two interviewees who came from extended working-class families, known to both police and social services. They lived on deprived urban estates and had irregular employment. Sexual abuse was just one aspect of a routinely violent home:

My brothers . . . [*pause*] . . . I would say Lee was the worst . . . Lee used to share my bedroom when I was tiny, and he saw my father abusing me, he saw my mother abusing me, I'm talking about in the house not in the woods, and so that was his prerogative, that's what he could do. And when I started secondary school he was in the fifth year . . . he could smoke, you weren't allowed to smoke, and he used to stub out cigarettes on my back. I mean he used a pump, he used a bicycle pump one day and put it up my bum. That's what he was like. Just an evil bastard. And my parents used to go out all the time during the week. They never had any money but they could always go out every night of the week. And he used to tie me up, literally tie me up and throw me over the settee . . . The neighbours used to bang on the wall when I'd scream 'cos they could hear everything . . . They were just evil bastards, they just used to fight. I mean Lee and Mark they broke the front room window about five times. They used to knock each other through it. It wasn't just like normal rough and tumble, it was a lot more aggressive. And some of the things . . . My mother, my mother used to be there in the front room when Lee was um . . . We used to have a settee, this orange and brown settee, and like we had a television and we'd all be sat in the room and he'd sort of like put his hand up my skirt, and I'd be sort of like kicking him, but my mother would see it and then she'd come over and slap me over the head because I was trying to like stop him doing it.

(Sophie)

Despite this apparent chaos, Sophie – along with interviewees from more orderly and apparently respectable backgrounds – believed that some of the abuse she suffered within the family, particularly at the hands of her grandparents, was deliberate 'grooming' for abuse in other contexts:

And then it wasn't like just sexual abuse as such, it was really sadistic. That's the only way you can describe it. While they were doing it they'd like call you names and . . . it was like being indoctrinated . . . if you showed any pain, if you screamed, then you'd get smacked, if you

didn't show any pain then you'd get smacked. So you couldn't win.
It was like as though you were being completely desensitized, it's the
only way I can describe it. Against sort of like pain in particular, so
you were getting used to it. So I'd have my grandfather on top of me,
my grandmother down at my mouth and then I'd have her rubbing
me up and down as well. I'd have them both biting me, and him
putting himself on top of me as well. It's like if you try and shut your
mouth you just can't do it, you just can't do it.

(Sophie)

The varying levels of different women's involvement in the familial abuse
described – some being very active in 'transmitting the culture of abuse' and
others far less so – is similar to that described by Faller (1991) and Cleaver
and Freeman (1996). However, ritual abuse memories were still deeply entwined with those of everyday domestic life for most interviewees. Lynn,
Kathleen, Sinead, Gene, Natalie and Sophie all described home lives saturated by abuse which they believed to have been a way of preparing them for
their 'correct' participation in ritual. In addition they thought that their
mistreatment had been intended to instil in them a view of themselves as
both innately 'evil' and 'special': chosen for the privilege of extreme degradation. Each recalled being trained not to cry or respond to pain, being
deprived of water, food and sleep, fed noxious substances and, in the case of
younger interviewees, given drugs. Such abuses sometimes intensified during
the run up to important ceremonies: their own birthdays, Easter, Beltane or
the Solstices. Lynn described such a period of preparation:

From about three days before you'd be either starved apart from
maybe excrement or blood or something . . . I wasn't being fed and I
was kept in the dark. So all in all I knew what was coming off, but I
was also very confused and disorientated. When you get really thirsty
and hungry you start to get spacey anyway.

(Lynn)

Interviewees described how loneliness, discomfort and lack of stimulus in
their preschool years had led to them learning how to 'switch off' and 'disappear inside their own head'. Two recounted how they could use a naked
flame or hyperventilate in order to 'trance out' at will. Such dissociative
practices are the same as those described by prisoners and torture victims in
their efforts to overcome pain, hunger and cold (Herman 1992). All recalled
the anxiety that suffused everyday life, the dread of returning home from
school or of being called downstairs, and went on to describe the kind of
constant vigilance that Elaine Hilberman refers to in battered women as the
'chronic apprehension of imminent doom' (Hilberman 1980: 1341). Kathleen
described some of these features as they connected everyday life and her
family's involvement in ritual abuse thus:

When you got up in the morning it didn't matter what had gone on
the night before, you had to behave as if nothing had happened. And

that could be difficult to achieve, for Mum could be washing the
blood off the walls or whatever and at the same time carry on and get
your Weetabix out, you know. It's hard. There was always so much
tension and you had to be careful about everything. But we did like go
to school, and if it was an OK day we would get fed and stuff. But if I
came home from school I used to go and hide under my bed and not
come out. I think I was probably hoping they would forget about me
until next morning . . . Ten o'clock was the watershed, if anything was
going to happen it would start by ten. If you got past ten o'clock you
were going to be left in peace.

So what if they did call you down?

. . . I'd be fed, but I wouldn't get the same as them. If I was going to
be fed there was a cupboard in the kitchen that was mine. Bridget
[my sister] had food in her room and it was different. I suppose what
you'd call quality, good food, that you might choose to eat. And I
was supposed to be . . . I would have infected or contaminated their
things . . . I often got dog food.

(Kathleen)

The isolation resulting from distrust and the deliberate manipulation of sibling relationships was an issue in a number of interviews:

I've said before that sexual abuse became so repetitive it just became
a normal part of my life. Well equally it was just an ordinary part of
my life that I was played off against my sisters. Oh, May could do oral
sex better than me so that makes her better than me . . . Constantly
feeling you were in competition with them, and they were the goodies
and you were the baddy or vice versa. And sometimes if they did
something bad you had to punish them for it. So they didn't feel they
could trust you, and I didn't feel I could trust them either.

(Lynn)

Gillean, Elizabeth and Kate also had sisters who they remembered as being
treated in quite different ways from them. They also had mothers with
ambivalent or contradictory relationships to the abuse in their families, who
each invested heavily in a pretence of domestic normality that seemed to go
beyond simply keeping up appearances to be something in which they themselves at least half believed (see Chapter 4). Neither Elizabeth nor Kate recalled their mothers attending ceremonies. In their accounts ritual abuse
memories are less integrated with those of 'ordinary abuse' in everyday life.

Beth provided a more complete exception to the pattern of very early
conditioning to both sex and pain within the family. Beth was sexually
abused in early childhood only by her uncle. Beth describes a careful 'grooming' process and a nurturing of attachment and dependency that is quite
different from the brutalization recounted by other interviewees. Beth described herself as a lonely, needy child who was easily seduced by the attention and affection lavished on her by her abuser. Her uncle's behaviour fits

descriptions given by sex offenders of 'breaking in' a child for sexual abuse (Conte *et al*. 1989; Wyre 1996) – a process that was clearly unnecessary for the parental and grandparental abusers of most interviewees.

Abuse outside the family

From the perspective of survivors it is not always easy to differentiate between abuse for different purposes. For example, interviewees were abused when there were cameras present; they might be later made to watch a film or look at photographs recording their abuse and believed that this was the sole purpose of the recording. In other instances, they were aware that the abuse was primarily 'for the camera' and that some set-ups were more professional than others. Awareness that money changed hands under some circumstances did not necessarily alter the experience of abuse for its victims. Their descriptions are more inclined to differentiate between whether they were expected to smile and 'perform' as if they were willing participants, ensure 'satisfaction' on the part of a particular abuser, or whether physical acquiescence was all that was required. Most interviewees thought their prostitution began at around the same time they started school. Kate remembered her family's return to England from abroad when she was about $4\frac{1}{2}$ years of age:

> I know that around that time I started seeing other men. He [my father] started taking me to other men. He used to just sit and watch or go in another room while the other men abused me. We'd go to their houses or their offices . . . wherever the meeting point was . . . hotels. I remember one and asking my dad what B&B meant. [*Laughs*] I realize now it was bed and breakfast, I didn't know at the time.
>
> (Kate)

Lynn described how prostitution became a more regular feature of life when she was 10 and her family moved south:

> And prostitution was a big thing from when we moved down there. It had been a big thing before but from then it became a very regular thing, every single week. Usually taken to the barracks, the army barracks. My father was still involved in the military at that time. Most of my clients were army, army men, and I actually had regulars at that age. There was an awful lot of prostitution going on from then until I left home.
>
> *In such an environment weren't little girls an unusual sight?*
>
> Ner, not really [*laughs*], we just used to go in, up the stairs. It depends on who I had, I mentioned before I had one guy, the only thing he wanted to do was actually urinate on me. I thought he was wonderful. And yet that in itself is appalling, but it was so easy and quick I thought it was great. There was another guy used to give me sixpence

and I used to have to hide it . . . Sex was an everyday part of my life anyway, so it was like these were the bonuses, sixpence or a sweetie or whatever.

(Lynn)

Interviewees used the language of adult prostitution – 'my clients', 'seeing other men' – to describe their experiences rather than a vocabulary of abuse. However gross the men involved, their behaviour was often experienced as benign compared to the terror and pain they experienced elsewhere in their lives. Sinead described a particular experience of being taken to Amsterdam by her parents and sold repeatedly as 'a virgin' in a brothel specializing in young girls:

I've done a lot of work in Amsterdam. Working in a sort of Madam's house. Er . . . fairly near Amsterdam airport I think is a red light district. Now let me think this time . . . I was 9. Between 9 and 10 . . . I remember this time these two guys came in. One of them must have weighed 28 stone, about 50, hideous. I'm surprised he got up the stairs . . . He looked like a whale, it was horrendous, he had folds of flab you wouldn't believe anybody could have. He got hold of me and said: 'You're a virgin right?' . . . All of a sudden he got my head and shoved it down . . . made me take him off orally . . . it was like he hadn't washed, he stank . . . O, god . . . I spent about three hours with them and they had sex with me about six times each. One would finish and the other one would start. The other one would play with himself and get him ready and get back on. There was bugger all I could do.

They went and somebody else came up then. This went on . . . I must have had sex about thirty times that night. There were streams of them . . . and each one was told that I was a virgin probably. So that was Amsterdam for you. They loved it . . . a 9-year-old. The other times were similar. They could make six or eight hundred pounds, a thousand pounds an hour for that. They could make twenty grand in a night for me. It was well worth their going over. They'd get it paid in drugs. But rather than shipping it over here they were given it here when they got here. Less risk. Crack cocaine, ether, all sorts, sedative drugs as well.

(Sinead)

There has been very little research on child and adolescent prostitution. The most comprehensive study is that by Mimi Silbert and colleagues (Silbert and Pines 1981, 1984) in which the youngest interviewee was 10, and 70 per cent of those interviewed were under 21; 60 per cent had been sexually abused before 'entering prostitution' and for most this had occurred when they were under 16. Silbert found that 38 per cent reported that they had been used in pornography as children – information that was not solicited by interviewers. In reporting on a Canadian replication of this research, Christopher Bagley (1997) discussed 'trick pad houses' where in 1993 the fee to have sex with a 'virgin' was between $500 and $1000:

These are girls with little evidence of secondary sexual development, and they may be resold as 'virgins' 20 or 30 times. Once they are well known in one city, they may be sold to a pimp in another city and shipped to another Canadian Province.

(Bagley 1997: 108–9)

Prostitution is generally conceived as something involving individual men, who are likely to be secretive about their activities. However, interviewees described occasions on which they were abused by men in groups. Gene said that her parents held 'paedophile parties' at their house, Sinead was regularly delivered to a house in a nearby town where a group of her father's golfing friends abused her, while as a young teenager Kate was required to 'service' her father's Masonic friends:

Yeah [*laughs*] I laugh because the way I see it is that I was the after dinner whatever. They'd all have their big meetings and they'd eat their meal and everything and I'd be available in a back room somewhere. And throughout the evening they'd pop in. And they'd leave money that I put into a bag, looked like a make-up bag, but it wasn't; and at the end of the evening I'd give my father the bag.

(Kate)

Group abuse often took the form of 'fun and games' which deteriorated into gang rape and was clearly remembered as deeply humiliating. This was particularly true for Gillean, whose memories of abuse included only this one occasion when her father clearly received payment:

It was a school. And there were square-topped tables and a big bunch of men meeting in this room. They were dressed in ordinary clothes and they were drinking and they were smoking and . . . Oh, it was terrible. There was me and there was another girl, long hair, about the same age as me.

How old were you?

I was about 12. [*Long pause*] And we were the night's entertainment basically. They put some of the tables together and they made us get up on the tables and dance and strip for them. And all the time they'd be calling out things, criticizing our bodies and . . . I was not particularly . . . I certainly didn't have breasts . . . Dad was there. He was the only person in the room I recognized. And he was just standing back watching and laughing. Folk were making a big deal of him 'cos he'd brought along part of the live entertainment for the night. And they did this auction kind of thing. And then they held me down across the table and they took turns at raping me. There was at least three of them but there could have been more 'cos after that I don't think I was really noticing terribly much.

(Gillean)

Elizabeth, recalling abuse by a group of her grandfather's friends in the late 1940s, was unaware of any money changing hands:

> That my grandfather used to come back, soppy drunk from the pub, and everyone else was in bed and he used to bring his friends and they would go down into the cellar, eight, ten people, friends. And they would get me out of bed and take me into the cellar and pass me round to suck these men, give them what they wanted.
>
> (Elizabeth)

By contrast Gene was clear that prostituting her was her – officially unemployed – father's 'business':

> Well I was kept off school lots of times because I was like rented out for sex to other people, sometimes in other parts of the country and for long periods of time. That was their big business. Apart from that I was kept at home a lot . . . it was part of . . . I wasn't allowed out too much . . . That's about it.
>
> . . .
>
> But people used to actually come to the house as well . . . big groups of business men . . . came for kind of parties.

Do you remember any of those people?

> Yeah, there was one guy I actually quite liked. He used to sit and talk. Not much else . . . bit [?] that way I suppose. I quite liked . . . he used to bring food for me and cigarettes. He was a sad guy. He couldn't have been that nice I suppose . . . Scruffy business man type . . . one of those.
>
> (Gene)

Pornography

In the regular Sunday night 'parties' held by Kathleen's parents, money did change hands, and the abuse was sometimes filmed:

> I know there were about half a dozen on any particular occasion. Sometimes more, there never seemed to be less. After a while I really lost all awareness of what was going on, who was doing what to me even. There were men and women, but the only woman I remember being assaulted by was my mother, the rest of them were all men. I don't know how long it used to go on for, it felt like an awful long time. And it was often filmed. A cine camera thing with a projector screen.

Did you ever see any film?

> O, aye, I had to watch it. Mum and Dad showed me.
>
> (Kathleen)

Debbie also remembered abuse being filmed at home and I asked her if she knew what happened to the films. The multiple purposes to which the pornography was put was echoed in a number of accounts:

> My Gran used to send them to Holland. I think her brother used to take care of things over there. I know they kept some . . . I know they had stuff because they used to watch them. There was plenty of porno videos, snuff videos, ones of which I was there at the time. It was just . . . it seemed a normal thing to sit down to a video of that . . . I can't remember a time . . . There were certain films I didn't want to watch and they used to make me. They'd turn my head and say if I didn't open my eyes that he would slap me and all, do worse and that.
>
> (Debbie)

Sinead gave an account of what she believed was a 'first time' in relation to pornography. Her father's best friend was involved in this as in so much of her abuse:

> I remember . . . I don't know how old I was, quite little . . . the first time I had full sex. I must have been not long at school, I started as a 3 year old. My mum had taken me up to the bedroom in the evening and put a dress on me . . . took my uniform off, put me in the bath and dressed me in this . . . I remember the vivid colours, it was a very deep purple smock dress, which was very short, little frilly lace on it. And she'd pulled my hair up into what I call a 'palm tree' on the top of my head, standing up with a waterfall effect, 'cos it was quite long. Put a purple ribbon in my hair, and then put this nappy on me. Took my knickers off and put a nappy on me. Little white socks with lace on and a pair of T-bar sandals . . .
>
> [*Her father's friend collected her and took her to a house with an attic studio*]
>
> He carried me to the other side of the room where they had cameras and spotlights, and he stood me on this platform . . . and like you'd pose a doll I suppose, clasped my hands in front of me first and put my legs together and just stand there and look at his hand over the camera. And he said: 'Smile for me', and I smiled and I remember this big flash coming at me and it made me jump. Then two of the other men came over, one of them stood behind me, and towering over, lifted the front of my dress to reveal my nappy. And the camera went again. I was then told to lift my hands above my head and he lifted my dress up, but not off, so it was covering my face. Through the material I could see the flashes going. He then removed my nappy, and took pictures like that. He then took my dress off . . . This is the first time I remember having full sex. There were some photos of him giving me oral sex. Then . . . I was somehow put on top of him so that his penis went inside me and he had control of lifting me up and

down. But the first time he went inside me the cameras didn't go and they must have switched the camera off, because I screamed and started to cry. I was immediately slapped and shook . . . And they started again. And it was the first time that they showed me being raped.

(Sinead)

Lynn also described a specific occasion on which pornography was being produced. Her family lived abroad during her early childhood and she recalled a picnic on the beach with her parents and another family:

It was my mother, this woman, her son and me. And I was told to run in and out the water, and I was being told to smile and laugh, and of course you do. And the last photo my dad took with his snap camera was of me coming out of the sea, and I have that picture today, and I'm laughing and splashing in the water and it looks just normal. But what happened is that I was made to come out, up the beach and the pornography was about me and this little boy on the two women . . .

Was this a new experience?

No, because I'd had pictures of me taken before, sitting down, opening my legs, using my fingers, playing with myself. The reason I think this memory made such an impact on me is I have several like this where it looks so innocent to the normal eye. Like I have that photo of me coming out of the sea, and it looks so normal, and within three minutes of that photo I was being horrendously abused and made to abuse other people, that little boy and the stuff with dogs and that's on video, film I mean, cine as it was then.

(Lynn)

With the exception of Beth and Elizabeth, all female interviewees spoke of being used in pornography. For some this was apparently limited to 'home movies' and photographs taken by their father or 'a family friend', others struggled to describe different levels of production:

like when we used to go on like trips abroad, they were completely different you know. It was . . . they talked . . . they were much sort of like . . . I don't know, the only way to describe it, not posher, a higher . . . level . . .

Class?

Yes, a higher class definitely . . . Like you have a . . . the room has got like a big double poster bed. You know what I mean? A four . . . a poster bed . . . It's just completely different stuff and all the equipment that they've got is much posher as well.

Where were you taken abroad?

Amsterdam, round Holland. Another place you know is Brussels, and Belgium as well. But that stopped as I began to develop. That stopped. But I didn't begin to develop until I was about 14 literally. So it

completely changed. Even at 15 I looked like I was 12, but my body
had changed so I was no use then. That's what they wanted you know
– they wanted and they needed children's bodies . . .

most of the time [in England] it would actually be the same person
that was doing the film. But they also had . . . one of the worst bits of
it was . . . you had to do things to other kids, and you had to sit there
and watch it. So it was a way they could keep you under control. You
were actually shown the pornography that we were actually in, and
shown it . . . because you get drugged, whether you get injections,
whether you get a drink beforehand . . . you know if you're told to
smile you do it. It makes you look . . . and because it's . . . because of
what happens to your body it makes you feel as though you're
enjoying it.

(Sophie)

Sinead describes similar experiences except that she remembered being increasingly used in pornography in her early teens:

By the time I was 11, I was 5 ft 4. I haven't grown much since then.
My hair was very long and I was being used more and more in
pornographic videos. I was being raped and used with three, four, five,
sometimes six or seven men at once – back, front, mouth and the rest
holding and touching. Being tied up, having sex with animals. One
session I remember, they used the Karma Sutra, and I had to do all the
positions in this. It took about two weeks to get this done, on various
nights. It was to be sold abroad. I also had to have sex with babies,
children a year old, 2 years old, for the videos. I mean that was . . . I
didn't . . . I wasn't at all happy about this. That was what the punter
wanted I was told. To be giving oral sex to an 18-month-old male
is . . . is something you don't ever get used to . . . and using quite
large vibrators on a 12-month-old girl . . . And the screams on these
kids . . . I could handle myself in the videos. But not the kids in the
videos with me. I didn't get used to it. But, this is what the punter
wanted, so this is what you had to do. They also used two kids
together, male and female, and made one . . . O, gosh . . . made one do
things to the other . . . however you make a year old child . . . That got
worse around 13, 14. That came around more and more.

(Sinead)

Over twenty years earlier, Lynn had also found that the requirements of
pornography changed as she shifted into adolescence:

But most of the pornography switched into very sado-masochistic
stuff, very sado. I was involved in lots of that, being tied up, being
beaten . . . and I think that was also 'cos I was getting bigger. I think
that's why I'd moved into a different market if you like.

(Lynn)

There have been only limited content analyses of child pornography. However, these have reported the use of children as young as 2, 'provocative' posing and genital exposure, as well as recording sexual acts involving adults and other children (Ennew 1986; Tate 1990). Reporting on child pornography seized and held by Scotland Yard's Obscene Publications Branch, one observer remarked that: 'Sometimes the activities – when they involve the apparent use of drugs, restraint and severe abuse – appear almost life-threatening' (Hames 1996: 202). Examining material from the same files Catherine Itzin describes various scenarios depicted including:

- A woman placing a girl (aged about eight) on top of a man's erect penis.
- A four or five year old girl performing oral sex on an adult man
- A man urinating on several children of both sexes.

(Itzin 1992: 51)

Conclusion

This chapter shows that the accounts my interviewees gave of abuse within multigenerational abusive families, wider networks of family friends, 'conventional' paedophile rings, and in clearly commercial contexts confirm and extend our rather scant research-based knowledge of abuse in such contexts. It is therefore possible, even for those most sceptical about *ritual abuse*, to accept that the majority of survivors' memories of abuse are plausible. The question then might become whether it is possible to strip away the 'bizarre' ritual elements from the more mundane experiences. It is interesting that my informants consistently separated 'the ritual stuff' from other forms of organized abuse, not in terms of their memories, but in terms of the clear distinctions made by their primary abusers who were involved in both. I asked Lynn whether pornography was ever made of ritual abuse:

No. Only simulated stuff, window-dressing. Or for showing *you* that you enjoyed it, particularly around the eating or drinking blood: 'look you like that, you're enjoying it'. And it doesn't matter whether you did, and you probably can't see your whole face but that's really difficult, and they're saying: 'Look that makes you one of us'. It's all about controlling you . . . But there is a market in the fake-satanic stuff, pornography with occult trimmings. Well there's a market in everything.

(Lynn)

Survivors may distinguish clearly between ritual and non-ritual types of abuse and the perpetrators involved in each. They may assert, as Lynn did, that the everyday abuses that took place in her own home and were perpetrated by her parents were far more devastating of her childhood than her drugged participation in a ritual murder. However, as the chapters that follow demonstrate, in survivors' lived experience of childhood and adolescence, 'ritual abuse' was constituted of events that were deeply entangled with the relationships and realities of their everyday lives. There is no easy way of filleting the 'ritual abuse' out of these narratives and transforming them into something more digestible.

Note

1 The life-histories of the three men I interviewed in the USA are discussed in Chapter 5. Their experiences of ritual abuse were also facilitated through their families but involvement was episodic and limited to their pre-teen years. The accounts given in interview were less specific and less integrated into their overall narratives.

4 | The **flesh** and the **word**: **beliefs** and **believing** in **ritual abuse**

> People have what they *take* to be 'spiritual' experiences without having
> to hold religious *beliefs*. (Indeed, it is precisely because of this outlook
> that those concerned can draw on beliefs or rituals which the modernist
> would keep apart). And this results in a form of relativism: religion
> beyond belief is religion where 'truth' is relative to what one takes to be
> involved in satisfying one's requirements.
>
> (Heelas 1998: 5)

This chapter is concerned with believing and beliefs in the experience of
ritual abuse described by my interviewees. As can be seen from Chapter 2,
the issue of whether any abusers who use ritual could possibly *believe* in their
performances or might merely dress up to frighten the children has been
significant to the discourse of disbelief. When Jean La Fontaine referred to
the three cases of abuse in her survey in which the use of rituals was 'substantiated', she emphasized that: 'In these cases the ritual was secondary to
the sexual abuse which clearly formed the primary objective of the perpetrators' (La Fontaine 1994: 30). In the 'non-substantiated' (satanic) ritual abuse
cases: 'Their defining characteristic is that the sexual and physical abuse of
children is part of rites directed to a magical or religious objective' (La Fontaine
1994: 30). In this chapter I am going to take up some of the puzzles about
belief present in the accounts of survivors, and suggest that what might be
needed in order to make sense of these is a complex understanding of what

constitutes belief systems as discourses of legitimation. I shall suggest that what is required is a model of 'believing' which gives embodied experience a central place in shaping beliefs. I shall also suggest that the different contexts in which beliefs become pertinent or irrelevant may be crucial to understanding survivors' accounts. An overly simplistic concept of belief as 'all or nothing' contributes to scepticism about the possibility of contemporary ritual abuse. Although my interviewees did not describe theologically sophisticated creeds taught them in childhood, they did insist that the way in which occult legitimations permeated their abuse deeply affected their experience even when specific ritual meanings remained obscure.

As I pointed out in Chapter 2, the question of what ritual abusers might 'believe' in relation to acts of rape, torture and killing is one of the most controversial of the discourse of disbelief. Even the very sceptical accept that the occasional group of paedophiles with a taste for sadism may dress up and act out rituals to scare the children. Where most draw the line is at the idea that anyone, apart from a lone psychopath, might develop or accept a religiously styled belief system that legitimizes or demands such practices.

The existence of various forms of occultism and satanism are not denied by sceptics; it is the connection with organized child abuse that is believed to have been invented by evangelicals and feminists. In addition to individual abusers occasionally claiming to have occult powers or involving children in rituals in order to instil fear, sceptics also accept the existence of self-proclaimed individual satanists. A small number of these commit crimes 'in the name of Satan' but are dismissed as either 'teenage-dabblers' or very disturbed *individuals* who find the writings of Aliester Crowley amenable to their paranoid/sadistic fantasies. Finally, there are public satanist groups, the Church of Satan being the best known, which preach a doctrine of personal liberty and individualism, but whose rituals involve nothing more harmful than standing naked in circles. Such organizations may even attract rich and famous members seeking the glamour of transgression and access to secret knowledge. The very existence of these cynical, deranged or 'Hollywood' satanists seems to suggest that it is unlikely there are any more serious varieties to worry about.

The conviction among sceptics that the organized practice of ritual abuse was 'impossible' lead me to consider what kinds of beliefs about contemporary society, religion and individual motivation might produce such certainty. The moral panic perspective contains a particular view of modern societies as being transparent to the sociological gaze but considerably more opaque to 'the masses' – who may be easily manipulated into paranoid fantasies. Oddly enough, it suggests that people in general are vulnerable to believing all kinds of extreme and unsubstantiated things at the behest of the mass media. At the same time – in relation to ritual abuse – advocates of moral panic explanations deny the possibility that organized paedophiles might embrace occult beliefs that legitimize the sadistic abuse of children.

The discourse of disbelief appears to share a widespread view of modern, industrial societies as characterized by increasing secularism and the triumph of scientific rationality over the ignorance of religion and superstition. Such a characterization is as old as modernity itself, and while we know that all religion has not withered away, the secularization thesis has a strong hold on western thinking such that religion and superstition are often characterized as 'survivals' from a premodern period. The early development of sociology as a discipline was deeply entwined with concern about the effects of the loosening ties of religion upon the social order (Turner 1991). In addition sociology has tended to develop a somewhat cosy, individualist view of contemporary western religious belief as a source of personal comfort or 'personal growth', a 'sacred canopy' (Berger [1967] 1990) or provider of community, and to emphasize the 'decline of the supernatural' (Bruce 1995). There is little wonder that stories of baptizing babies in satanic rituals in Richmond and Runcorn are hard to swallow.

The **sociology** of **cults**

Sociological assumptions about secularization were challenged by the emergence in the 1960s and 1970s of a host of new religious movements, and sociologists were concerned to explain their attraction and meaning for those involved. Studies of 'conversion careers' (Richardson 1978) provided insights into how group membership, self-identity and moral/political beliefs might interact to produce an 'I' which shared a universe of meaning with the 'we' of Divine Light Emissaries or the Children of God. The conclusion of most research was that cult members were ordinary folk finding different but none the less comprehensible answers to the questions of living that we all struggle with (Barker 1989). As with most sociology of 'deviant' groups, the task was to show how the activities involved made sense within the framework of those involved.

Overall, the sociological research on cults has tended to emphasize what such organizations apparently offer to individuals who join. Popular fears about physical and psychological coercion have been debunked, and the relatively free and frequent voluntary leaving of cults has been described (Barker 1989). Sociologists generally argued that the more dramatic portrayals of escape from cults, involving the 'necessity' of active 'de-programming' from cult 'brainwashing', is a product of 'exit counselling' groups with a financial and political investment in propagating such stories (Bromley and Richardson 1983; Beckford 1985).

Most of the sociologists who have contributed to the discourse of disbelief concerning ritual abuse do so from within this tradition of work on new religious movements: James Richardson, having been a prominent 'anti-anti-cult' sociologist since the early 1970s, presumed that his old right-wing Christian adversaries were behind 'the satanism scare' (Richardson *et al.* 1991). Prior to this, response to concern over the ritual abuse of children there was little sociological interest in satanism except in order to differentiate it from various pagan and wiccan groups frequently maligned by association. In one of the few studies of a satanic group, Edward Moody (1974) concluded that satanism could be positively beneficial for the individual and society. In *The Encyclopedia of American Religions*, Gordon Melton (1989) makes the following distinction between types of satanist:

As one studies the contemporary satanist scene, two distinct realities emerge. On the one hand are what are frequently termed the 'sickies'. These are disconnected groups of occultists who employ Satan worship to cover a variety of sexual, sado-masochistic, clandestine, psychopathic, and illegal activities . . . These groups are characterized by lack of theology, disconnectedness and short life, and informality of meetings. Usually they are discovered only in the incident that destroys them. On the other hand are the public groups which take satanism as a religion seriously . . . While, theologically, the Christian might find both reprehensible, their behaviour is drastically different and the groups should not be confused.

(Melton 1989: 145–6)

There is an odd assumption that disorganization and incompetence necessarily accompanies abusive and antisocial behaviour, such that the idea of 'organized crime' in the context of satanism becomes an oxymoron. The reports of survivors of ritual abuse challenge such assumptions, for the groups they describe are *both* extremely abusive *and* organized, they may or may not be liturgically sophisticated but they are often described in terms of group membership being relatively stable over some years.

In *Speak of the Devil*, La Fontaine (1998), following in this tradition, describes the occult 'scene' in contemporary Britain, concluding that there is nothing to link the ideas or practices of those involved with the abuse of children. In addition, she maintains that there is little that links the various descriptions of ritual abuse by 'believers' or survivors with the philosophy or rituals of serious occultists:

Despite the greater amount of information from survivors, the beliefs or doctrines of satanists that make them a distinctive cult are still not clear . . . Even those who claim that they were being prepared for high office within the cult do not give a coherent account of its gods or its theology.

(La Fontaine 1998: 153)

Accounts from survivors

My research largely confirms La Fontaine's view that no picture of a single cult with a coherent doctrine emerges from survivors' accounts. For La Fontaine, this is taken to indicate that whatever other forms of abuse children and adults may have experienced, occult beliefs and associated ritual practices are likely to have been grafted on to their accounts 'after the fact'. While not denying that this can indeed occur, I conclude that there are alternative perspectives to that provided by the sociology of cults which do not render the presence or absence of a 'coherent doctrine' central to assessing the validity of survivors' accounts. Indeed, the very lack of coherence within individual accounts suggests a synchretism which is common among occultists as it is more generally within the 'self-spirituality' of the New Age movement (Heelas 1996). Tanya Luhrmann (1989) provides a detailed description of groups practising *'ad hoc* ritual magic' in her anthropological study of contemporary English witchcraft. Here she describes the construction of rituals borrowing themes and symbols from Egyptian, Celtic and Greek mythology:

> they develop their talents with a loose collage of pieces of magical manuals, previous rituals and myths. Their creativity lies in the pastiche of cultural symbols and myths from different periods and places, through which their own ideas emerge.
>
> (Luhrmann 1989: 70)

Survivors' references to an eclectic collection of deities, symbols and ceremonies seem far less bizarre when considered in relation to such accounts.

Of course it is possible that an *ad-hoc* collection of occultish practices and beliefs could be 'grafted on', not through interactions with social workers and therapists, but by abusers themselves, aiming to increase their hold over children. Such a theory fitted with my personal inclination to minimize the significance of 'occult trappings' and to assume that any religious veneer could be lifted from the surface to reveal the 'raw' rape and torture beneath. I explored this possibility in interviews with survivors. However, what emerged was a more complex picture of the beliefs – and the beliefs about beliefs – of those involved.

Another possibility that emerges from the above is that belief systems develop in large part as legitimations through which those seeking authority naturalize their power by linking it with 'symbols of justification'. As C. Wright Mills points out: 'Intellectual "conviction" and moral "belief" are not necessary, in either the rulers or the ruled, for a structure of power to persist and even to flourish' (Mills 1959: 41). However, 'legitimations that are publicly effective often become, in due course, effective as personal motives' (Mills 1959: 37). From this perspective one might anticipate a continuum of conviction among those involved.

La Fontaine believes the moral panic over ritual abuse to be a 'contemporary witch-craze' similar in dynamics to the witch-hunts of medieval Europe analysed by Norman Cohn (1975), and drawing on the same culturally available stories of infant sacrifice and intercourse with the devil. In other words, accusations are made against poor and marginal members of communities which stem from the psychology and theology of the inquisitors. Carlo Ginzburg's work modifies Cohn's claims, suggesting that in some instances the witch-craze collided with remnants of pre-Christian religion, and in doing so provides a method for examining the accounts of survivors of ritual abuse in terms of the possible origins of the beliefs and practices they describe. Ginzburg searched for anomalies in the testimonies of those accused of witchcraft, arguing that: 'the more a detail strays from the stereotype, the greater is the likelihood that it brings to the surface a cultural stratum immune from the judges' projections' (Ginzburg 1990: 77). Stephen Kent (1993a, 1993b) has adopted a similar methodology in analysing the accounts of survivors of ritual abuse.

Survivors' accounts

I originally made contact with most of the survivors I went on to interview through the distribution of a questionnaire which included a question about what their abusers had believed, or claimed to believe, or convinced them to believe. I received five questionnaires from survivors who clearly identified a specific non-satanic belief system claimed by those who had ritually abused them and used to justify their abuse; these were Mormonism, Roman Catholicism, Fundamentalist Christian, Masonic, neo-Nazi and Pagan witchcraft (one stated that she had been abused in two different ritual contexts). As the main focus of the research was on the controversy inspiring abuse which appeared to involve satanic/occult rituals, I did not interview any of these informants.

Putting these to one side, the remaining 32 answers to this question clustered in three groups: those who stated that they were afraid to answer the question (4) or considered it irrelevant (2); those who referred to Satan and other deities (20) and the 'don't knows' (6). Fear was typically expressed thus: 'I don't want to think about this/I'm terrified of this part/I can't tell – I'm afraid of the consequences'; resistance, thus: 'Whatever crap they think excuses what they do – I don't want to think about it'. 'Don't knows' typically replied that they 'had not been told much' or 'did not know what their parents believed – only what they did'. Although two respondents wrote simply 'Satan is God', others gave more fulsome responses:

Satan is Lord of this earth. Lucifer and other deities can intercede for you.

The devil, and they worship certain gods too.

I don't know if they believed in Satan or used that as an excuse.

We were Satan's followers but there are 666 gods who are the devil's generals.

Baphomet, Baal, Jeopah and other deities.

Satanists believe they have chosen to know reality as it really is – that humanity is basically cruel and all else is deception. Other gods were invented by Satan to make the 'sheep' easier to control.

In addition, the following beliefs were the most frequently mentioned by respondents: Satan/evil is all powerful, Power is the (ultimate) goal/aim, Rituals bring power, Power is gained by eating flesh/drinking blood, Energy is released by death/sacrifice, They know everything you say/do, You will die if you tell/disobey, Good is evil/evil is good, Pain is pleasure/strength.

During interviews the same kind of picture emerged. On the one hand, references were made to the same general themes of power, while on the other, specific abusive rituals were described, but no standard liturgy or creed became apparent. It must be remembered that survivors were well aware that these were the least believed aspects of their experience, as well as being those which they perhaps least understood themselves. Kathleen became anxious and silent when I asked about the meanings of rituals she mentioned. Sophie and Sinead were most concerned to protest their present disbelief, while the otherwise articulate Beth stumbled over her words and drifted off the subject. In their responses to my questions, interviewees variously distanced themselves from any interest in the beliefs they or their abusers might have held:

What were you taught?

Well I was taught you weren't allowed to use Jesus' name, weren't allowed to keep crosses, not allowed to read the Bible. And he'd get me to learn bits by heart [from books] and copy stuff down.

Do you remember what the books were?

They were just books of stories, a bit like the Bible. How we are living in a dark age and how the devil will come back and rise up and stuff. I don't put much stock in it now but it was powerful at the time.

(Gene)

Back then, what did you believe?

I believed he was Satan! He was my master and I was to obey him. Anything he demanded or commanded was to be done, no questions asked whatsoever. And that it was an honour to be chosed by him. You know if he came forward and out of all these kids he touched you or looked at you, it was an honour and you were supposed to be well proud about it. [*Laugh*] And that if we obeyed him we would live forever, with all the power we could want. Except we had to prove that we were fully dedicated to him before we would get that.

(Kate)

A **formal creed**

Interviewees emphasized that their knowledge was limited concerning any belief system surrounding their abuse, and what understanding they did have was based on their particular experiences. There were only occasional references to any more structured learning. Gene referred above to 'copying things out', Lynn to 'learning by rote', and Sinead to 'classes' in which she was taught the fundamentals of 'the faith'. From the way these are described in the following extract, I assume that this formal teaching relates to a fairly early period in childhood:

Do you remember being taught explicitly about their beliefs?

O, yeah. I used to have what they called 'religious lessons' . . . They'd teach me about the rights and wrongs of living. How it was that Satan

was the master, but because he occasionally lost his temper and wasn't
very nice all the time then a lot of people in the outside world didn't
like Satan and chose to worship God. But this was wrong and they
would eventually learn that Satan was the master and then it would
be too late and they would burn in Hell.
  . . .
    Tolerance [sic] was always a key attribute, you would be able to
tolerate any form of punishment in the name of Satan. It pleased him
if you were able to be cut and beaten without screaming. Satan didn't
like noise. If you screamed during punishment that would make Satan
angry and he would punish you, if he punished you then you'd die,
and you didn't really want to die because he'd sit you on top of fire
and roast you for ever, very slowly and you'd be in constant pain and
never die.
    That's what it was about: learning to be obedient. Learning to have
a Master and know who your master was and do as you were told –
his word was law, he took his instructions from Satan.

(Sinead)

Confusion between Christian and occult beliefs for children who were taught
both in different contexts was described by Sophie:

> It's a joke. 'Cos on the woods it's like Dagon and Satan and Baal
> and Malach [sic] and all this business, and then you've got God is
> wonderful, God is brilliant! It's like what is going on. It makes
> you . . . I mean that's another reason you block it off, you soon realize
> it's two lives that you actually lead and they are both completely
> separate to one another.

(Sophie)

In some interviews I gained the impression that occult beliefs and practices
were routinely 'blocked out', along with their accompanying trauma, in the
young lives of interviewees. At the same time, the concentration on surviving everyday abuse, coupled with the 'closed' nature of family life, led to
limited awareness of the wider social and political world. This gives a time-
less quality to many of their accounts so that childhoods, from the 1950s to
the 1980s, sound very similar. Lynn provides a rare historical reference in
locating her parents' religious beliefs alongside their political aims:

> They used anything negative throughout the world as proof of their
> powers. The other thing in this case particularly is that my mother
> actually believed it as well. I remember I told you that I remember
> when Martin Luther King had died. Not because I knew a thing about
> that man, never heard of him, I only heard of his death. Of course the
> reason I heard of his death is because we celebrated his death because
> we'd created the power. The only thing I knew about him is he must
> have been OK or we wouldn't have been celebrating. I've got books

about him now, just to find out who it was we supposedly created so
much energy for.

(Lynn)

If what the survivors who wrote and talked to me had to say about the
formal creed they remembered were limited to such material, it might be
legitimate to conclude that the sole purpose was to frighten children. The
descriptions are child-like, the beliefs they report lack any theological sophist-
ication, and they seem unlikely to have been shared by the educated professionals who were sometimes among their abusers. Interviewees were certainly
aware that they had been deceived and tricked:

The image of Satan was . . . I realize now but at the time . . . even up
to when I last went to a gathering it was what 1993 . . . it took me to
then, which sounds pretty pathetic really, to realize it wasn't Satan
that was in the room: it was a man dressed up with a massive ram's
head mask, or a different one. But because you don't have fluorescent
strip lighting in those places, it was all very dark, smoky, a lot of noise
going on, movement . . . it took me till a couple of years ago to realize
that it wasn't Satan, it was a man . . .
    We all did what we were told and got everything right as best we
could, because there was also that fear that if we did anything to
offend him or didn't do what he wanted he would kill us. Which they
very willingly demonstrated on animals. I suppose looking back on it,
it was pathetic really because they had this dog. And this dog was
told, by Satan, told to sit, and of course the dog sat didn't it . . . it was
trained to sit . . . and stand, and the dog stood, lie and the dog lay.
And they asked the dog to do something, I can't remember what it
was, turn around or something which isn't normally in the dog's
trained vocabulary, and he didn't so they killed him. But as kids, the
dog sat and it stood, but when it didn't turn around when Satan
demanded it, crrch! they killed it. Looking back on it now as an adult
who can distance themselves, that was a very pathetic but clever way
of making little 'uns believe that he had power. Whereas in realistic
terms – ridiculous. But that sort of thing happened.

(Kate)

However, interviewees did not conclude on the basis of 'debunking' such
deceptions that this was the end of the matter. There were two apparent
reasons for this: the first was based on their observations of those involved
which suggested there might be a continuum of belief/disbelief among their
abusers. Second, their own embodied experience of involvement in rituals
led them to conclude that beliefs could not necessarily be entirely understood as a set of stories deliberately constructed to frighten children.
    At the same time, interviewees were wary about claiming or naming a
generalized belief system. Within the discourse of disbelief there is a common assumption that ritual abuse claims concern abuse supposedly organized by an international conspiracy of satanists. The survivors I interviewed

made no such claims, rather they emphasized that they had little knowledge about how their abusers networked with others.

A **continuum** of **belief**

In answer to questions about what they thought their abusers had believed in relation to the ritual abuses they practised, some interviewees chose to describe two different individuals. One of these they regarded as having been a cynic, motivated almost entirely by 'greed and lust', and the other who they thought had taken their occult beliefs seriously. This distinction was often gendered – a mother or grandmother being characterized as a 'true believer', while a father or uncle was a presumed cynic. Debbie's account is typical:

And what was this all for, were you told what any of this was meant to be about?

Well I was told it was for Lucifer, but I was never told in great detail, apart from about eating the flesh. 'Cos my Gran thought she would be immortal if they ate human flesh. That's proved them wrong 'cos my grandad died this winter.

Was there any attempt to teach you . . . [unclear]

I think just before I left they had started to. But I wasn't really a willing person I didn't want to know. I didn't want to understand it. And I don't really believe . . . even though they are satanists you get the type where they're the satanists and that's their first belief, and partly the abuse is just additional to that. 'Cos I think my Gran took the satanic side seriously, but people like Butch, the abuse was the main thing and the satanist bit was additional to that. So it's like you get those that are the abusers and those who are the satanists – even though they are doing it you know. But Butch I just think it was that he could get his rocks off on it, 'cos I don't think he believed as much as the others.

(Debbie)

In some adult abusers, the relationship between cynical involvement and belief was seen as complex, even confusing. Kate describes how a friend of her father's, who was 'into' the most appalling sadistic abuse, and clearly influential in relation to profane matters, surprised her in a ritual context:

And he had an incredible ability to make other men copy him, to join in, even though you can see there is that hesitation. I don't know what he had over them but they joined in.

But he wasn't, you said, someone who was particularly senior within the cult group.

No, he wasn't that high up at all. And in some ways he was . . . I don't
know where I get that from but . . . he isn't all he was made out to be,
he wasn't as macho as he appeared. I remember at one [meeting] he
had to kill the lamb, and he nearly made a complete balls-up of it. He
was in such a nervous state. It seemed very strange to me that this guy
had incredible power and influence over a lot of people, was going to
balls up on something I could have done. It was a very simple thing
yet he was going to make a mess of it. He wasn't very high up in it,
my father was higher up than he was, and yet my father bowed to
what Andrew said and wanted . . . to a point. It was only when my
father said: 'I think you should stop, she isn't breathing' or whatever,
that Andrew would stop.

(Kate)

Kate also comments on the evident terror of the occult practices evinced by
men she assumed had been recruited into the group as adults:

I have memories of when I was an old hand at it really, standing in
front of new recruits, or new men, and seeing absolute terror on their
faces, complete fear. I can remember quite young thinking 'Oh, he's a
new one! Hasn't been here before'. But where the transition of them
accepting what was happening . . . it was all great and this was part of
everything, and when they were first introduced to it – I don't know
where that transition came . . . or how they were introduced or
anything like that. But I do remember absolute sheer terror.

(Kate)

In her interview, Lynn takes up the same theme, suggesting that even within
individuals there may have been no clearly fixed position, but a more context-
specific relationship to belief. Talking about illusionist tricks incorporated
into rituals, she said:

The weird thing about it is that it was done for the children. Some
adults did believe it as well. Yes, they did. I don't know if they were
being deliberately naive or if they had no knowledge. But even people
like my father, who knew they'd done it, also believed it was also
happening. And I know what it is, when I hear people talk about God
and they say 'God works in mysterious ways'; and I might say 'but
you've just done that' and they'll answer 'Yes, but He gave me the
facility to do it'. And my parents would do exactly the same. So even
if they did it, it was because they were doing it with his knowledge.

So they were making something that really existed concrete?

Yes. Well, 'He' was in them wasn't he? Rather like the person who
creates the miracle. Like I said I'm not sure my father really believed
anything much. For someone like my mother she has to believe that
very deeply: that she was 'His' vessel, in order to carry on.

(Lynn)

Interviewees rejected the deception/true belief distinction and did not claim to know whether or not 'the ritual was secondary to the sexual abuse' (La Fontaine 1994: 30) in relation to their experiences. In an article on contemporary superstition, Colin Campbell (1995) develops a concept of 'half belief' to explain people's denial that they hold particular beliefs while still practising such activities as touching wood in order to ward off misfortune. The details of his argument are not relevant here, but the idea that people manifest belief through the enactment of rituals which verbally they would deny is interesting in two respects. First, it led me to consider that beliefs may not be things that are 'always with us' as essential aspects of our deepest sense of self, and second, that what we enact through ritual behaviour may be an important dimension of belief which is separable from a linguistically articulated commitment to a particular creed.

In relation to the accounts of ritual abuse survivors concerning the beliefs of their abusers and themselves, a concept of half-belief, as mobilized by Campbell (1995), may be useful in terms of the internal contradictions of individuals and might be used to describe a particular position on the continuum on which individuals involved in ritual abuse may be ranged from 'true believer' to 'spiritual cynic'. However, such a continuum is one along which *individuals* may also move over time, a factor that is particularly relevant to the process by which interviewees escaped from their abuse, physically, intellectually and 'spiritually'. In order to capture this complexity and to account for the context-specific demonstrations of belief such as those of Lynn's father, who only seemed to 'believe' when her mother was around, or of the 'macho' Andrew, who quaked at performing a ritual sacrifice of a lamb, we also need a concept of 'contextual belief'. Half-belief and contextual belief, along with an understanding that beliefs and actions may be synchronous or desynchronous, can be seen as dimensions which need to be taken into account in making sense of the varieties of belief interviewees describe in relation to both their abusers and themselves.

The **embodiment** of **belief**

The survivors I interviewed were far more concerned with the 'abuse' in ritual abuse than with its rituals, and some declined my invitation to describe a specific ritual in which they had been involved. However, it was in the 'thickness' of descriptions of ritual practice that some survivors were able to give me that their sense of the significance of beliefs seemed to be embedded. As Clifford Geertz argues: 'it is primarily at least, out of the context of concrete acts of religious observance that religious conviction emerges on the human plane' (Geertz 1966: 28).

The project of my research was not to collect and analyse specific ritual accounts. However, one sociologist who has done precisely that is Stephen Kent (1993a, 1993b). He believes that the sociology of religion is an appropriate intellectual tradition from which to examine ritual abuse accounts because it takes seriously the reality of religiously motivated behaviour, and that much of the content of ritual abuse survivors accounts makes religious sense, in addition:

the religious sense that they make often presupposes a degree of esoteric theological knowledge that appears to be beyond the educational or experiential horizons of the people who recount them and the professionals who work with these clients.

(Kent 1993a: 231)

In the course of my interviews, three survivors made reference to being forced to act like dogs: having to bark, eat from the floor, walk on a leash, and suffer sexual abuse involving real dogs. Kent also refers to three accounts, collected in interviews with three Canadian survivors, of such dog-like behaviour being enforced in a ritual context. The survivors interviewed by both Kent and myself interpreted this treatment as deliberate degradation – 'they wanted to break me down' (Kent 1993a), but Kent goes on to provide a number of scriptural precedents for an understanding of dogs as enemies of God (Philippians 3.2, Revelation 22:15, Deuteronomy 23:17–18).

Kent's work is interesting because by a quite different route he confirms my view that there is a substantial gap between the beliefs of which survivors appeared to have formal knowledge and their 'thick' descriptions of rituals which suggest a complex cosmology. My interest was in how survivors themselves understood and explained this gap, and indeed whether it appeared as a problem in their accounts of their lives.

Interviewees recognized their lack of formal and detailed knowledge about the 'real meanings' of rituals they had experienced. Some, like Kate and Sophie, explained that they had imbibed a belief system through its practices.

But it's like . . . you're not sat down and you're not taught things, you learn as you go along, you learn not to do this, you learn not to do that.

(Sophie)

Do you recall having any sense of what all this was about?

In the UK – at that first memory – I didn't know what it was all about, but it was almost like I knew what was coming next. In the Middle East I mean I guess I learnt from the older girls and boys, just watching them and I suppose in turn, I taught the younger ones without realizing it. Just like when you should kneel, when you should stand, where you should move to. When you should . . . they don't call it a mug [*laughs*] . . . the chalice. When you should pick that up, when you shouldn't, and at what part of the chanting you do what and what you expect the men to do.

(Kate)

Others, like Kathleen, emphasized how they believed as children they had attempted to 'take in' as little as possible of what was going on at ceremonies: Initiation rituals were described in two different interviews and provide some insight into the implicit beliefs that might be found in rituals:

There was an animal on the altar, the animal was sacrificed and then cut open. I was, I had to do most of all that. I didn't cut the animal open but I don't know if I'd have had the actual physical strength to do it, the animal was a goat again you see. The animal was opened right down the middle and then opened up. That's when you really know it, it smells high as a kite, a horrible smell. The intestines were then taken out, parts of that were passed around. They drained the blood and I was made to drink and eat. I was then made to lay in the carcass of the body. At that point anyone had a perfect right to come and take parts, what's classed as taking parts of my body, which is actually just abusing someone. My mother sat on my face, my father entered me vaginally. So all this is going on, the carcass is just sort of crushed by now, the intestines are laid all over you what remains, and it's been put in your mouth. It's awful, pretty awful and it goes on for hours. Other children will be made to come up and perhaps push bits of intestine in your ears or up your nose, stick it internally. And that's part of . . . and some of them will be told to draw a symbol on you and some of the children will have symbols put on them to show their age and what they're coming up. Lots of other things. It's also I think the way they get the adrenalin going.

Did you have any idea as a 6 year old what any of this was supposed to be about?

Then I did because they were saying what was going to happen. That er, that er . . . I had given up my body and the devil was now inside me and the fact that my father had raped me there meant that he had placed the devil there. So the devil was inside me and was alive, so my body was no longer mine.

(Lynn)

Lynn described how this ritual was later followed up by a fake operation apparently intended to reinforce the belief that her body was not her own through further embodied experience:

They told me that they were taking out a bit of the goat's intestine that had accidentally got in when the devil had gone in. Now I know that's impossible and they just had some intestines there. But at 6! And they said they had to remove some of my intestines too so the devil had a bit more room in there. You believe those things, I don't think you have a choice. How would you know they weren't true anyway? But they put a lot of effort into convincing you . . . Now as a teenager I saw that happen so many times to other people so I *knew*, but even then if you'd tried telling me looking back on my own that it wasn't any different, I wouldn't have believed you. I'd have thought 'mine was different, mine was real' and 'they're doing this to confuse me'.

(Lynn)

Sophie described a series of three 'initiation' rituals in her early childhood. The second of these also involved an animal:

> 'Cos you know one of the gods they worship is Dagon. It's really sick. Because my father was a master I was a devil's daughter, and this was over an Easter time and they had a bull. It took four of them to drag this bull . . . [*unclear*]. And they cut it open, sliced open the stomach, and I was hung upside down and basically immersed into it. And that was their other initiation, it was like they were re-giving birth to me. That was their logic behind it. I didn't get told so at the time obviously, 'cos I didn't know what was going on. But it's like you can't move, you can't do anything 'cos you're just paralysed, your legs are paralysed, you can't shout . . . if you shout you get something put in your mouth. You know you can't show pain, you just can't do anything, you've got no choice. And I actually thought I was going to suffocate. I really did, I thought I was going to suffocate. I mean animals are just like one of their favourite tricks you know . . .

> *And were you told anything about what this was all about?*

> No. You were just taken. You knew that something was going to happen because beforehand you'd get . . . starved and no water, preparation begins.

> (Sophie)

That 'believing' is intimately connected with embodied experience is explicit in Lynn's discussion of manifestation. However, her account also suggests some of the ways in which believing may be context specific and therefore vary within individuals at different times, as well as between individuals:

> They believe there's seven levels to manifestations, and one of the first levels is pain, hurt, fear, lust. It gives you some idea of all the things that have to happen in the room in order for manifestation. They believe, these create such a strong form of energy . . . But there's not many survivors you're ever going to talk to who will not tell you that the room was vibrating. If you get that many people in one place having so many fantasies fulfilled, and the adrenalin is going, and they're chanting and they're doing all the other things, then it'll happen . . .
> It's like that energy becomes a door. A door that opens to manifestation. And it feels like that. Many times I've said it, the room was moving, I don't mean physically moving. I mean it was alive . . . At the high point of this one there were three. And it was quite weird. The reason for that is it was the run up to Christmas and it was very much the anti-Christ stuff. But it was also the . . . I forget the [name] . . . the serpent thing . . . The one that's supposed to come from the core of the earth? They had the weird[est] plans you know. Their plan was that this serpent, coming from the core of the earth,

that they were going to manifest then could start to destroy the earth.
Eat away at the positive energies.

(Lynn)

The relationship between embodied experience and 'the sacred' has been
explored by Mellor and Shilling (1997). Their historical argument is that
Protestant reformers successfully promoted a version of religion based on
commitment to scriptural based beliefs (a 'reading' religion) displacing the
'carnal knowing' which in medieval Christianity took the form of 'communities of bodily interaction bound together through ritual eating' (Mellor
and Shilling 1997: 16). They claim that the late twentieth century witnessed
a retreat from the cognitive and rational and a resurgence of 'sensual solidarities'. While drawing on Maffesoli's (1996) vision of 'postmodern tribes'
'keeping warm together', they emphasize the fact that the 'need for meaning' can just as easily incorporate envy, violence and hate. The 'warmth' of
common identity can be generated through the shared 'pleasures' of persecu-
tion, gang rape or the 'joy of killing':

> The sacred can be nasty, unpleasant and terrifying, as well as glorious
> and salvational. If life is generally brutish and short, then intimations
> of the totality of that life, through the collective effervescence of the
> sacred, are likely to reflect that reality.
>
> (Mellor and Shilling 1997: 176)

In trying to describe a 'sensual solidarity' based on a 'left sacred' (Hertz 1960),
they specifically exclude the 'victim':

> The subject of an exorcism is not always willing, and the coercion in-
> volved in this activity is complemented by the violent rupturing of the
> body from itself brought about by the ritual practices associated with
> this event. In the case of compulsion, exorcisms might be viewed as
> sensual solidarities only insofar as they involve the exorcists.
>
> (Mellor and Shilling 1997: 184)

Mellor and Shilling's interest is in the 'collective effervescence' (a sort of
naturally bubbling search for meaning) from which 'sensual solidarities' spring,
and they fail to theorize power, hierarchy and coercion and the different
kinds of relationships to 'the sacred' these might introduce.

Interviewees can be seen as *both* victims and members of ritual abuse groups.
From their perspective, it seems that what is most important in terms of a
carnal knowledge of an occult sacred is the 'naturalization' of bodily experience, so that concepts, theories and beliefs gain authority through what
Elaine Scarry (1985) has termed 'analogical substantiation'. Scarry argues
that beliefs of a religious sort, which have no basis in the material world, can
borrow from the compelling reality of the sensorially experienced body. For
Scarry, it is part of the 'civilizing process' that alternatives have gradually
been provided to this bodily form of verification: human sacrifice is replaced
with animal sacrifice, which is in turn replaced with the Crucifix as a symbolic
representation of sacrifice. In times of crisis and uncertainty, the body's role

may return, providing as it does in torture regimes, proof of the power of the regime. For torturers, the vision of suffering is converted into a convincing spectacle of power – the realness of the pain is borrowed and its incontest-ableness is conferred on the power that brought it into being. The experience and infliction of pain are central to ritual abuse. The experience of torture is the bedrock of belief in survivors' accounts. As Scarry describes, pain is an absolute reality and certainty to the sufferer, it leaves space for little else. The structure of torture facilitates the leap from the immediate experience of pain to its objectification in the 'insignia of the regime', making the link seem natural and inevitable. What Scarry provides in her analysis of torture is a way of understanding the body in pain as productive of belief for both torturers and their victims, but in different ways for each. She argues that torture is always accompanied by words (interrogation usually providing an official justification for the practice). For the victim, the pain is hugely real and the questions and statements of belief unreal, while for the torturer the opposite is true. A number of interviewees believed that they began to be formally taught about an occult belief system in their mid-teens and that they resisted the teaching, associating such knowledge with an increasingly abusive adult role within the cult. In other words, they differentiated between the embodied believing produced through pain which they experienced as victims, and the more systematic, cognitive belief system they associated with their abusers – a system substantiated (made flesh) through their suffering.

Power operates upon and through bodies. In ritual abuse an occult belief system becomes naturalized as 'self-evident' through torture, but also, less dramatically perhaps through numerous body based claims. For example, the presumed relationship between left-handedness and evil in many cultures is well documented (Hertz 1960) and some interviewees mentioned being taught to be ambidextrous, or that their 'natural' left-handedness had provided proof of their 'belonging'. For girls and women, the incorporation within ritual practices of their menstrual blood and breast milk as potent secretions tied their bodies to the very production of occult power.

Such an analysis of the relationship between abuse and belief helps to make sense of reports by a number of interviewees that bodily incapacities limited their participation in producing the words which often accompanied ritual abuse. Speech or hearing difficulties were claimed as a source of pride and differentiation from their abusers:

> I could write backwards without any problem, but I could never
> speak it backwards. I couldn't do it. I remember Uncle John saying to
> [*unclear*] 'she's left-handed'. I remember thinking what on earth has
> that got to do with it. And whether or not it had anything to do with
> it I do not know.
>
> (Beth)

The **adornment** of a **secret**

Beth did not know what occult meanings might be associated with her left-handedness. Among my interviewees 'not knowing' was linked in one direction with not wanting to know, with rebellion and rejection. In the other direction it was linked to the secrecy and exclusion deliberately practised by their abusers. Interviewees agreed that nothing had made them more anxious and afraid than 'not knowing':

> [From the age of 13 we] were told more about the significance of certain things rather than being told that things were 'just because you had to'. You didn't . . . They told you just enough to get you ready for it but not too much so you . . . You're scared of what you don't know about really. If you know about something you can maybe do something about it or at least get your head round it. [*Pause*] It's maybe what I didn't know that scared me. There's not a lot I did know really.
>
> (Gene)

Beth makes the same point:

> I think there was a lot of fear . . . because it was never explained. I know there were times when I did ask Uncle John questions, I don't know what they were but I know I did question him. He didn't ever really give me a straightforward answer.
>
> (Beth)

The sociology of secrecy has not attracted a great deal of interest, but if Georg Simmel (Wolff 1950) was correct then secrets are a crucial aspect of power in the modern world and are intimately connected with 'evil':

> although the secret has no immediate connection with evil, evil has an immediate connection with secrecy: the immoral hides itself for obvious reasons even where its content meets with no social stigma as, for instance, in the case of certain sexual delinquencies. The intrinsically isolating effect of immorality as such, irrespective of all direct social repulsion, is real and important beyond the many alleged entanglements of an ethical and social kind.
>
> (Simmel in Wolff 1950: 331)

Simmel argues that secrecy is both a means to desirable ends and attractive and valuable in its own right (we can think of adultery or gambling in this respect). The exclusion of outsiders from the secret leads to a powerful sense of the value of possession: what is denied to others must have special value. From this we might suppose that within a group which has appreciated the value and attraction of secrecy enough to cloak itself in such, there would be further layers of secrets. In the most extreme cases there might be members of a secret group who had no idea of some of its purposes, activities or beliefs. As part of the pleasure of secrecy, in Simmel's formulation, is the power of deception, then such duplicity would provide the greatest satisfaction.

When secrecy has been discussed in relation to cults, it is generally assumed that its importance is as a barrier between the cult and the outside world, rather than as an integral part of an internal labyrinth of abusive networks and hierarchies. However, membership of all kinds of entirely non-abusive occult groups is often progressive, with 'secret' knowledge and access to 'mysteries' supposedly gained at each stage. In traditional witchcraft covens there are three 'degrees'; the third, involving symbolic or actual ritual inter-course and the incarnation of the Great Goddess or Horned God is shrouded in secrecy and only undertaken by the most committed of practitioners.

Belief and escape

Most people appear to leave cults because they decide the way of life is no longer for them, or because they become disillusioned with the beliefs and practices. This does not mean there is no pressure to join, or remain in-volved in, such groups; attention and affection may be involved, as may the stimulation of guilt. However, the processes differ little from those that occur in the family, school, army, or some traditional religions. As Eileen Barker notes: adult conversion to the belief system of most cults involves less control by others than that which is involved when a child is born into a family with a strongly held religious tradition (Barker 1989: 19).

With the exception of Beth, all my interviewees had been born into a sexually abusive family and were ritually abused by their parents and/or grandparents. Their isolation from peers made the development of alternat-ive points of reference slower than it is for many children. The survivors I interviewed described their own beliefs as changing over time, from being terrorized and tricked as a small child, through being 'in two minds' in adolescence, to whatever degree of scepticism they currently held. Four in-terviewees expressed their continuing fear, uncertainty or 'open-mindedness' about the supernatural implications of some of their experiences, others were strongly invested in an entirely material understanding of their abuse and deeply suspicious of all 'religious stuff'. Escaping their abuse appeared to be intimately related to developing at least a degree of scepticism. As one survivor put it: 'The cult was in me quite as much as I was in the cult'.

Leaving a cult is generally described in the sociological literature as an event with a clear 'before' and 'after', the exception being those people whose leaving is forced (kidnapped by family and anti-cult 'counsellors') and who later choose to return (Beckford 1985). The division between cult and non-cult worlds is clear cut: involvement in a cult is generally considered to mean distance from one's family and previous everyday life. Leaving cults is described as an absolute step; no part-time or secret membership seems to be common. This is by stark contrast to the experiences of many of my respondents, some of whom lived 'a double life' for some time after their apparent escape. (To a question about the age at which escape from abuse had been possible one questionnaire res-pondent simply wrote: 'It wasn't like that'.) In interview Gene described how she got herself taken into care aged 14, but that this did not end her abuse:

> the enormity of what I'd done came home to me . . . hit me after
> about the first week of being in care. I thought 'O, god, what have I

done'. So I went back [home] . . . there'd be trouble . . . so I went back and um . . . which was a pretty stupid thing to do 'cos once I went back I was well into it again.

Tell me what you mean.

It's like once you get back into it, I mean I'd only been away a week . . . you just get back into it again. Even that short a period of time – a week it's like: 'Ah, there is something else to do' . . . it's like there is a possibility. But when you get back into it the first time it's like there isn't. It knocks your confidence back. It's doubly hard to get out the next time . . . you've got to stay away for longer than a week if you're going to get out!

And was staying away hard in itself?

Yeah. It was like . . . I was scared I'd get into trouble all over it. Based on stuff I'd done . . . I was quite old by then . . . I wasn't that scared of like the supernatural, but I was in a way, like I said I've got an open mind. Just basic things like that really. It was like a compulsion – I had to go. No one was there to stop me because they didn't know what my problems were. I couldn't do it on my own.

And do you understand that compulsion now?

Just so . . . so . . . you know . . . I'm sure someone somewhere would have an answer to that but to me it's just like . . . when you've been to it so long . . . it's so like . . . [your] way of living is just so like that . . . it's really scary or you're scared of something anyway, you can't stop doing it all of a sudden. It was just too hard to resist really. It was so scary that they'd come and get me or something like that, especially when they were opposing Care Orders and that . . . [So I thought I could] kinda have my cake and eat it. I'd appease them by going home every now and again. After the initial trouble of me going into care and them being mad about that to start with, it calmed down a bit and like got into a routine. So I'd do both. I had actually to be home like specific dates . . . over Lent stuff like that.

(Gene)

Kathleen described a very similar period where she 'hid out' at a friend's house for three or four days at a time before she 'really felt she had to go home'. Her extrication from her family was slow, difficult and at the time of our interview still incomplete. Sinead, however, put a more positive spin on the six months or so that she led a double life:

I think that went on for six, maybe eight months? Seeing you and living with them. I think that's what helped me get out . . . because I needed the contrast of home living and a life outside . . . but still going back, and not making any direct confrontation with them until I was sure the outside life was what I wanted. Until I was sure people outside were safe. I could have run away there and then, but I think I

would have ended up going back to the group again if I had – because
it would have been such a culture shock if you like . . . I think if you'd
said to me after three or four visits that I had to come away: 'We
don't want you to see your mother or speak to her', I couldn't have
done it.

(Sinead)

It is certainly fear rather than 'faith' that most informs the ambivalence and
complexity survivors described over 'getting away'. However, the two cannot
be entirely separated for what is described is the difficulty of extricating
themselves from a family and subculture in which they had been almost entirely absorbed: violence, sex, drugs, perverse rituals and pan-theistic occult
beliefs were tangled together with the rest of everyday life.

Conclusion

In our early days with Sinead, I briefly considered exploring the theological
background of the rituals she sometimes described. The result is that I am
now the proud owner of a book on Teutonic Magic – a subject which seemed
to be a source of particular fear. None of us ever read the book. For a while
I assumed that Sinead knew more about the occult beliefs and symbols she
referred to than she was willing to say, that fear or superstition combined
with the need to be a bit important and mysterious kept her silent. It quickly
became apparent that this was not the case. At one time Sinead's dreams
were briefly haunted by an image of the 'Eye of Horus' pouring blood.
Apparently it had decorated the altar cloth at a particular ritual, but Sinead
knew nothing about its mythological context beyond the fact that it was 'all
seeing', and that it was somehow linked with the Egyptian deities Set and
Astoreth. The fear and distress associated with the symbol were real enough,
but the symbol itself mattered very little.

The question as to whether ritual abuse related belief systems can in any
way be regarded as authentic which arises from the discourse of disbelief, has
I hope been displaced by the discussion in this chapter. From the perspective
of survivors, some inhabitants of their ritual abuse worlds chose their beliefs,
others had beliefs thrust upon them. That the beliefs of ritual abusers are
self-serving does not mean they may not be 'real' or cannot 'act back' as an
influence on their lives and practices.

The Marquis de Sade believed in the 'rightness' of the abuses he fantasized
and enacted,[1] and justified them by reference to his own 'natural inclina-
tions', which he regarded as continuous with Nature in all its cruelty and
violence.[2] Other philosophers have regarded nature as 'red in tooth and
claw' and have emphasized the importance of dominating this destructive
force, but Ariès in his history of death suggests:

The Sadeian tendency has certainly been more widespread than has long
been believed, but in forms more socially acceptable and less aggressive.
We find it in the new forms of satanism. The new Satan is the man who

has espoused nature, like the monstrous creature of Frankenstein. The modern temptation tends rather towards the superman, the successor of Satan. For certain types of strong men who have understood the Sadeian system of nature, there is no more 'legal order'; everything is permitted.

(Ariès 1981: 392)

The occult beliefs apparently espoused by ritual abusers and absorbed by their victims cannot be simply separated off from the whole constellation of beliefs and practices to which they are connected. The rape of children and the desire for wealth and power may be bound together with the hope of immortality, providing a tolerable fit between beliefs and practices. A view of beliefs as often being partial and contextual is useful in understanding the spectrum of investment in the supernatural that survivors describe as existing both between and within those involved – including themselves. Beliefs might be usefully regarded not so much as 'mental' convictions but rather as something evidenced within ritual practice and known through embodied experience. They might not necessarily be diminished by ignorance of a formal creed, but rather enhanced by the adornment of secrecy.

La Fontaine considers the reports of beliefs and rituals in accounts of ritual abuse unlikely because they do not conform to any single, recognizable belief system. She suggests that accounts therefore do not emphasise the importance of 'correct performance', precision and detail normally so universally important in rituals (La Fontaine 1998). However, the accounts of survivors discussed in this chapter describe an anxious emphasis on 'doing things right' in a ritual context. Some interviewees, describing how major rituals were meticulously planned and rehearsed, also mentioned rare moments of aesthetic or sensual pleasure in wearing beautifully made masks and costumes. At the same time, such rituals and their associated deities inhabited an eclectic, 'world-raiding', self-justifying 'belief system' in which 'ecstatic' experience was for most participants more important than the coherence of tradition or creed. I have shown that this 'pan-theistic occultism' developing rituals based on a variety of traditions has a non-abusive counterpart in groups which practise *ad-hoc* ritual magic. In addition, recent discussions of late-modern or postmodern religion in general suggest that both eclecticism and a focus on 'the self' provide a general form in relation to which the beliefs and ritual practices described by my interviewees are rendered a little more believable.

Notes

1 As Jean Goodwin (1994) has pointed out, the 600 sadistic practices described in de Sade's ([1789] 1992) *120 Days of Sodom* correspond with practices described in contemporary ritual abuse.
2 There are two types of naturism simultaneously appealed to here: the natural as 'in nature', and natural as in 'the natural order' and therefore morally right (see Jackson and Scott 1996).

5 | The **gender** of **horror**

Much of this book engages with aspects of ritual abuse which have been central to the disbelief the subject has aroused. In US day care and UK family network cases involving allegations of ritual abuse (Finkelhor *et al*. 1988; La Fontaine 1998) and in the life-stories of survivors (Smith and Pazder 1980; Coleman 1994), women have been routinely numbered among the accused. The involvement of numbers of women as active perpetrators of ritual abuse appears to contradict the view of women who sexually abuse as an exceptional minority among incest offenders, paedophiles, traffickers in child pornography and others. Although the issue of women's involvement has not often been a specific target of the discourse of disbelief, I believe that it has been fundamental to the general incredulity with which accounts are often received.

Men who sexually abuse children can be 'made sense of' in relation to the dominant discourse of masculinity. Feminists have insisted on the importance of explicitly doing so, but implicitly 'common sense' and tabloid culture does the same. On those occasions when women have been publicly identified as responsible for the sadistic abuse of children, their 'right' to be understood 'as women' comes into question. In the case of the 'moors murderers', Ian Brady was considered no less a man, however 'evil' his crimes; it was Myra Hindley who was deemed to be 'unsexed' by her 'unnatural' involvement. Men may become monsters while remaining men, but women who commit certain acts cease to make sense as women. The gap between their crimes and hegemonic femininity threatens fundamental beliefs about 'what women are'. Feminists have of course identified as a patriarchal myth the 'natural' woman, tied to her children with bonds of love and responsibility but even they have not been entirely immune to its lure, or to the claims to moral superiority it allows. Like any revolutionary movement, feminism prefers those whose interests it represents to behave well and has sometimes banished particular women to a place 'beyond the pale' of feminist understanding. My aim in this chapter is to demonstrate both the plausibility of women's involvement in the various forms of abuse described by my interviewees, and to show that discursive constructions of gender do not evaporate at the threshold of sadistic abuse. Rather they continue to construct hierarchically the activities and identities, roles and relationships of those involved.

When asked about the roles of men and women in ritual abuse, the women I interviewed insisted on their equality in terms of status and their equal perpetration of acts of cruelty and violence. Having explored the evidence for such claims to equal status within the overall life-histories, I suggest that they pertain more to the formal creed and ceremonial practice of ritual abuse groups than to everyday life. An emphasis on the same 'acts' being performed by both men and women may serve to obscure the gendered contexts, meanings and relationships that surround them. However, I do not dismiss these claims to equality merely as a strategy by which men 'con' women into lifelong participation in ritual abuse, for they also form part of a discourse within which some women located themselves as both 'women' and 'abusers', and within which they enjoyed a sense of competence, status and power. By marked contrast with the responses of women interviewees, a very strong awareness of the significance of gender was apparent in the three interviews I conducted with male survivors. The key issue that arose from their abuse was that of finding an alternative masculinity to that of their abusers. There was no need for an equivalent search for a non-abusive femininity among the women: hegemonic femininity characterizes women as gentle, nurturing and non-violent and women's accounts of their rejection of ritual abuse frequently lay claim to such 'natural' qualities within themselves.

Gender and child sexual abuse

As I showed in Chapter 1, a feminist understanding of the sexual abuse of children as an instance of male power has been central to making sense of the prevalence of such abuse. Feminists have argued that a father's sexual abuse of his children is congruent with many aspects of what it 'means to be a man' in contemporary western patriarchal societies: where men have historically regarded their wives and children as property, where vulnerability is eroticised, pornography readily available, and male sexual 'needs', violence and domination are naturalized. The weakness of this argument lies in its failure to analyse the transition between such societal features and the individual men who may or may not 'choose' to adopt the identity they suggest.

The question of why some individuals sexually abuse children is frequently answered in terms of their own childhood experience predisposing them to children as a 'sexual object choice' or to the re-enactment of their own victimization. The inadequacies of simplistic 'cycle of abuse' theories were discussed in Chapter 1: in particular their failure to address the fact that while some men who have been sexually abused as children may go on to become abusers themselves, very few women follow an equivalent course. It is evident that what we need to understand is how children of both sexes make sense of having been sexually abused in a variety of contexts, and the different ways in which the meanings attached to such experiences are incorporated into their identities. All children draw on the (gendered) discourses concerning sexuality and the family that are available to them, and out of a mixture of private experiences and public discourses begin to construct the narratives of self which guide, inform and justify their course of life.

Analyses which have recognized a plurality of masculinities (Hearn 1990b), their stratification and their different relationships to violence, can help make sense of why some men do and some do not abuse children, and the particular versions of 'being a man' in which the identities of either are invested. Such work also points to the importance of the contexts of institutions and subcultures in generating particular masculinities and in their hierarchical organization such that in various contexts the basic pattern of domination 'feminizes' subordinate men. In relation to sexual abuse, male abusers provide one model of 'being a man' to any child they abuse. However, the possibility of investing in a similar form of adult identity is clearly available to boys in a way that it is not to girls. The three male survivors I interviewed talked of consciously seeking a version of masculinity different from that of their abusers. Their 'escape' from ritual abuse was described in terms of not having become an adult perpetrator. By contrast, women interviewees described their survival mostly in terms of the preservation of some essential capacity for attachment/trust/empathy which their abusers had attempted, but failed, to destroy. Their 'escape' was seen as being from a lifetime of male violence and exploitation as well as from the 'necessity' of abusing another generation of children.

In this chapter, I argue that making sense of women's involvement in ritual abuse entails understanding them as 'women' constructing meaning and identities out of a variety of contradictory materials. It is only if we anticipate that the dominant discourses which construct men and women as entirely different kinds of people map directly on to real life individuals that women abusers become incomprehensible. While there may be a hegemonic discourse of femininity to which girls and women are subject, it is by no means impossible to reject as well as reproduce its dictates (Moore 1994). This makes possible the development of resistant identities including those of feminism, but it also allows for the existence of numerous subcultural variations in gender roles and expectations which may be less than revolutionary.

The discourses of femininity and the 'ways of being a woman' these provide are also multiply differentiated by class, culture and subculture: 'femininity' has long been understood as being fractured into a plurality of femininities. (The demands of men for both 'Stepford wives' and 'Stepford whores' was one of the earliest issues addressed by the 'second wave' women's movement.) Attention has also been paid to the internal contradictions that beset different versions of femininity. For example, within traditional

Catholicism the elevation of womanhood to a quasi-saintly status occurs alongside women's actual subordination in both domestic and religious life. The Church has provided various outlets for women's skills and ambitions while ensuring that these do not directly challenge patriarchal authority (see Harris 2000). There may be some parallels between such a situation and that of women involved in ritual abuse.

There are female members of most deviant subcultures and their roles are often an odd mixture of faux-machismo and traditional femininity. Women bikers, for instance, may combine hard drinking and motorcycle maintenance with fulfilling dutifully the role of a sandwich-making, T-shirt ironing girlfriend. Their involvement in such a subculture distances them further from women outside than is the case for men, and they may therefore invest more in membership of the 'gang' and their own rebel status. However, their isolation and dependency may also make them vulnerable to abuse and sexual exploitation. This is a situation in some respects comparable to that of women involved in families and groups practising ritual abuse. The important differences are the extent of separation from the surrounding culture and the generational continuity that renders kinship as well as other forms of attachment internal to the group.

This chapter explores the discourses and practices of gender revealed within life-history interviews, showing how the mothers and grandmothers described by interviewees conformed in many respects to traditional gender roles and were subject to both male authority and male violence. However, I shall also show that, alongside this everyday culture of subordination, runs an occult discourse wherein women's magical/spiritual powers are considered equal or superior to those of men, and a Sadeian version of sexual liberation explains the natures of both men and women as finding their true expression in the fulfilment of perverse desires. For some women who had been brought up with the ritual expression of such ideas in conjunction with their own lived experiences of abuse, this discourse clearly provided both legitimation and identity.

Protestations of equality

The women I interviewed rarely pointed directly to the gendered nature of their experiences of ritual abuse, nor did they overtly stress gender differences between their abusers. On each occasion I asked interviewees about the position of women in ritual abuse, I was immediately told that men and women were equal or that women had as much power as men. My informants often went on to explain that a high priestess and high priest were 'classed as the same', as were a priest and priestess, and that women abused just as much as the men. I was frequently told that women were 'worse' than men in the cults: 'more into all the blood and guts', 'more spiteful' and that they 'had more imagination for punishments and stuff'. Given what I knew about other forms of sexual and domestic violence, prostitution and pornography, it seemed to me unlikely that groups practising ritual abuse were islands of equal opportunity, but it was impossible to encourage conversations beyond this assertion of gender parity.

There are a number of possible explanations for this being the case. The general disbelief in sexual abuse by women might fuel a need to insist that women are 'down with the worst of them'. The difficulty of separating from cult and family, and the need to differentiate between oneself and one's abusers, might encourage a binary divide between 'us non-abusers' and 'them', rather than a gender divide that would include victims and perpetrators on both sides. However, as I explored the descriptions of significant others, their roles in different forms of abuse and their everyday lives, I began to identify equal participation within ceremonies as the primary site of 'equality'. I recognized that formal, ritual equality might well serve to mask underlying power relations and help to convince girls and women of their equal guilt and responsibility. Such an analysis fits with that provided by American survivor Elizabeth Rose:

> Ostensibly, women and girls were the center of cult activities. In my family's cult fertility and sexuality were the focus of many different cere-monies. Numerous sermons were devoted to woman's place in Satan's world. We were told that because Eve had accepted the fruit from the serpent, women were inherently more wicked and evil than men, and so more capable of carrying out Satan's work . . .
> In rhetoric, women seemed to be held in high esteem – but the reality was far different. Women were maligned, humiliated and abused. A woman's value in the cult was based solely on her sexuality: either her ability to have intercourse or to be fertile and bear children. The men in the cult dominated the women, physically and emotionally.
>
> (Rose 1993: 42)

No such analysis was proffered by the women I interviewed. Indeed, the protestations of equality I met with in asking about gender differences tended to terminate swiftly such a direct line of inquiry. One exception occurred in my interview with Beth, who was willing to struggle with my questions:

What was the difference between being an adult woman and an adult man in the group?

[*Long pause*] Um, males were more highly thought of . . . in some situations . . . I haven't really thought of . . . In some ways not an awful lot actually. I mean you had some roles that were female roles and other roles that were male roles – themed.

(Beth)

Beth did not find it easy to describe gender differences in the abstract: she said that 'she hadn't really thought about it', and she qualified some of her comments as she spoke. However, she went on to explain that men made the decisions, 'had first pick' and were 'individuals' in a way the women were not. Women were subject to the men's instructions and a division of labour that allocated them low status work such as childcare and candle-making:

> The women made the candles, the men wouldn't make the candles, it
> was beneath them . . . They assumed that you might be able to manage
> to make candles that smelt grotty or tasted foul or did whatever
> various things. And so they would trust you with the knowledge to be
> able to do that, but when it came to other things you had to have a
> man to show you how to do it.
>
> (Beth)

Ceremonies, in Beth's account as in those of the other survivors I interviewed, were always led by both a man and a woman, and victims of any age
and either sex might be sexually abused, tortured or 'sacrificed'. Within
ritual abuse groups, ceremonies are performances staged for the audience of
their participants. As in the production of pornography, a particular image
of gender relations may be projected, while what happens 'off-camera' or
back-stage might be quite different.[1]

The **division** of **labour**

The division of labour between men and women described by interviewees
was pronounced. The 10 interviews with women survivors in Britain contained 49 references to women performing traditionally feminine tasks, and
no references to men performing these functions. It has to be said that the
versions of 'childcare' and 'domesticity' were sometimes bizarre and abusive,
involving cleaning children after abuse, administering enemas, defrosting
frozen body parts and acting as abortionists, but they were none the less
recognizable as 'women's work'. Apart from references to violent outbursts
and sexual abuse, I found only six references to ritually abusing men 'at
home'. Two of these were described as regularly reading or watching the
news and two more were involved in doing 'business deals' with other men.

In Chapter 4, I described the involvement of mothers and grandmothers
in the preparation of toddlers for abuse and the perversions of the routines
of bathing and dressing these involved. Similarly, training children to swallow noxious substances without vomiting was a maternal task that had both
simple and elaborated forms. Urine being served as lemonade or faeces as
chocolate cake was mentioned in four interviews – vomiting being 'discour-
aged' by enforced re-ingestion. Kathleen was often fed dog food, while Sinead
recalled rotten meat complete with maggots. However, some women had
clearly developed the basic ritual-related task into a 'creative' activity in
which they took some pleasure:

> Like she [my mother] used to make a Yorkshire pudding. I thought for
> years and years that Yorkshire pudding was this white slime that you
> poured over your dinner. We had this white goo, and actually that
> was anything from fat to candlewax in that. It was horrible, absolutely
> foul, and it would all stick on the roof of your mouth. And that would
> be usually after a ceremony. Any fat that was left over, if they'd done

a burning or anything like that, and the candles that were left over, we'd have in our 'Yorkshire pudding'. Christmases and birthdays, like birthday cake, being told you are eating chocolate cake and you're eating shit.

(Lynn)

The specific *tasks* performed by women varied by both class and personal competence but the *responsibility* of mothers or grandmothers for the care and control of children was clear in all accounts. Middle-class mothers' specific role in relation to the public presentation of children and family to the outside world is demonstrated in the following account:

Basically my father insisted that my mother spent most of her time creating a perfect family image. Part of that was family snaps or any pictures, Mum would have to put them in a photo album and put comments underneath, you know 'jokey comments'. There would be one of me crying on a family outing and Mum would write underneath 'Kate having a tantrum, exclamation mark', where actually my father had just beaten me black and blue for something insignificant. When you looked at the albums it was a typical family album. There's a picture of me, I'm standing outside some sort of building and I'm looking decidedly lost and very small and tiny, and underneath my mum's put: 'The lost traveller, exclamation mark'. Well actually, I was standing outside a house, my father had taken the photo and we were waiting for the man to answer the door so I could go in and he could abuse me . . . And Mum was always baking cakes and having her women friends, who were selected by my father, over for tea. On family birthdays we always went to a restaurant or something, and photographs were taken. And the reality of it was it was just a big show, we all hated it, well I did, it was ridiculous.

(Kate)

In similar form, Sinead described her teenage mortification at her mother ostentatiously taking her hand when crossing roads, and the 'joke' of her decorating a lavish Christmas tree in the front garden when not a single bauble would be seen inside the house. Gillean was less certain about the fraudulence or sincerity of her mother's maternal efforts, wondering whether she might have believed in them herself:

It was all to do with surface niceness. Although I do honestly believe that on one level she was trying to almost compensate for the abuse by being loving. The effect that it had was to cover up the abuse and isolate you. I can remember her . . . I always had dreadful problems with constipation and my back passage, and I remember her kind of [?] treating my sore behind. I'm sure that was after I'd been abused and she would like clean it out . . . what she was cleaning out was actually semen which was pretty disgusting but . . . And anything that kind of hinted at the abuse would be strictly taboo. Like you were never allowed to talk about these problems and you were certainly never taken to the doctors for anything like constipation.

(Gillean)

The mothers and grandmothers of interviewees tended not to work outside the home even in the 1980s. Some claimed that their fathers explicitly prohibited this, others suggested that their mothers would not have been able to cope with holding down a job. However, two interviewees said that their mothers had briefly had jobs as 'dinner ladies' at their primary schools in order to keep an eye on them. A partial exception was Sinead's description of her mother's successful bid to work outside the home despite her father's opposition. (Trained as a nurse, she worked part-time for a couple of years with terminally ill children, a decision which is highly suggestive of her extraordinarily 'split' identity.) However, the primary role of Sinead's mother along with the other 'capable' mothers was the care and control of their daughters. In particular, they were described as monitoring their fertility and acting as midwives and abortionists. Frequently, they are described as policing their grand/daughter's femininity, and giving messages about the importance of virginity or chastity which were at complete odds with the abuse they were involved in:

I was never allowed to wear a tampon or a Lillet or anything. She thought it was dirty, to put something up you. Ironic yeah!

Did she have other attitudes like that?

Well, I had to have long hair. I couldn't wear trousers, especially jeans 'cos those were for boys and girls and ladies wore skirts, and I had to wear very short skirts.

(Debbie)

Elizabeth describes the double messages from her grandmother, who punished her severely for being a 'dirty little girl' when she tried to talk about her grandfather's abuse of her, but who also acted as her abortionist on a number of occasions. Here she describes her use of a Higginson syringe:

It is an old fashioned type of thing used for enemas, colonic wash out, which had a bulb on it. One end went into the soapy water and the other into the bottom and you squeezed the bulb and the water went up it. But she put it into my mouth and into my bottom at different times or at the same time . . . 'Cos this was her big thing, wash your mouth out . . . so I suspect I was complaining about what had happened to me and she was saying don't be so disgusting, wash your mouth out with soap. But then she also washed me out anally, so that must have been because she knew damn well what was going on – but I was the one that was wrong, and thinking about it, probably a straight thing from her own childhood . . . So it was a very convenient way of getting her feelings out by hurting me, by washing me out, cleansing me of my sins.

(Elizabeth)

Sophie provides a very clear account of her mother's role in managing her reproductive abuse, and the confusing messages she transmitted:

> And when I actually started my periods my mother went absolutely ape-shit, the fact that I'd started . . . she was so angry with me. 'If I got raped she'd kill me', and I was like 'I don't understand what's going on' you know. I just couldn't understand . . . there were so many mixed messages. She was just so angry it was untrue, she was really annoyed.

Did you know about periods?

> No, I had no idea. Even sex education at school we didn't get taught about them. I didn't have a clue what was happening . . . And I knew . . . 'cos I overheard 'fertile' and I didn't know what fertile meant. So I tried to hide my knickers when I came on and things like that – so they wouldn't find out. I just knew it was something dodgy, but I didn't know what it was about. But I soon found out. Because she kept on asking me, my mother kept on asking me, asking me and asking me whether I'd started; and me saying: 'What dya mean?' I didn't have a clue what she was going on about, 'cos like sex was never mentioned, it was just completely taboo.

And how soon after you started did you fall pregnant?

> It was quite soon, within a couple of months of starting. The thing was I didn't know, and because . . . my mother would count the towels that I had, and there was nowhere to hide packs you had had, if you hadn't used any packs you know. So she knew when I hadn't started, so when she asked I'd say 'no', 'cos if you lie you've had it.

So she'd have known when you were pregnant?

> Yeah, and there was like this . . . all I can say is jubilation.

> (Sophie)

The warnings against rape, which seem so bizarre, may suggest that these women were responsible for reserving sexual/reproductive access to their daughters for particular men at least some of the time. This fits with the memories of some survivors that at certain times only their father and/or the high priest raped them. Elizabeth, for example, remembered 'holidays' when she was raped repeatedly by her father well after the age when he had apparently lost interest in abusing her and switched his attentions to a younger sister; she therefore assumed the intention was to get her pregnant by him.

Beth's parents were not involved in her abuse; however, within the cult – to which she was taken by her uncle – she was provided with 'parents' who performed traditionally gendered roles:

So the group allocated you 'parents'? What was their role?

> Yeah, that's right. Um [*pause*] . . . I suppose in some ways to make me feel that I was special to them. And therefore if I was special they were

the ones who were going to do things and teach me things and show me things. Um . . . and certainly as far as the woman was concerned . . . she gave me hugs and cuddles and kisses that my mum never gave me, so I wasn't complaining . . . not to start with . . . she was the one who gave me a bath afterwards. You know it was more sort of practical things.

(Beth)

Other interviewees described being cleaned up, quietened and comforted by women in the group, and Beth later describes the cult's satisfaction over how good she herself was with children and their approval of her training as a primary teacher:

teaching was OK because I would have a really strong grasp of child development and you have to have people who know how children think. And boy, do they know how children think! And they know that what freaks a 3 year old doesn't freak a 5 year old, what freaks a 5 year old doesn't freak a 12 year old. Somebody is one step ahead all the time.

So being 'good with children' was useful in the group?

And that was certainly a skill that was utilized in the group. That was one of the things that I hated in some ways . . . was the sense of knowing that because children responded to me . . . I'd think 'I don't want them to respond to me' . . . People say: 'O, you're really good with kids', I hate it when people say that to me, I really do, 'cos it brings back so many things of 'Yes and because I was really good with children what happened to them?'

(Beth)

Kate was clear that her role as an adult woman was mapped out for her:

I knew that basically I would be an abuser . . . and I would be abused in turn by the men. I knew one thing my father was very happy for me to provide them with the babies. That's what he wanted. It was a fairly safe thing to have to do, because if they want a full term child then they're not going to kick you around for nine months.

(Kate)

This kind of perverse form of traditional 'women's work' may not be peculiar to those involved in ritual abuse. In a recent case of multigenerational family-based abuse, the mother was said to have played an important part through her dedicated performance of a perverse maternal role: scrubbing her children's genitals with scouring powder when bathing them, and keeping a calendar charting her daughters' periods because her husband had an aversion to menstrual blood (Davies 1998).

Three interviewees described training for ritual abuse which occurred outside the home undertaken by a 'master'. This was a 'special', dyadic, non-familial relationship which may have been primarily for the satisfaction of an ageing male abuser. Alternatively, such childhood relationships of obedience may have provided a model of emotional dependence on an abusive partner in preparation for the arranged marriages for which like their mothers these girls were destined. Sinead described such a relationship thus:

> That's what it was about: learning to be obedient. Learning to have a Master and know who your master was and do as you were told – his word was law, he took his instructions from Satan.
>
> *And who was the Master?*
>
> O, you had various masters, you didn't only have one. You could change masters according to what happened to the master really. Your master was a member of the group who was a sort of mentor, he would look after you. If you were being punished by someone else for doing something wrong he could stop the punishment, he could rescue you.
>
> *So who was your master when you were little?*
>
> [X] was one, he was old, 60-ish, but he wasn't an elder until later on. I had him for about three years and he quite often 'rescued' me from beatings. He was the one that taught me not to cry, not to show any emotion at all when someone was being beaten, when I was being beaten, when someone was being tortured or killed, or when I was being tortured. I wasn't to show that it bothered me. And he taught me that, through beatings, drumming it into me.
>
> (Sinead)

Masculinities/femininities

In each interview, I asked for descriptions of survivors' parents and primary abusers and in each case I was given descriptions that were contrasted strongly by gender. Three extremely abusive mothers were described variously as 'mad', 'weird' and 'twisted'. The unpredictability and 'wildness' of these mothers was contrasted with cooler, more rational fathers. One woman described her mother as having 'moderate learning difficulties'. In similar vein, Sinead described her paternal grandfather as 'a typical, big-mouthed Yank', while her grandmother, mostly silent except for occasional inappropriate comments in the middle of conversations, and with the black 'panda' eyes of the chronic anorexic, was said to resemble 'Frankenstein's monster'. Two women described their mothers as 'complete victims' who were brutalized and utterly dependent on their cold, violent husbands. It was these same mothers who were particularly active in keeping up a good family image for the outside world. The participation of these mothers in the active sexual abuse of their daughters was described as minimal.

In three families ineffectual, 'soppy', alcoholic grandfathers were contrasted with powerful, 'hard' grandmothers who were described as 'keeping the family together'. However, in most cases the *relative* normality of male abusers, and in particular that of fathers, was emphasized by most interviewees. These were largely perceived as confident and self-important men, braggarts and misogynists who their daughters often believed had themselves been 'spoilt' as children. Gillean was one of several interviewees who described her father as a 'golden boy':

> He was the youngest child in the family and very much the petted, spoiled, favourite, youngest son . . . I know that he was spoiled and petted. I know that the contrast between how he was and how his older cousin was, is incredible. The cousin was brought up in the family and should really have been treated like a sibling, but she never was . . . Poor soul she's so self-effacing and apologetic that she can hardly speak. She has never married or had a decent job or got on . . . And I feel some of the dynamics in their family were repeated in mine. Where the oldest child of the generation, which in this case was Mary, and in my case was me, was the scapegoat.
>
> (Gillean)

Lynn's father seems to have relied more on self-aggrandizement than family praise. His claims about himself included having been a movie stunt man and having broken records for parachute jumping. Lynn described her parents as operating within separate spheres. She thought her father was more interested in 'public power', wheeling and dealing rather than staying at home and beating the children, while her mother's satisfactions in life were based on children, kitchen and religion. Lynn believed her mother was probably 'too bizarre' to get by in the outside world:

> He's a very sane, logical thinker, cold, calculating, but he's also a charmer. People fell for that, but I don't know if it was then charm or what it was; power? Or just that he seemed to have all the answers. People get very sucked into 'this is a very intelligent man' . . .
>
> Now my mother [*laughs*] she's a completely different kettle of fish. Out of the two, I'd say it was my mother who was far more the intelligent, but in a totally different way. My mother could tell you anything about plants, herbs. She should have been a scientist . . . In her case she was probably too fragmented to hold it together. The mother part of her would do the ordinary sort of things, housework stuff, but I've never in my whole life seen her show compassion, caring, anything like that, nothing, never. She was very dedicated to her beliefs, strongly, and that overrode everything, completely in her life . . .
>
> She was actually a very scary person to be around normally. And yet I know when we were all coming through this we used to wonder if she was insane, but the more I've thought about it the more sure I am that she wasn't. I think she was just deeply committed to what she believed. Whether I understand it or not is not the point, and I'm not

trying to condone it . . . She wasn't insane, it's no good me trying to
say she was, that would be just trying to find a cop out . . .

   My father is very money orientated and power orientated, I reckon
he was on a big ego trip. There was times he said he believed, and
maybe he did for that short time. And particularly around my mother
he said he believed, mind you, you wouldn't dare around my mother
say you didn't [*laughs*] . . . My mother was very into magic. She
believed there was a power that she could tap into. And that went
along with their religion, they believed there were seven doors to hell.

(Lynn)

Abusing parents were frequently contrasted in terms of belief: a number of
fathers were described as cynics or non-believers in terms of the occult religion surrounding the abuse, while the four mothers/grandmothers described
as most active in ritual abuse were all considered to have believed in Satan
and in their own occult powers.[2]

Lynn also described the husbands and sons of her eldest sister (the only
one of the five sisters to remain involved in ritual abuse as an adult) and
compared the competitive ambitiousness of one of these young men to that
of her own father, who had fought for his position in the group by terroriz-
ing his elder brother into semi-retirement. Such descriptions of the operations of power and competition were reserved entirely for men:

   Her first husband was an immensely horrible cruel man, the second
   one was just a drip. The first one was very like my father, I remember
   him. I can remember him in my abuse, 'cos they used to come home
   regularly and she had children. Now, she had Andrew when Mum was
   having Norma, so he's nearly the same age as me. We believe that he
   was being trained to take over my father's job and should have done
   so. But he had a younger brother, only a few years younger than him,
   and he was very competitive. Rather like the feud that had gone on in
   my father's family and he had won over his elder brother, that was
   going on there.

(Lynn)

Most of the men described by interviewees were seen as consistent, as people
who 'added up' or 'made sense'. The only exceptions were the 'soppy' grandfathers who were described as being more 'split' between their abusing and
passive, 'fireside' roles, and descriptions of them were generally 'more feminine'.
However, *all* of the primary female carers/abusers were at some point described as being 'split', 'contradictory', 'unpredictable', 'volatile' or two-faced.

   In addition to fathers and grandfathers, a few other men were described as
being primary abusers. These men were most often uncles, or a best friend/
lover of the survivor's father. In the four interviews in which such abusers
appeared, their extreme practices, devotion to sadism, twisted humour and
enjoyment of risk make them stand out in survivors' memories. These 'extreme' men help to normalize the fathers and grandfathers who are central
to these accounts. In the working-class households inhabited by Debbie and
Sophie, brothers and uncles brawled and were arrested by the police on a

routine basis, but each identified one tormentor who 'didn't know when to stop' and whose access to them would occasionally be limited by a mother or grandmother. Kate describes her father's friend and business partner as an abuser whose enjoyment of risk made him more dangerous than the rest:

> Um, putting it simply he's completely evil. I fear him more than I fear my father. Because at least my father knows how far to go, Andrew doesn't, he has no boundaries, and unless there's someone there to put a hold on things he can get very dangerous. And he's always the one that comes up with new ideas, 'O, let's do this, why don't we try this?' And if Andrew's around there's always a camera around, he's very proud of what he succeeds in doing.

> *And what did his tastes run to?*

> He would do anything and everything really. [*Pause*] I mean anything that took his fancy that he could think up . . . Anything . . . what he liked seeing was terror, I think that's what I worked out that he liked seeing. Um, . . . they took great fun in strangling you, to the point where you blacked out. There was always that fear that they wouldn't stop in time, this is it and you die. They loved doing that. Andrew was quite . . . he liked electricity as well in a very bizarre way. You know, he used to use stun guns and enjoyed giving kids ECT, which wouldn't have been so bad if they'd used an anaesthetic but they didn't, which wasn't very nice. We'd end up biting our tongues and our muscles were always really aching and I couldn't remember what had happened before.

> (Kate)

Andrew's difficulties with sacrificing a lamb (described in Chapter 3) make clear that he had not been brought up with ritual abuse. As with Alan in Sinead's life, his power was within the strictly secular realm. What both descriptions suggest is the dual systems which men were involved in, and the possibility of being extremely powerful in terms of the secular, abusive, criminal world, but ignorant and insignificant in a ritual context.

Marriages made in hell

No one described their parents' marriage as a happy one. Mutual dislike was not unusual, expressed in regular violence in which women ranged from passive punch-bags to active antagonists. These were, however, unusually stable relationships. Only Debbie's parents had split up, and then only after her mother had a 'breakdown' and fled the country. Debbie was one of three interviewees who thought their mothers might have 'married into' ritual abuse families without having grown up in such families themselves. However, other marriages may well have been 'arranged' between families deeply involved in ritual abuse. Sinead described photographs of her paternal grandparents with her own parents together as children, and wondered whether they might be related by blood as well as marriage. Elizabeth described her own 1960s marriage to her cousin as having seemed 'inevitable' despite the lack of enthusiasm on either side. This sense of 'destiny' or inevitability under-pinned Gillean's mother's acceptance of her husband's cruelty and violence:

> She believes there is one man in the universe you are destined for, and he was the one for her. And um . . . she is almost addicted to him in a . . . she is very self-sacrificing and she thinks that self-sacrifice is love. And she will put up with almost any amount of verbal and emotional abuse from him. And I think over the years he more or less crushed who she really was, by his verbal abuse. When I was younger he used to hit her as well, sometimes in front of us.
>
> (Gillean)

Lynn describes her parents' marriage as one in which, although there was no love lost, there was complementarity of roles and a shared 'life project':

> I don't think there was any love between them. But I don't think that was an issue for either of them anyway. I don't think it ever crossed their minds either is what I'm saying. It was just like they had lives to lead, and they had things to do with that life . . . I think they spent a lot of time working together, and for two people who obviously didn't like each other to me it shows an awful commitment . . . What else can I tell you about them? They were both very competitive but in different ways so they didn't clash. They were competitive in relation to different needs, so in that sense you could say they were very well matched. Like she was into the potions and drugs side and it was him that cared about heading up a major cult. So in some ways they actually complemented each other.
>
> (Lynn)

Gillean explains her mother through contemporary discourses of addiction and co-dependency, while Lynn makes sense of her parents' marriage in the cult terms she presumed were relevant to them. However, both accounts suggest a premodern version of marriage: 'one man in the universe you are destined for'. The importance of a notion of 'destiny' has also been noted by Jacqui Saradjian in her interviews with women perpetrators of ritual abuse, one of whom she quotes as saying:

> It was my right to be there. It was my destiny. I was special. I wanted everything to happen to me . . . That's why I was there . . . it was my destiny.
>
> (quoted in Saradjian 1996: 174)

Feminine identity

I have so far focused on women interviewees' gendered descriptions of their abusers. I now turn to the contradictory meanings that being female had for them and the ways in which these provided a pattern for becoming an adult perpetrator *and* the possibility of rejecting such a future. It is important to remember that ritually abusive families and groups do not exist outside the mainstream of society but are in constant reaction to and interaction with the surrounding culture. As children, interviewees were taught that the values normally associated with 'goodness' constituted nothing more than a 'slave morality': chastity, meekness, love and sympathy for the weak constituted the cant of fools, hypocrites and Christians. In fact such values are identified as 'feminine' quite as much as they are associated with a 'gentle Jesus' form of Christianity; this meant that within the abusive system girls were taught to revile precisely those moral qualities most closely associated with women 'outside'. At the same time, they had considerable personal experience of the inauthenticity of femininity. Their fathers were at least consistent; it was their mothers who sometimes faked maternal concern and domestic virtue. From the earliest age they too had been required to put on 'girlish charms' along with 'sexy' underwear for the benefit of cameras and customers.

A great deal of the physical and emotional abuse which interviewees remembered most clearly from early childhood seemed to have been focused on the eradication of any traces of the 'feminine-Christian' virtues through the destruction of any tendency to attachment and the awakening of rage. This might, as in Debbie's life, involve permitting or encouraging an attachment for a short period, which was cut short by the death or disappearance of the person concerned. At an earlier age, the same attachment-followed-by-traumatic-loss scenario might be arranged in relation to a pet, as it was with Sinead's cat Suki, or later with a litter of Gemma's puppies, whose dead bodies were given to her gift wrapped on her tenth birthday. Each of the women interviewees who had sisters – Elizabeth, Lynn, Kathleen, Gillean and Kate – describe the profound alienation fostered between them.[3] Lynn describes the way she and the two sisters she grew up with (the elder two having left home when she was a toddler) barely acknowledged each other's existence. Though they were all profoundly abused, they were each encouraged to think that the others were being favoured above them and to see them as competitors. The impact of such experiences on victims of torture is captured by Judith Herman: 'Commonly the patient has the fantasy that she is already among the dead, because her capacity for love has been destroyed' (Herman 1992: 194).

Through such strategies, empathy, trust and affection were rendered too dangerous to be readily risked and the only safe relationship to others was indifference. Such experiences are of course extremely destructive to any child regardless of gender. However, because these characteristics are marked as feminine the particular impact upon girls is to deny them ready identification with others of their sex. The idea of women as 'naturally' gentler and more emotional than men still underpins much discourse about gender difference. To be 'unsexed' in this respect therefore involves a kind of social death: to be a woman as constructed within hegemonic femininity is apparently incompatible with girls and women's experience of ritual abuse

Interviewees also described experiences that appeared to be intended to awaken such rage that they would commit violence against others 'of their own volition'. Being mocked and ridiculed frequently accompanied abuse. The soundtrack of laughter was described to Jacqui Saradjian by the four women she interviewed:

> Each of them also described how they made children perform abusive acts on each other. The children were highly praised for their abusive behaviours, being told that they chose to do it, enjoyed doing it, and were very good at it. During all torturous acts the pain of the children was laughed at, ridiculed and denigrated. One woman described someone within the group whose specific role was to laugh when a child was hurt.
>
> (Saradjian 1997: 165)

Gillean described a memory of a 'gathering' where she was baited and goaded into such a frenzy that she stabbed someone. Lynn spoke of children being set to fight each other and men laying bets on the outcome as they might at a dog or cock fight. She claimed never to have believed that she was 'one of them' except in such moments when the 'proof' seemed to come from her own hatred and rage. Sinead had been led to believe that her 'wrath' was the true core of herself and that anger rather than love defined her relationship to others. The official discourse of gender that accompanied ritual abuse and which claimed women's equal propensity to violence and sadistic pleasure was verified through such experiences as it was through the experience of abuse at the hands of women. Discursive claims about equal propensities for abuse are 'given body' through such experiences, their veracity is felt to be proven by the undeniable truth of pain and rage.

Struggles over the body

Research on torture and captivity has emphasized victims passivity and the co-option to the beliefs and values of their abusers which dependency, fear and trauma often brings about (Hearst and Moscow 1982; Strentz 1982), and Judith Herman has eloquently described the similarities between the experiences of political terror and domestic abuse (Herman 1992). The role of the body in lending reality to the political discourse of regimes which depend upon torture and terror is analysed in the work of Elaine Scarry (1985). Through 'analogical substantiation' the structure of torture facilitates the leap from the immediate experience of pain to its objectification in the 'insignia of the regime', making the link seem natural and inevitable. Both torturers and their victims learn the truth and power of the regime through torture, just as battered women and their abusive partners both gain embodied experience of patriarchal discourse through each violent episode.

Feminist theory, from Firestone (1979) onwards, has highlighted the significance of the body and bodily processes for the oppression of women. Gendered social practices appear 'natural' and inevitable through their apparent roots in biological differences between the sexes. For girls and women who are ritually abused, sexual pleasure and orgasm, menstruation, lactation, pregnancy and childbirth all take place within an abusive schema which 'steals' them from the female body and appropriates them for the 'benefit' of the group.

Physical changes linked to reproduction such as menstruation and lactation are widely assumed to have 'natural' meanings. In late-modern societies, girls at menarche are generally told some variant on the story that monthly bleeding is part of their body's preparation for them becoming a mother (or even 'becoming a woman'). Ritual abuse groups do not appear so much to destroy such 'natural' meanings as extend and pervert them. Interviewees described having to drink breast milk from other women, having their own drunk by the group and the incorporation of their menstrual blood into rituals. The female body appeared to 'naturally' produce secretions with occult significance, thus it was co-opted into the abuse system.

In my interviews with male survivors, sexuality was a central theme, with women it was discussed only peripherally. However, some women described the way in which sexual arousal had been linked to pain throughout their childhood and had impacted on their sexuality. Their own bodies had produced the 'evidence' of their complicity and the 'truth' of their masochistic desires:

> The thing about human bodies is, treated in a certain way over a long period of time they respond . . . in one particular sado-masic [*sic*] film I'd been tied to a table. I'd been horrendously beaten and abused with pins and needles stuck in my body, and I was in chains . . . Afterwards that was one of the ones I was made to watch regularly: 'Look, you really enjoyed that, you get off on it don't you? You need pain don't you? You want pain.'
>
> (Lynn)

One survivor described a rare moment of honest communication with her mother who, some time after her daughter had extricated herself from her family and its networks, had asked her: 'But don't you miss the sex?' Interviewees had usually continued to be sexually exploited in a variety of contexts as long as they maintained any relationship with their abusers. However, once they began describing their lives after puberty narratives focused on reproductive rather than sexual abuse.

In survivors' accounts, it is possible to see how the patriarchal discourse of ritual abuse was lent reality by the particular abuses of women. However, some women also developed a narrative of resistance out of that same bodily experience, interpreting it through their encounters with the outside world in which a different discourse of female nature and the 'truth of the body' were prevalent.

In Chapter 6, I show how a number of the survivors I interviewed located a particular experience of giving birth, and the subsequent death of their infant, as central to their stories of practical and moral escape from the world of ritual abuse. For any teenage girl to be pregnant and give birth is to enter into certain discourses of maternity. The ritually abused teenager is not immune to the values of her peers or ignorant of the discourses of gender in the wider culture. The occult discourse which for their abusers was given flesh in these experiences was resisted and rejected by my interviewees – the evidence of their bodies was that the regime was wrong and they did not belong within it. However, this is not the only time that the body was described as a locus of resistance to ritual abuse.

Resistance to ritual abuse often involved survivors acting upon their own bodies in ways that ranged from shaving their heads to attempting suicide. As a small girl, one interviewee recalled trying to stain her blond ringlets green by rubbing them with grass, as she associated her 'Shirley Temple' appearance with her abuse in pornography. Debbie described piercing her ear with a safety pin as a defiant statement of her early teens. Some 'body rebellions' were more double edged: Sinead described a rare instance of complicity with her mother that involved them 'cutting up' together. Starvation and vomiting were both enforced as punishments, and practised by survivors as providing some measure of control and experience of personal power. One woman claimed to have been able to keep her body weight so low in her mid-teens that she ceased menstruating and could not fall pregnant.

In addition to these self-directed acts of resistance, interviews also contained a number of descriptions of bodies failing to fully participate in the business of ritual abuse. The 'involuntary' limits to participation set by speech or hearing difficulties were claimed as a source of pride and differentiation from their abusers. The organs of speech and hearing were in turn engaged as sites of rebellion by survivors who could not join in the chanting at ceremonies because they had problems 'voicing', or had a hearing impairment. Beth's account (previously quoted) is typical in the link it makes between bodily incapacity and resistance to knowledge and co-option:

> I could write backwards without any problem, but I could never speak it backwards. I couldn't do it. I remember Uncle John saying to [?] 'She's left-handed'. I remember thinking what on earth has that got to do with it. And whether or not it had anything to do with it I do not know.
>
> (Beth)

Sexual abuse by women

In Chapter 1, I pointed out that the question as to when/whether women abusers are abusing in the absence of male coercion has been central in the literature. In relation to my research, however, it is not a straightforward matter of either/or. The survivors I interviewed had lived within male-dominated families and ritual abuse groups, but, within that overall context they described women abusing at the behest of men *and* independently. In studying their accounts it is possible to distinguish between sexual abuse as training or punishment focused on the body of the child, and abuse as sexual gratification focused on the body of the woman abuser. The former was related to the preparation of children for involvement in pornography, prostitution and ritual abuse, involving the correct performance of both abuser and victim; the latter seemed essentially private. There was no simple division between domestic and public space here, for training and performing for the benefit of others occurred in both contexts.

Both Sophie and Kathleen described being abused by women in domestic space, but in terms of cult intentions and purposes. Sophie claims that if her grandmother was by herself she would not abuse her, but that with Sophie's brothers or her grandfather present she would participate in sadistic physical and sexual abuse. Kathleen recalled that throughout her early childhood she would be sold for sex on Sunday nights to men who came to the house. Her mother always finished the evening with a private ritual:

> She used to finish it. They had candles and stuff in the room, and she had, well I hope it's a very idiosyncratic method of putting the candles out, which was on me or often in me. And that's how it would finish.
>
> (Kathleen)

By contrast with Sophie's grandmother who 'wouldn't bother' to abuse her when no one else was around, Elizabeth remembered sexual abuse by her aunt and mother as very much for their personal pleasure:

> Staying in Oxford, my Auntie Jane had . . . her husband was away in the war and she had an abortion . . . miscarriage, abortion. And I was quite fond of her, used to visit her a lot, taken to stay there. I must have been 4, 5. I . . . she used me to make herself feel better 'cos she hadn't got a baby. Um, this was a recovered memory. That I had to actually suck her breasts, although I was long past that age to be doing that . . . And another memory like that is playing hide and seek and I was with her in Gran's house. And we hid in a bedroom under the covers and we were doing it then as well. And yet another memory of abuse by her was . . . where I was enjoying it, because she was so loving towards me and I didn't get much of that. So she was being really, really . . . holding me and hugging me and then she got me to touch her, and I was licking her as she'd taught me to do – and I was used to it by then so it seemed all right. And then we sort of fell together on the bed with great excitement . . . and she was so pleased with me . . . she was saying: 'That's lovely'. Well you can imagine that she was obviously having an orgasm, as an adult. And really, really pleased with me. And I felt really pleased that I had pleased her . . .
>
> This was between the ages of 3, 4 and 7 or 8, before she had her own daughter. But I particularly remember that I was doing this because she had a miscarriage. She was giving me a reason: 'This is because I don't have a baby, you be my baby' . . .
>
> And I remember that Mum also used to do this. She also had a miscarriage between me and Sally. So this is again around 2 or 3, where she used me in exactly the same way to suck her breasts. Then it got much worse than that . . . with Mum it was much more . . . I've half read about this since and I can't really make myself believe that she was really wanting to use me as a . . . [*pause*] . . . object to express

her sexual feelings. It was either that or it could have been even
worse, that she really wanted to hurt me, and hurting me was turning
her on. I can certainly remember being tied to the bed while she was
doing things to me . . .

   Mum did incidentally tell me that she could never get the sexual
relationship together with Dad, she told me that in my teens, they
couldn't do it. Dad always used to wake up at 5 in the morning and
expect her to do it and he'd go back to sleep again. She wanted it to
be something more, but they couldn't sort it out. So yet another
memory of that time is they used to get me out of bed in the middle
of the night, take me to their bed and push me down under the covers
and use me as a go between for their sexual intercourse. So I would be
licking Mum and Dad would be putting his penis into my bottom.

                                                              (Elizabeth)

Mothers and/or grandmothers were generally the survivors' earliest and most
consistent abusers. Even those remembered as passive victims had still col-
luded in and covered up their daughter's abuse, to identify with them in any
respect would mean identifying with women who remained involved in such
practices. Some interviewees remembered their mothers being pregnant at
times when no sibling was born, and therefore assumed that their mothers
had produced babies/foetuses for the group as they themselves had been
forced to do, and Elizabeth recalled having to take a foetus aborted by her
mother to a cult meeting. This did not, however, suggest to them any sense
of shared exploitation. One very partial exception emerged in Sinead's interview describing a fleeting moment of identification which I quote for its
rarity value in these accounts:

   He [my father] was a big shot and everybody knew it. Mum usually
   kept into the background then . . . didn't sort of want everybody to
   know . . . I suppose a bit like me, didn't want everybody to know who
   she was and what she'd gone through.

                                                                 (Sinead)

Interviewees spoke of themselves as being forced to sexually abuse other
children in both ritual and pornographic contexts, these memories were
clearly very painful and no one wanted to dwell on the subject. However, they
acknowledged that as children such occurrences had been routine and they
had mostly been too concerned with their own pain to dwell on that of others.
The survivors I interviewed had understood growing up as involving moving
increasingly into the role of an abuser: as teenage girls they were often
responsible for 'minding' younger children and keeping them in line. At the
same time any attempts to develop non-abusive relationships were thwarted.
Sinead described the appalling double bind which forced her to sexually and
physically abuse a young woman to whom she was greatly attached:

   I always felt it like it was happening to me, because I could always see
   the pain on her face but she wouldn't show it. She would always wink

at me or smile, when I knew she was hurting and it was me that was
hurting her. It was a case of : 'If you don't do it we'll do it, but we'll
kill her afterwards.' And: 'If you really love her you'll hurt her'.

(Sinead)

Sinead also talked about making pornography in which she had to 'have sex
with babies, children a year old, 2 years old'. For Sinead, these were the least
tolerable memories, the most stubbornly painful. She made clear that coming to terms with her victimization was an entirely more straightforward task
than dealing with her role in the abuse of others:

I think I'll always carry that, and I'll always remember the screams
... more so than the screams in a ceremony. Because these kids were
not used within a satanic group. Their mothers brought them along
and were paid a lot of money to have their kids used. I think often
about those kids and the effects on them. I mean I was 13, and no
one was holding a gun to my head ... not that day at least.

(Sinead)

The **men's stories**

Before I began this research, my contact with survivors of ritual abuse had
been exclusively with adult women and teenage girls. From survivors I learned
that boys had been abused alongside them in pornographic, paedophile and
ritual contexts. From research on children's experiences of organized and ritual
abuse (Finkelhor *et al.* 1988; Hudson 1991) it seemed that the abuse experiences of young children were similar regardless of sex. Given this information about the abuse of boys, it seemed important that I numbered male
survivors among my interviewees. However, this did not prove straightforward.
Out of my initial questionnaires only four were returned by men, three were
British, although one of these was resident in Germany, and the fourth was
from the USA. These questionnaires were rather sparsely filled in, and two
respondents wrote specifically that they did not remember much about their
ritual abuse experiences. Through therapeutic networks, I attempted to make
contact with other male survivors, and having failed to find men in Britain
willing or well enough to be interviewed, I finally undertook interviews with
three men in the USA.

Unlike the women I interviewed in Britain, these men had been involved
in ritual abuse only during a particular period of their childhoods. In two
cases, ritual abuse had been facilitated by one member of the family while
others were apparently non-abusive. Gerry was ritually abused during the
years he lived with his mother and stepfather – from age 6 to 10; Sam was
sexually abused by his paternal grandfather and taken to rituals by him until
he was 11 or 12; Erik visited his mother's family on the other side of the USA
three or four times in his pre-teen years, and his only experiences of sexual
and ritual abuse were on these visits.

The differences in the amount of abuse, its timescale, and the extent of family involvement, are the clearest differences between interviewees in terms of gender. Interviews with these three men were apparently gendered in terms of content and focus, sometimes in ways that I found surprising. The biggest difference was that there was far less detail in their accounts, specific stories were both fewer and more fragmented. Daniel and Thompson (1995) have discussed the gendered remembering of men interviewed as adult children of stepfamilies. They describe men's accounts of childhood as less 'full' and 'rich' than women's, and as taking more coaxing to extract. Male interviewees were described as presenting accounts in a more 'sewn up' way, and to frequently deny remembering much about distressing events. The men I interviewed were 'good talkers' but the accounts they gave of their lives tended to the general, with relatively few recollections of specific events. With one exception, the women I interviewed told their life-stories through a series of specific memories.

Considerably more time was spent talking about adult experiences, particularly of sex and relationships, and how these had been affected by past abuse, than was the case in my interviews with women. Indeed the central theme of each interview was that of finding a different version of masculinity from that of their abusers. Unlike the women I interviewed, Gerry, Sam and Erik were absolutely clear about the patriarchal nature of the family and cult backgrounds they described. While their descriptions of the relations between men and women in their families are consistent with those given by women survivors, their explicit discussion of these in terms of male power is quite different. It is clear that neither their own abuse by women, nor women's participation in ritual suggested to them any real gender equality.

All three men clearly differentiated themselves in interview from the patriarchal inheritance of their families. Gerry describes his paternal grandparents as follows:

Grandma was very subservient to Grandpa. They were hardcore Southern Baptists, of the mind-bent that women belong in the kitchen, barefoot and pregnant, and if a woman steps out of line it is perfectly OK for a husband to beat the daylights out of her. In that environment – my dad being the baby of the family and the only boy, and the last of the male line – he could do no wrong . . . And the same basic mind-set existed on my mother's side: that women were there to serve, the men were there to rule.

(Gerry)

Despite the fact that it was through his mother and maternal grandfather that his ritual abuse occurred, and despite her abuse of him, Gerry provides a sympathetic, if disturbing, portrait of his mother. He described the domestic violence she suffered from his father and later his stepfather, who he believes kept his mother drugged for years. Similarly Erik and Sam described mothers who were subject to husbands and fathers, and to whom they apparently attached little blame. In each account, sisters are objects of concern and regret rather than the estranged and suspected figures who feature in a number of my interviews with women survivors.

There is one picture [of my mother] that is really frightening . . . She's
holding me up in the air, and her eyes are very sunken, black circles
under them, and the look on her face is like something out of *The
Exorcist* or something. An almost possessed look. She looks, not
physically sick only, but mentally sick. It's really a frightening picture
– I wish I'd brought it. And several of the pictures are like that. There's
one where I'm sitting on the couch with toy gun holster and cowboy
outfit. And she's sitting on the couch just resting her elbows on her
knees and her chin on the palms of her hands. And the look on her
face is: 'What the hell have I gotten myself into?'

(Gerry)

Gerry described his earliest memory of being sexually abused by his mother.
He places this in the context of both her continuing relationship with her
father (who he believes abused her from birth), and of preparation for ritual
involvement:

She started out by having me touch her breasts, the vulva . . .
explained what each part was for. I guess she was rationalizing to
herself that she was teaching me about sex. Then she demonstrated
what the male organ was for by taking me in her mouth. I later found
out that my stepfather was doing the same thing to my sister. It must
have been about a month later that I found out . . . all during those
years my mother still was in contact with her father . . . visited him a
lot . . . he took us to a house where a coven was meeting and forced us
to take part in an earth mother type ceremony. My mother was naked
on the altar. And my sister and I were used to represent the seed of
the earth. We were placed between her legs and my grandfather was
dressed up in a robe and a cowl. The same as life precedes from the
earth, takes fruit, life has to be fertilized, to recreate [*sic*] . . . and I was
brought to an erection by him taking me in his mouth and forced to
have intercourse with my mother and with my sister, and my
stepfather sodomized me, raped my sister. When I tried to stop him
I was knocked flat. That was the beginning of the beatings. I was
forced to stimulate my mother orally and the women in the coven
orally . . . And they were involved in a paedophilia ring. We'd get
rented out to other adults. My grandfather would pick us up and drop
us off at somebody's house. And we were told that if we were to
completely obey the adults, if we didn't we'd get beaten and they'd
demonstrated that. Then they learned a nice little trick to get me
completely compliant, they wouldn't beat me if I resisted, they'd beat
and rape my sister and my baby brother.

(Gerry)

Gerry disclosed his abuse to a social worker declaring that he did not care if
he was killed for it, as at least he might give his younger siblings a chance
that way. When they were all taken into care, he fought not to be separated
from his sister, and later when older foster sisters abused him, he managed to

prevent her involvement. With great sadness Gerry described his sister as having become a 'cabbage' as a result of a failed suicide attempt in her twenties. Sam similarly expressed considerable concern over two of his sisters who had long histories of mental illness and had been Lithium dependent throughout their adult lives.

As young adults both Sam and Gerry turned to religion, and seemed in part to be seeking through Christianity a way of being non-violent, non-abusive men. Gerry married his first wife when he was only 17, beat her up and seriously thought about killing her after she sexually humiliated him. Sam became involved in a Christian 'cult' as a young adult and entered an 'arranged' or at least approved marriage which lasted only a few years. Both men described problems with sex and intimacy. Sam feared sexual addiction as the likely alternative to his chosen celibacy and described how compulsive masturbation had accompanied his first flashbacks of abuse.

Erik's immediate family appears positively ordinary by comparison with many described by survivors of ritual abuse. However, the same patriarchal divisions are described. His grandfather took a second wife after the death of his first in order to have someone to look after the children, and treated her as a servant throughout their married life. Erik describes his father as 'smooth and sophisticated', 'violent', obsessed with keeping up an image of himself and his family, and convinced that 'to feel anything is a symptom of mental illness'. His mother he described simply as 'depressed'. It was, however, through his mother that sexual and ritual abuse occurred, for her father and brothers apparently continued to exercise control over her despite her having married outside the cult and moved to the other side of the USA.

Erik described only two memories of abuse in the context of rituals, but one of these included involvement in an infant sacrifice:

I remember being held on the table and raped by my grandfather. And you know as I try to deal with 'what did the room look like?', I wonder if it was maybe a Masonic Hall, my uncles were Masons, or whether it was a small room in a synagogue. Because the Jewish star and the Masonic . . . it's not so different. And in those days the interiors of those buildings were all dark wood and . . . that's just how it was. And I remember other men standing around watching and then I remember being thrown in a corner. I don't have something that comes before that or after that, I have that. And I have a memory sometime after that of being in a similar room with men and women. I remember an altar . . . this is fairly typical satanic kind of stuff, I remember candles and incense burning. And I remember being pretty woozy and I remember being naked and sitting in a chair and a baby being brought to me, and a knife being put in my hand, and my eldest uncle holding my hand with the knife and disembowelling the baby. [*unclear*] That's . . . like to talk about it is like it's real, like it's happening right now, I could feel the blood on my body, I could feel the organs coming out. [*Pause*] My sense of it is that I was not in danger, that I was being initiated. In the ritual abuse survivors group I went to for a little while, they were all women in that group except for me, they were all scared of what was going to happen to them; I didn't think that something was going to happen to me. And that may be a big difference in their recovery from my recovery.

(Erik)

Erik's story of remembering and recovery is intimately tied up with issues of masculinity. Unlike Gerry and Sam, Erik described himself as a successful man. Having had a worthwhile career in education, he dropped out in his forties to care for his second son, who had learning difficulties, and to build a house. It was during this time when, as he put it, he 'dropped the image' and became 'a housewife of sorts', that memories of his abuse returned. The memories came chronologically, and seemed to be linked to his son's age at the time. This is a common experience of women survivors, where a daughter reaching the age at which her mother's abuse started triggers memories. However, for Erik there had clearly been something 'feminizing' about remembering his abuse that was problematic to him:

I was ashamed, I was humiliated, I was frightened. I also wasn't productive like I'd been all my life. I wasn't making a lot of money, I was doing kinda odd jobs carpentry stuff, because the consulting stuff with the foundations was kinda hit and miss. I suppose I had my past that I was hanging on to, I had some real estate investments, I had a relationship, I had kids . . . That seemed real different from these [women in the incest survivors group I joined] . . . who all seemed barely hanging on. I didn't know if I belonged there, I didn't know if I trusted them, I didn't want to become like them . . . For the people in the group it was their life, that's who they were, that's what they hung their hat on, that was their identity. I didn't want that identity, I wanted to deal with it but . . .

(Erik)

Erik moved on from the survivors' group in which he was the only man, to a men's group with a focus on exploring masculinity through rituals, and to martial arts and a relationship with an Aikido master. In addition, he reflected on the importance during his childhood of an ex-Marine who used to take bunches of boys on camping trips and teach them survival skills, and who had provided a model of self-sufficient masculinity for him. In similar vein, Gerry talked of a native American Scout group which had taught him tracking and hunting skills, self-control and self-respect. Ritualized versions of masculinity continued to be important to each of these men, providing alternative ways of living to those of family and cult.

Sam described his involvement in ritual abuse as having been facilitated by his paternal grandfather. Sam said that he suspected that his father, like himself, had 'tasted and felt what it was like to be under someone above him'.

Well, so, the first memory was kind of rough with my grandfather – painful. Then with this other place that came into my life, things worked out much better because they were really professional, they were really slick, they played a lot of sexual games, they sexualized you a lot and made games out of it. That's basically what happened for a while, maybe a two-year period. A lot of sexualizing, and comforting and training. Giving you pleasure, a lot of pleasure.

(Sam)

Sam expressed considerable confusion about the 'pleasure' he had experienced in the context of abuse. As he recalls he had the chance to become a perpetrator, but he refused, and from then on was treated like a girl and abused mainly by women. His account is not easy to follow. However, since interviewing Sam I have come across another male survivor who had been 'treated as a woman' throughout his adolescence. As an adult this man dressed as a woman and described himself as completely addicted to pain:

The later years went from oral sex to anal sex, then there was the exchange, dressing as a little girl and being prostituted. Going and doing 30 people in whatever time schedule, few hours, 10 minutes with each man. They were just silly, in that little realm for such a short time and probably paid a thousand bucks. This was 7, 8, 9. By the time I was in my teens it was over pretty much . . . Adolescence was coming on and you're not the sweet, little sexual object they want any more. So you're put out to pasture . . .
  In the cult family, because of my grandfather's strength I had the ability to experience the pleasure of being a perpetrator. To be raised to know where I was going and to go there. One of the things was women took the brunt of . . . I've seen them cut up men, I've had strong association with having to chew on somebody's penis in a hot dog bun in a pornographic film of some sort . . . But, so . . . I was there and saw them cut up women from top to bottom, bottom to top. I feel like I was being structured in that way but I said 'no'. I had four older sisters, and the training I got at home and something unconscious in my own life outside of . . . I wouldn't do it, and from that point on I was feminized, subjugated to be a woman. From that point on like . . . oral sex with women was the main food for my life quite a bit. Then the feminization of my own mentality, perspective . . . I just had this tremendous memory the other night of oral sex in a bathroom with a man. This whole thing of him grabbing my face and holding my jaw open, biting down and being smacked . . . it was a really clear memory. Men were rough, men were dicks, fuckers. Women were very appreciative . . . of their orgasm, they were gentle. The first few years in my memories there was heavy trauma, the wickedness. And then this feminine part opened up.

(Sam)

Conclusion

Only in my interviews with male survivors were the subjects of women's oppression and gender identity explicitly and enthusiastically discussed. The women I interviewed spoke primarily from the perspective of survivors abused by both male and female adults. From their perspective, gender differences were not of primary import, as they were not equal to a distinction between abuse and safety, or between cruelty and care. In women's accounts of adolescence, this began to change. As they grew nearer the adult world of women – particularly through experiences of pregnancy, childbirth and infanticide – connections were made between their gender and their future. In recounting their lives, it was at this point that identifications were made with 'female universality' – a topic I explore further in Chapter 6. The conflict between continuing upon 'the path mapped out' and rejecting an abusing lifestyle, was in part expressed as a contradiction between becoming 'a woman' and being an abuser. To stay in the cult into adulthood would be to 'unsex' oneself in terms of socially dominant discourses of gender. This had no direct parallel for the men I interviewed. This may be because being a ritual abuser is an extreme point on the continuum of hegemonic masculinity. Men's rejection of abuse therefore provoked the problem of how to be a male survivor and how to be a man.

Through analysing the everyday divisions of labour and patterns of relationship that were described by interviewees, alongside abuse perpetrated by women and their overt ritual equality with men, I have shown the male-dominated character of the groups and families in which my interviewees were abused. However, rather than regard women interviewees' claims about gender parity as a simple matter of 'false consciousness', I have suggested that they were identifying a 'feminine identity' within the abusive subculture in which women might be partially or whole-heartedly invested. The discourse of abusive occultism which operated largely in relation to the organization and performance of rituals, rendered women and men equal in the pursuit of power and pleasure. A more everyday discourse of 'subordinate femininity' in which women's place was prone or at home and which demanded obedience to father or husband coexisted with their ritual elevation. The two seemed to be linked by a notion of 'destiny' which combined an abject acceptance of abuse and the absolution of responsibility, with some sense of power and identity gained through its fulfilment.

According responsibility is an extremely complex business when an entire life, and an entire family, is permeated with abuse and its legitimations. It is further complicated when we consider that the women discussed in this chapter lived through periods of social change when the possibility of women's self-determination increased dramatically and the power of fathers and husbands declined. Elizabeth described her family as 'steeped' in abuse. Her grandmother was born at the end of the nineteenth century and her great-aunt took one of the few routes out of a middle-class family then available to women when a diagnosis of 'religious mania' led to the asylum. By the 1950s Elizabeth was able to leave home to train as a nurse 'forgetting' her abusive childhood; in the 1960s Lynn (ten years younger than Elizabeth) could run away from home at 17 saying only enough to convince her future mother-in-law that her father was 'a dirty old man'; while in the 1990s Gene, Sinead and Debbie sought and found support, counselling and asylum while still in their mid-teens.

Few interviewees had any detailed knowledge of their parents' or grand-parents' histories but many believed they had been similarly abused. If this is so then ritual abuse had provided an apprenticeship in torture to which in turn they had indentured their own children. Children of both sexes were required to be prepared for sexual use in ritual and commercial contexts from infancy and women's responsibilities for childcare therefore included training in the toleration of physical pain, and appropriate 'sexual' behavi-our. Later they would be responsible for policing their daughters femininity, fertility and reproduction for the cult. However, to argue that the sexual abuse of children within the family was written into women's gender role, or to acknowledge that some had been trained in it from infancy, is not neces-sarily to 'excuse' women involved in ritual abuse as 'only following orders'. Women did not only abuse when there was a gun at their heads. Like Sophie's grandmother, some engaged in sexual acts only when there were other people around, but others inflicted physical, emotional and sexual abuse because it gave them pleasure to inflict pain, or comforted them in their own griefs.

Notes

1 A specific example might be that described by one interviewee who told me that lesbian relationships were completely taboo within her group, but that sex between women, and the sexual abuse of girls by women, was a regular feature of ritual activity as it is in pornography.
2 Gene is the exception here, for she describes her mother as 'weird and depressed' but her father as the 'true believer'.
3 Gene had a half-sister with learning difficulties who stayed with the family occa-sionally but was otherwise in residential care.

6 | Making death meaningful

Survivors of ritual abuse recall being routinely proximate with death in ways which are extremely rare in late-modern societies. This chapter explores the ways in which stories about death are both important for understanding the experience of ritual abuse, and form a central feature in survivors' narratives of resistance. For the survivors I interviewed, the death of someone with whom there was a personal connection – however fleeting – was often invested with great significance. Most particularly each of the women described having endured pregnancy followed by a forced abortion, or the birth and subsequent ritual killing of their baby, more than once during their teenage years. In describing their adolescence to me, many laid particular emphasis on the importance of a late-term baby, whose birth seemed to have represented a turning point in their rejection of the ritual abuse culture within which they had been raised.

Survivors' memories of witnessing and participating in violent deaths have probably aroused more incredulity than any other feature of their life-stories. I shall suggest that this automatic disbelief originates in contemporary attitudes to both death and religion such that 'ritual sacrifice' is always already consigned to a distant time or place. Killings which appear to have resulted from a search for sexual gratification or pecuniary gain, on the other hand, make sense within contemporary understandings of human motivation. At the same time late-modern societies shelter their citizens from death in ways that make the death-saturated life-stories of ritual abuse survivors extremely alien to most people's experience. Taken together, the attitudes towards and experience of death and religion among the audience for survivors' accounts is crucial in understanding their reception. This is a point readily accepted in terms of explaining the predisposition of evangelical Christians to *believe* accounts of ritual abuse, but the hegemony of scepticism has generally placed it beyond reach of equivalent considerations. Before exploring this further, however, I shall outline my own encounters with the issue of death in relation to ritual abuse, locating my belief in my experience as both a carer and researcher.

When I first began caring for Sinead, I remember how contagious her terror could be. On numerous occasions on a bus, in the street, or talking at the kitchen table, fear would clutch at my innards and fill my mouth with a salty saliva which my throat refused to swallow. What I absorbed was per-haps a homeopathic dose of the terror I regularly saw in Sinead's rigid jaw and dilated pupils. Through this second-hand experience, I felt her dread to be of a world-shattering kind which rendered our life together no more than a fragile fantasy – one that might be ripped away at any moment to reveal the inescapable reality of ritual abuse. Her terror was of death: Sinead feared that her abusers might kill her or anyone connected with her. Early in our acquaintance, when she herself was 'on the run' and sleeping rough, she had her much loved dog put down in order both to protect her from the parents who had abused them both and to ensure that threats to harm Gemma could not compromise her own determination to make a new life. If it had not been for the intensity of her determination and evident anguish over this decision I might have found this a melodramatic gesture on Sinead's part. Only later were some of the experiences on which her fears were founded shared with me. In other words, my acceptance of the 'truth' of Sinead's memories was grounded in my acceptance of the emotional truth of her terror. Her flashbacks were vivid, visceral and exhausting and the events she described made sense of the nightmares, self-hatred, despair and rage which was the stuff of our daily lives.

As I have already discussed, this kind of knowledge about ritual abuse is embedded in relationships. It is the foundation for the claims of therapists and foster parents certain that what their particular client or child has told them happened really happened. Such knowledge is gradually accumulated over time – belief engenders confidence and as trust grows disclosure gradually increases (see Sinason and Svensson 1994). Hearing accounts of witnessing death from other survivors whom I interviewed for the research was a very different experience. For the most part we met as strangers careful to maintain some emotional distance from the 'material' and from each other. From this position the scepticism that haunts most public responses to stories of undis-covered ritual murder seemed a natural attitude. There were after all some bizarre and confusing memories which interviewees could not explain and could not disentangle from the effects of drugs, pain and terror. From the standpoint of most interlocutors it might not be surprising that such memories – severed from the contexts of whole lives – could be dismissed as the nightmares and delusions of the severely disturbed, and considered to require no further explanation. However, I recognized the need to expose to critical scrutiny the assumptions behind the 'common-sense attitude' that awakened incredulity to some stories rather than others. First among these seemed to be contemporary ideas and experience of both death and religion.

Death in late modernity

Birth and death are both in decline in late-modern societies. My mother tells a story from her childhood in the 1920s. There was a woman her mother knew who sometimes stopped to speak. It seemed to the child that each time she did so she had the same tale to tell, and it always began: 'Eh, Lizzie, I've buried another 'un.' The image my mother conjured up of this woman digging another in a row of infant graves (coupled with her tendency to comment meaningfully on my mother's 'mawky paleness') gave her nightmares. The story is one of my mother's markers that differentiate between 'then' and 'now'; the past is a foreign country populated by dead babies and we do things differently these days. Infant mortality rates have declined dramatically over the eight decades dividing then from now. But the dead babies of my grand-mother's friend no longer exist in another sense. For the death of a baby in twenty-first-century Britain is a tragedy encased within well-developed med-ical and therapeutic discourses. There are specialist organizations dealing with the aftermath of cot death, stillbirth, children with cancer, support for parents of murdered children, miscarriage, meningitis. The thing itself has become rare; para-professional advice for those affected by it is plentiful.

Despite the development of a bereavement industry and the clamour of those repeatedly breaking the taboo on talking about death, Philip Mellor (1993) is one of many sociologists who have argued that modernity 'system-atically sequestrates' death along with whatever else runs counter to its own projects of reflexively constituted knowledge, order and control. Such an argument makes sense of the way in which modernity has increasingly re-moved death from everyday life and placed it in the hands of specialists (Hockey 1990; Walter 1991; Bauman 1992; Clark 1993), so that even our dearly loved departed are no longer welcome in our homes as corpses. Viol-ent and horrific deaths may be the constant stuff of media fantasy and 'news' but we no longer attend public hangings. Actual deaths are only rarely encountered by most of us in late-modern societies, a fact that encour-ages our reception of the stories of ritual abuse survivors as fiction rather than actuality. The contradiction between this and the emergence of a dis-course of bereavement is more apparent than real, for the focus of the latter is the survivor engaged in readjustment to life after the loss of a significant other – part of the fully modern project of self-making.

It has often been claimed that the key function of all religion is to make death meaningful – linking through litany and ritual the finite individual with the infinity of God, nature and the social order (Berger [1967] 1990). In general, this seeking of meaning in religion in order to avoid the dread of death is regarded as benign and functional; while the secularization sometimes sup-posed to be inherent in modernity is seen as a challenge to human abilities to cope with mortality. The result dovetails with the sequestration referred to above such that our lives are increasingly turned away from death, which even in its meekest forms threatens our faith in the meaningfulness of life.

The ready everyday rationality which renders so much about ritual abuse counter-intuitive dismisses as 'impossible' stories of contemporary human sacrifice. This may result in large part from the hegemony of an evolutionary account of sacrifice in both anthropology and religious studies. The covert influence of the Judaeo-Christian heritage on anthropologists from Hubert and Mauss ([1899] 1964) through Evans-Pritchard (1965) and beyond has led to a focus on the progression of sacrifice towards a higher (symbolic) form. Other commentators describe the centrality of the crucifix and the sacrament of 'blood' and 'flesh' in Christianity as having replaced earlier and more literal religious practices (Maccoby 1982). Such analogical substantiation is widely assumed to be part of a one-way civilizing process. 'Other' world religions may still condone the stoning of women taken in adultery, the infibulation of pre-pubescent girls or the ritual decapitation of cocks and hens but religiously motivated brutalities seem unthinkable in late-modern societies. When such apparently do occur (the Manson murders, the Jonestown massacre or the Heaven's Gate suicides) we seek where possible an 'explanation' in terms of a charismatic (and psychopathic) leader and beyond that dismiss them as weird and incomprehensible.

The idea of the psychopath killing for pleasure or the gangster doing similarly for profit provides a residual category of mad, bad and dangerously damaged *individuals*, but it does not fit with survivors' insistence on the collective practice and identity of their abusers. According to survivors, animal and human life is ritually destroyed to enhance the 'power' of those involved. It is supposed to bind together the 'faith community' in a shared experience of transcendence. Such an idea of absorbing the 'energy' or spirit substance of an animal or human sacrificial victim is attested to in many premodern cultures, and in some – such as the Ancient Greek cults of Attis or Dionysus or the Human Leopard Society of Sierra Leone – it has also been a 'mystery' rite binding initiates together through the solidarity of illegality and the ownership of a 'secret' which places them outside the ordinary social world (Girard 1977; Burkert 1983). Human sacrifice bears the horror it does only in a context where all death is a scandal against the drive to mastery which constitutes modernity.

Ritual abuse survivors' experiences of death are difficult then in a number of ways: the kinds of deaths they claim to have witnessed are to the rest of us 'media experiences', confined to horror films and the 'dying rooms' of Chinese orphanages; immediate contact with the dead and dying is unfamiliar to most of us, and any experience we do have tends to be confined to 'good, clean deaths' (Ariès 1981). In addition, our ability to believe or make sense of the deaths in accounts of ritual abuse is curtailed by the hegemony of the grand narrative of modernity. Within this, the particular view of the evolutionary progress of religion (such that embodied experience has been replaced by symbolic depictions of sacrifice) and the apparently inevitable progress of secularization renders religious motivation largely irrelevant.

The existence of powerful narratives about the civilizing process which emphasize the ascendancy of the abstract over the literal, rationality over superstition, and mind over body lend a particular flavour to our relationship with death and exclude from easy consideration life-stories that contradict such a narrative thrust. However, as Bauman notes, such a tendency is rarely totalizing: 'Human reactions to death are ostensibly too complex and perhaps also too stubborn to be successfully channelled by any culture in a universally acceptable fashion' (Bauman 1992: 23). Just as groups and individuals may borrow from other epochs and cultures in their efforts to deal with mortality, there are equally varied sociological and anthropological insights into death and religion which illuminate the accounts of ritual abuse survivors suggesting their interconnection with rather than dislocation from the world we know.

Death, meaning and doubt

Anthony Giddens (1990), in considering the meaning of death in high modernity, shares with Peter Berger a belief that death always provides a window of opportunity through which 'ontological insecurity' may enter – for death is the point at which all our self-makings, our strivings to control, beautify, protect and develop our bodies and ourselves, come to an end. Berger ([1967] 1990) argued that the major motivation behind the human production of the social world is that of avoiding the descent into meaninglessness which consciousness of mortality threatens. He claimed that although all social realities are human products, they are externalized and objectified so that people regard them as social facts. These 'facts' are in turn internalized and become part of subjective consciousness, but the process is partial only: 'Consciousness precedes socialization. What is more it can never be totally socialized – if nothing else the ongoing consciousness of one's own bodily processes ensures this' (Berger [1967] 1990: 83). This means that there is always the possibility that people will recognize the human-constructedness of social reality, and death can provide a powerful kick in this direction. 'In other words, death can threaten the basic assumptions upon which society is organized, as well as opening up the individual to the dread of personal meaninglessness' (Shilling 1993: 178–9). Or as Bauman expressed it: 'In the light of mortality, all meanings of life look pallid, wan, insubstantial' (Bauman 1992: 31).

The sociology of death offered as a hypothesis the idea that death potentially disrupts individual's unquestioning acceptance of the inevitability of social arrangements: nature rips the social fabric showing it to be a human-made backdrop. So when I began examining the various reports of deaths in my interviews, I had an idea that they might represent 'fateful moments' during which the stability and inevitability of the social worlds inhabited by survivors might be undermined. If this were so, I imagined that what would 'break through', in the realization of the human constructedness of all meanings (Berger [1967] 1990: 23), would be the particular human construction of the particular social world of ritual abuse. The recognition – 'It doesn't have to be like this' – would be likely to be bound up with moral judgements – 'This is wrong'. One factor that more easily permits the judgement of extreme 'wrong' in this context is the availability of an alternative set of meanings in the wider social world surrounding the ritual abuse cult. What solidifies this understanding of some deaths as 'wrong' is an active, if not always wholesale, rejection of the belief system of ritual abuse within which they took place. In other words, this 'threat' to taken-for-granted meanings was one which some of the ritual abuse survivors I interviewed appeared to have transformed into an 'opportunity' to escape the discourse of their abusers.

The occult beliefs attached to the ritual abuses reported by survivors apparently operated to make some deaths more 'meaning-full' than others. In at least one report (examined later), there is a full description of a 'good' satanist death – apparently meaningful to the dying man and his community. However, I shall argue that the reports of survivors suggest that multiple meanings can be generated in relation to different deaths and that certain types of death – those most marginal to the ritual system and those most emotionally and physically personal – may serve most readily to allow oppositional meanings to be generated.

Throughout this book I describe ritual abuse as occurring in opposition to, but also inside and continuous with, the societies of late modernity. Understanding this is crucial to making sense of survivors' lives. The illegal international markets in pornography, drugs and child abuse with which ritual abusers are involved are twentieth-century creations. In addition, it can be argued that the very machinery of modernity – the increased mobility, anonymity and privacy of the individual, the separation of work, family and leisure (at least for a large number of middle-class men), the hiding away of death and violence from everyday life – may all enable abusive and secretive groups to thrive. At the same time, those practising ritual abuse form rigid, hierarchical, patriarchal secret societies which are violently opposed to many aspects of late modernity – most particularly of course to any advances towards the emancipation of women and children.

Types of deaths

The survivors I interviewed described young lives lived in the shadow of death. I began each interview by asking survivors whether they had been told anything about their own births. A number recalled having been told that either they or their mother had almost died, that their mother had tried to abort or kill them, or in three cases that they had been born a twin, and the twin had died or been sacrificed at birth.[1] Others remembered being alerted to the suicide or arranged demise of a member of the group who had attempted to leave. However, there were three main types of death which survivors reported actually witnessing or being involved in and it is these with which this chapter is concerned. I have categorized these deaths as incidental, personal and ritual, and will explore the significance accorded to each in survivors' accounts. It is interesting that, with the exception of occasions when an interviewee related the sacrifice of her own baby, the least emphasized of the three were deaths which had taken place in a ritual context. This is not to say that other ceremonial killings were not spoken of, but these tended to be generalized as 'what sometimes happened at ceremonies'. The deaths discussed in most detail were those which were 'personally meaningful', all of which had in various ways resulted from abuse but either had no ritual element or were related in ways that downplayed the ritual context.

Certain experiences of death appeared to provide the survivors I interviewed with 'moral opportunities', and some used memories of particular deaths as personal 'fables' through which to explore the moral meanings of the world of their childhood. The complex process of adopting and accommodating to an alternative morality, the desire to claim it as an essential aspect of the self ('I always knew it was wrong') and the shifts in identification with, and dissociation from, previous significant others, will be addressed in this context. I suggest that for girls and women the experience of enforced infanticide may provide both a significant 'moral opportunity', and conflicting identifications with the women they number among their abusers, and with women in the wider society.

The other theme emerging from interviewees' accounts of death is that of the complex and contradictory meanings invested in the self-as-flesh as the body moves centre stage in accounts concerned with birth and death. Throughout this book, I am concerned with reports of bodies *in extremis*, with accounts of torture, rape, starvation and the body as the focus of control within the abusive regimes of childhood. In these the bodily self is sometimes characterized as Judas to the moral self: as when orgasm results from unwanted sex, or hunger overcomes the utmost repugnance. However, it may also be experienced as a locus of resistance. In almost a reversal of 'The spirit is willing, but the flesh is weak'; it is the body which may be described as finally balking at the requirement to hurt or harm another as if morality were somehow rooted in the body.

Incidental deaths

It would not be appropriate to call the deaths I want to discuss first 'accidental', for it suggests a mistake, something to be regretted. Rather these deaths were consequences (not always intended) of abuse, and appeared to have been inconsequential to those who caused them. They are all examples of marginal deaths, the deaths of people that 'did not count', except to the women who remembered and chose to 're-count' them as part of their own life-stories. None of these was a ritual killing, they were not punishments, they were not rendered to survivors as meaningful in any way. The intention of the actions of the perpetrators was their own 'pleasure' (or in the last case, possibly profit); that they cost a person their life was incidental.

These 'chaotic', undisciplined and inadvertent deaths best illustrate the constant presence of the fear of death in survivors' lives. These were often deaths which no amount of obedience or self-control could ensure protection against; deaths in which interviewees expressed their identification with the victim whose place they could so easily have occupied. Elizabeth reflecting on the murder of a young man she witnessed as a teenager expresses this as follows:

> Seeing people killed, particularly this young man, and thinking: 'well what did he do that we're not doing all the time. What's different about what happened that time than when I'm getting raped'. And when I saw *Schindler's List* it was something that was said to the housekeeper: 'You will always be afraid of death – it was the chap that was her boss – that he might kill you because you don't know why he kills people. He kills people at random'. And that's what it was like in the cult. People were killed at random, it seemed to a child and even a teenager, no rhyme or reason why someone would suddenly be killed. It was their turn. So you never knew, what was it you might do that meant next year you'll be dead. And I grew up with that. I lived my whole life with that fear, until I started to do this work. Like what is it you have to do that makes people kill you? And so I always had to be really, really good. Really well behaved, never put a foot out of line, never say what you want, never say: 'I don't like that, I don't like you doing that', because they could kill you.
>
> (Elizabeth)

Despite the equally evident randomness of a child's death remembered by Kate, her account still emphasizes the importance of self-control in guaranteeing her own safety. Kate insists the little girl's death was an aberration, if only she had obeyed the rules and not cried out it would never have happened. Kate knew not to cry; she believed her own survival depended on it. This was therefore the sort of death she thought she could avoid for herself. This is the mind-set Bauman (1989) describes among Jews in the Warsaw ghetto, obeying the rules, convinced the rules would save them.

> She was at a ceremony with her father and I was with mine. Afterwards . . . I don't know where her father went . . . but there was me and my dad and a couple of other men and the girl. I know that one man was having sex with me, one man in the kitchen, and my dad was having sex with this little girl and she was crying. And if that's one rule that you learn very early on is you do not cry. Come hell or high water don't cry. You weren't allowed to, if we did we were punished. And my father got very angry with her and I remember him throwing her against the wall, and picking her up and really shouting at her telling her not to cry. He took one of the knives off the wall, 'cos there were racks, and he stabbed her and took her off down to one of the back rooms and I had to go and look after her. I was told to stop the bleeding and I couldn't. She was still crying and I remember saying to her: 'Don't cry, you mustn't cry', because I was so frightened they'd come back in the room and do something more. And in the end she stopped crying. At the time I thought 'O, good, she listened to me, wonderful'. Looking back on it I realize she just went unconscious and she basically bled to death. I remember

covering her in a green towel, and this man just coming in and
picking her up. Literally carrying her out under one arm. And I never
saw her again. I was left with this massive pool of blood. That was it.

(Kate)

The story emphasizes the lack of significance that Kate's father, and those
with him, attached to a child's death. Kate's indignation falls on the way the
girl was carried away under some man's arm as if she was just something
to be disposed of. By contrast, Kate herself had covered the body with a
green towel and a moral universe yawns between the two actions. This death
mattered to someone, and allowed Kate to identify a clear distinction between her abusers and herself. It seems it was the very meaninglessness of
the death that allowed space for the creation of meaning.

Beth uses the accidental death of another little girl as a way of differentiat-
ing between two different ritual abuse groups which she attended with her
uncle. The group involved in this incident abused children in group 'games',
shared a taste for sexual sadism and were described as practising small-scale
rituals, but they did not go in for human sacrifice as did the 'more professional' group she would later encounter:

in the hut was the first time that I saw [*pause*] . . . the first time that
I saw a child was killed, but I think it was an accident because it
was . . . all hell broke loose . . . But that's me thinking back on it.
There were the water butt things there and outside of the hut, and
you'd get your head shoved under the water and all that kind of
stuff . . . which was how long can you hold your breath for? So if you
could hold your breath for one minute and ten seconds then that was
one minute and ten seconds they could do things to you. They'd
hang you from a rafter, from a beam in the hanger and I think they
basically got it wrong, 'cos when they took this kid's body down she
just went limp.

(Beth)

The death of a child was not an unlikely, if in this case an unintended,
consequence of ligature. The abusers who Beth remembers were apparently
playing with death but were clearly not quite prepared for the consequences.
The account is unusual among those of interviewees only to the extent
that she remembers that 'all hell broke loose'. Other respondents reported
incidents where things had probably gone further than intended, and an
unplanned death or injury occurred, but the attitude towards these was that
they were of no significance.

Beth was the only woman I interviewed who recalled a 'first time' in
relation to witnessing a death. Her relatively late introduction to ritual abuse
– unlike most of the others she was not born into a generationally involved
family – probably explains this. This absence of a 'first time' in most survivors'
stories of their lives points up the fact that death, like sex, was an ever present
feature of life. Death incidents were not presented as significant stories because
they were incidents of death, but because they were important to people's

attempts to account for themselves. This is true even in Beth's case, for the 'point' of her story is the constant proximity of death in the course of her abuse. The water butt in which she was herself submerged, and the deadness of the other girl, are fused in this account, thus making it clear that the threat and possibility of her own death were always close by.

The last example I want to take of an incidental death is a report given by Debbie of the death of a tramp, killed in the making of a 'snuff' movie.

There was plenty of porno videos, snuff videos, ones of which I was there at the time. It was just . . . it seemed a normal thing to sit down to a video of that . . . I can't remember a time . . . There were certain films I didn't want to watch and they used to make me. They'd turn my head and say if I didn't open my eyes that he would slap me and all, do worse and that. So . . . and I used to have terrible nightmares from them.

And did you say you'd been there or were in some of them?

Yeah, the 'snuff' ones. The house . . . there was a tramp that they brought in. He was very drunk, he was laughing and everything, and everyone else seemed to be laughing as well. I was even laughing 'cos it seemed quite a jolly thing. I didn't know what was going to happen. And er . . . they laid him out on the table, where they used to cut up animals and kill any . . . whatever the sacrifice was . . . and er, they cut him from his stomach, just sliced him right open. He was screaming for so long, it seemed like he was screaming even when he was all open up. And er . . . they started pulling out all these intestines and everyone was eating them. We were made to eat them. [*Pause*] I feel so guilty 'cos a lot of the times I used to just do it, I wasn't even made, used just to . . . you know . . .

. . . get on with it?

Yeah. [*Pause*]

And that was something that was filmed that you were made to watch?

Yeah. We were made to see. And they seemed to zoom in on his face a lot. Which . . . was . . . horrible. I still wake up, just seeing his face. I don't remember, like in the dreams, anything else apart from his face.

(Debbie)

The horror and guilt that Debbie feels in relation to this death are juxtaposed with the laughter of those involved at the time. Death is treated with levity, the death of a tramp is inconsequential. It is the film, whether produced for use in the group or for wider distribution, which turns a real death into a horror fiction. There is a horrible irony here, for the stories of ritual abuse told to foster parents and social workers in cases such as Congleton, Manchester and Nottingham, were frequently blamed on small children having watched horror videos.

Other interviewees said that they knew or assumed that adults killed in rituals were 'tramps' or homeless young people; however, the one specific account of such a death is of a non-ritual death occurring in a ritual space. Debbie refers to the table where sacrifices were normally conducted being used – and thereby makes it clear that this was not an example of one of those ritual deaths.

It seems to me that these incidental deaths were available for the inscription of meaning by survivors *because they were so meaningless*. Ritual sacrifices seem to have been far harder to rewrite, being as it were already full to the brim with the significance of an occult cosmology and a set of ritual practices. Survivors comment on the attention to detail in the rituals they participated in, the rehearsals, detailed organization and participants' dismay at the smallest variation or mistake. Such meaning-full deaths leave little room for ontological insecurities, which, it seems, were far more likely to creep in by the back door of incidental deaths. Maurice Bloch makes a related point in a discussion of rituals and millenarianism:

> rituals are occasions on which such individual doubts are not usually in evidence since, in ritual, the behaviour of the participants is as if orchestrated by a shared score. Furthermore, the formalization of ritual speech, song and action itself makes individual expression of dissent very difficult to express within the medium.
>
> (Bloch 1992: 85)

Personal deaths

The incidental deaths described above were those of strangers, but some survivors also suffered the deaths of significant others. Emotional attachments within ritual abuse groups were described as extremely rare. Children often did not know each other's names, and self-isolation was a survival strategy commonly embraced in the face of suffering over which they had no control. Personal deaths were therefore most often the deaths of women's own babies. In the context of the Holocaust, Bauman (1989) has argued that no matter how insidious intellectually the stereotype of the Jew was to many 'ordinary' Germans, its applicability ended where the sphere of personal intercourse began: ' "The other" as an *abstract category* simply does not communicate with "the other" *I know*' (Bauman 1989: 188, original emphasis). If distancing and dehumanizing are factors which make possible the witnessing or taking of actions against others which we would not choose to endure against ourselves; then proximity and responsibility are the factors that make such actions unbearably painful. Using Stanley Milgram's (1965) experiments to illustrate the social production of distance, Bauman argues:

> Being inextricably tied to human proximity, morality seems to conform to the law of optical perspective. It looms large and thick close to the eye. With the growth of distance, responsibility for the other shrivels,

moral dimensions of the object blur, till both reach vanishing point and disappear from view.

(Bauman 1989: 192)

The use of long-range weapons, Milgram's experimental subjects being in another room from their 'victim', the minute divisions of labour through bureaucracy and technology: all these further distance those who are already strangers, already 'other'. The lack of a personal, emotional connection already renders certain people 'remote and barely visible' in moral terms. Most of the deaths that ritual abuse survivors witness, physically proximate though they are, are the deaths of strangers, categories of persons already defined as 'lives unworthy of life'. Little was said of these in most of the interviews: there were too many and they were too alike. They were unable to have the same moral impact as 'personal deaths'. However, 'personal deaths' appear to provide 'moral windows' through which the meaning of other deaths can be reinterpreted.

Debbie described being forced to witness the death of her friend when she was 8. The two children had been left alone in a room with books and candles and had started a fire:

And then we ran off, we ran out of the house and we ran down the hill, the grassy hill bit, and they set dogs out on to us and they caught us. And then they brought us back in. And I thought they would just tell us off . . . 'Cos I always thought if Ellie was going to be sacrificed it would've already happened. But this time it was just a punishment, it wasn't anything to do with a ceremony or anything like that. And, er, they got hold of her and put her in this big oven . . . it looked like a do-it-yourself oven, didn't look like a proper . . . but it was huge. And er . . . they turned it on. And my punishment was to watch her. But I loved her 'cos she was still defiant even at the end. 'Cos they wanted her to scream and they wanted me to scream, and I wouldn't 'cos she wasn't. But she wouldn't, she just looked out, she just . . . she was so pretty as well.

(Debbie)

Again the emphasis is on the fact that this death – though 'staged' by Debbie's abusers – was not part of a ceremony, and on the apparent disposability of Ellie's life in response to such a minor offence. Ellie apparently belonged to one of the categories of 'lives unworthy of life', and as such Debbie's personal connection with her is unusual. Debbie describes such children as follows:

They couldn't speak, they'd just make grunts and . . . The kids that were down could speak and could walk, 'cos a lot of them in the cages didn't walk or anything.

And you think that those caged children were kept there all the time?

Yeah, they were. They were brought up at the house, 'cos some of the babies were kept, some were sacrificed but some were kept and they would then be brought up at the house.

Why did they keep children?

Just to save them to a later age, just to kill them. 'Cos otherwise they've got to get children from outside which they'd consider risky.

Were they used for anything else?

Not really you know used for sex and things like that. That's it really. They were just thrown scraps of food. There seemed to be different degrees of the kids that were left there. I mean like Ellie, she would sometimes be dressed, sometimes not. But she was kept . . . not immaculate but . . . you know, a lot cleaner than the kids in the cages, 'cos they were left in their own mess and . . .

And Ellie you were friends with, so she talked?

Yes, there was a lot of them, say about half of them that could talk very well. And Ellie could read as well . . . yeah, she could read.

(Debbie)

Other survivors spoke of similar children, but it is only in Debbie's account that they become fully human. The death of Ellie is highly significant to Debbie because of the relationship between them. It is unlikely that such a relationship was allowed much time or privacy, but in the context of ritual abuse it counted as a personal relationship. The death of someone who had a name – even where the name has been accorded to them posthumously by the survivor – seemed to place them in a different category of moral response.

Some survivors described being deliberately encouraged to become attached first to an animal, which was then killed, and later to another child who subsequently disappeared or whose actual or staged death they witnessed. The intention attributed to this was that of breaking any tendency to make attachments: 'Anything I ever loved was taken away from me or destroyed. That's how they teach you not to risk feeling anything for anyone.' But whatever being forced to watch Ellie's death was meant to teach Debbie, the meaning she constructed from the experience was quite different:

For a while I was just very numb about it. And then I thought 'no' . . . I mean this is part of the reason I talk to people now, is because I know she would have done it. And we always said that we would get out. That we would run away. But we planned to do it together. But there was one time when we said if we didn't do it together we would still want the other one to be free. And she is free in a sense. The way I see it is this life is only short. So . . . you know . . . It is bad what happened, but it's not the be all and end all, there's something better that's going to come along for me. And she's already there. At least I know I've got someone up there on my side.

(Debbie)

Ellie's death is made meaningful by the inspiration that Debbie claims from it. Her relationship with the dead girl prevents it from being 'incidental'; indeed it is filled with a quasi-religious significance: 'she died that I might live'.

Hearing Debbie's story, I recalled the first time Sinead had talked to me about children kept in cages. I remember the shock I felt was not at the idea of caged children, but at Sinead's attitude towards them. Her description was flippant, as if they were vermin whose lives were of no consequence, as if there were no connection between her and them. Met with a horrified silence, she began shouting that such children were animals, that they were not human, that if anybody tried to rescue them they would only die because filth and cages were all they knew, and they could never be normal. Her rage subsided into violent sobbing, and afterwards she talked about her sense of guilt and responsibility towards those she had left behind. This was not directed towards the anonymous children she had described as 'not-human', however, but focused on two girls her own age, girls with names, abused within the same group as herself.

In Dachau and Bergen-Belsen, prisoners were rendered less than human by similar means. The stench of urine, the appearance of malnutrition, insufficient clothes for human dignity: all these factors help place people beyond the *universe of obligation* where moral precepts do not bind. In such circumstances some are earmarked as 'we', others as 'not us', non-people. When the 'killed is not *Tu*, the murder is not a murder' (Bauman 1992: 39).

The **death** of **one's own baby**

The personal death involving a friend is unusual in these accounts. The exception to the anonymity of the deaths witnessed, or participated in, are the relationships that female survivors claim with one of their own babies. Although pregnancies of various duration had been numerous in the lives of most of the survivors I interviewed, five women highlighted one birth-and-death as particularly significant. Invariably this pregnancy ran to term or was induced only a little prematurely.

The focus of much child death discourse is the grieving mother. Where a child has been killed the grief is mixed with rage. An extreme presentation of this is Anne West, the mother of Lesley-Anne Downey (killed by Ian Brady and Myra Hindley), who has been invited to revisit her grief in the mass media for nearly 30 years. News, soap operas and self-help guides all emphasize the naturalness of a mother's grief and the necessity of expressing it. But at the same time the 'grief' expresses the 'mother', confirms her goodness, her proper affections, her sisterhood with other women and her place within humanity.

This is the discursive context into which survivors of ritual abuse must speak their stories of repeated births followed swiftly by sacrificial deaths. Such stories do not readily fit the available discourses of birth and death; contradicting what we 'know', they are met with widespread disbelief. However, accounts must still be constructed of extreme as of mundane aspects of our experience and survivors have little choice but to borrow what they can from available accounts of infant death, in order to make sense of their experiences to themselves as well as to communicate them to others. Ambiguity is not ironed out in this process: those shaping their experiences to fit what can be said, may also indicate an incomplete 'fit'. Clues about different versions are present in those told.

It would not seem unreasonable to suggest that there can be no more intimate experience of death than that of an infant who was part of one's own body but a short time before. Mary O'Brien suggests that: 'For women, giving birth is a unity of knowing and doing' (O'Brien 1981: 14), that reproductive consciousness is tied to the body. O'Brien argues that reproductive consciousness, as awareness of bodily processes and potentialities, is universal to women. While criticizing those who attempt to attach a 'natural' feminine or maternal character to such knowledge she believes that:

> These involuntary, feminine moments of reproductive experience are symbolically important in the development of female universality.
> (O'Brien 1981: 51)

The accounts considered here suggest that it is through the experience of pregnancy and childbirth that ritually abused girls may come to think about themselves as women, and therefore as members of a category of persons continuous with others outside the cult. At the same time, it is within these experiences that a 'mother' is born – a person subject to the discourses of maternity. If death is a site of ontological insecurity, birth can be thought of as a location of physiological connectedness with implications for the development of moral judgement. Drawing on Levinas, Bauman (1992) describes moral relationship – that of responsibility for the Other – as pre-ontological, pre-intellectual such that proximity equals responsibility. Certainly these accounts suggest experiences in which a particular experience of proximity to another – in this case their own child – provided a fateful moment in the development of a moral self.

The women who attached particular importance in their life to the loss of a single late-term baby described these experiences as having helped them to get away from their abusers, enabling them to define themselves as different from those who had abused them, and providing a focus for their anger and pain. These babies were invariably named by their mothers, an action that may have been informed by two different strands of thought. First, within the world of ritual abuse, survivors describe names and naming as significant and powerful. To give a dead baby a 'secret' name is therefore a subversive act. Second, in contemporary discourses of bereavement, naming even a stillborn baby is considered a 'healthy' thing to do. According individual identity to the baby is meant to facilitate the expression of grief, rendering the loss more real.

I was reminded listening to these accounts of echoes within my own family. My mother had four miscarriages before giving birth to my elder sister. The last of these was a baby she carried almost to term, a boy she named 'David Andrew'. He 'stood in' for all her losses which had ended each period of hope that 'this time it would be different'. She regularly referred to this non-existent brother of ours, and reminded herself how old he would have been had he lived. Perhaps because of this, the extraordinary 'ordinariness' of these stories, despite the horrific circumstances surrounding them, has always struck me.

Lynn described the birth and death of her baby daughter as *the* pivotal event in her escape from her abusers. Her account, which I quote at length,

also makes clear her abusers' deliberate encouragement of her attachment to
the child:

> I had three other children, at various stages I should add . . . The third
> one was a full-term pregnancy. Funny enough, it was about the time
> I ran away each time, so I think there was a deep inner knowing of
> what was going on. Even if I didn't want to really announce it to
> myself, I believe I knew . . .
>
> And what happened to this was that she was induced and she was
> born within a few hours. And she was a normal healthy little baby
> girl . . . And when they brought her back and I was holding her, there
> was a lot of 'Would you like to keep her?' and 'Was I worthy of
> keeping her?' I had to prove that I was worthy of keeping her and
> look after her. And if I promised to be good, and really, really try,
> they would give me a chance, and these were things I would have to
> do. And that was OK, and I agreed to all those things and I believed
> them. You know, we have a deep-rooted need to be loved, but we also
> have a deep-rooted need to give it back too, and I believe that this is
> what was happening here. I really wanted, more than anything, not
> just love this baby but look after her . . . Throughout that whole week,
> a lot of abusive things happened . . . And there were other things going
> on, preparations, things if I had wanted to I could have seen, the
> things I was making myself not see. Because I believed I was protected
> then. And I . . . between, as I would go back and in this bedroom,
> there she was, and what they'd done is they'd converted the bottom
> drawer for a sideboard into her bed and I would take her out and love
> her and nurse her and I would bath and clean her and feed her. And
> for the first time in my life, I really believed it was going to be OK.
>
> . . . I was encouraged by other people. 'Yes, you really love her, don't
> you?' and 'Oh, look at the way she looks at you'. And so there was a
> lot of . . . and there was a relationship growing there. And I suppose
> some people would say that's a natural bonding going on there, but
> it was there nevertheless . . . And this continued the whole week till
> Friday. Then on the Friday they came and removed her and I think
> I knew then . . . And I was drugged, there was a lot of abuse around
> that. On the Saturday, I was picked up and . . . I was taken to a
> church, an old church, and because it's my baby, I was supposed to
> have the honour, only I think I was getting really rebellious . . . there
> was my mother and father at the altar, they were high priest and
> priestess, and my little girl . . . At the end of it, what was left of my
> little girl was put in my arms and I was taken out and made to lay her
> in a grave, and it was shortly after that I decided this . . . and that was
> how I got out. Her name is Melanie and I can share that. I find it
> really hard to . . .
>
> And anyway that night she died, and I think a huge piece of me
> died with her, and yet she gave me the right to be free. That seems
> kind of hard, that my child died, but if it wasn't for her I wouldn't
> be here . . .

Tell me why.

After that night, I'm pretty certain that they didn't care whether I died
or not that night. That in many ways they knew I'd become a danger
to them. And I think they thought: 'well if she dies during this we'll
find a way of explaining it, and if not . . .' I was very badly beaten
that night, and tortured. And although I did survive it, I survived it
in a place that told me I had to run . . . But also my dad had started
saying things, and my mum mentioned like. One of the girls in our
group had committed suicide about a year and a half before this by
jumping in front of a moving train. She kept saying that if I did that
it would be all over, all over in minutes, never know a thing about it.
My mum put loads of pills by the side of my bed and said: 'Well you
can take them if you want, you'll never wake up again, it'll never
happen again' . . .

There was so much going on at home. Lots of morbid, sick stuff
about where Melanie was. And they would talk about her dying
moments of agony. Real sick, sick stuff. So I actually just ran. I knew
that I'd reached my limits with them, that if I didn't run they would
eventually get me to kill myself.

(Lynn)

Lynn refers to 'a deep inner knowing' in relation to her pregnancies and the
impending horror they signified. This idea of knowledge, or of an alternative
moral order, being located in the body, a secret opposition that 'grew inside
me', appears in more than one interview. Her baby, once born, represents
this knowledge of otherness in external form. Melanie is described as a
'normal healthy little baby girl'. She is the 'normal', 'natural' outsider to the
world of ritual abuse.

Lynn was 'tricked' into allowing herself to love her baby. On the other
hand she acknowledges that she allowed herself to believe in the possibility
of 'this time being different'. She refers to the fact that some people would
interpret her attachment to the baby as a natural bonding. In this way she
connects her story to a dominant model of motherhood, without actually
claiming this as true for herself. The details she selects emphasize both the
connection and difference between her experience and that of 'ordinary'
mothers. The baby's cot is a bureau drawer, and it is the remains of the little
girl which are put into the mother's arms.

It is Melanie's death which Lynn describes as the springboard for her bid
for freedom. However, her actual description of her parents nudging her
towards suicide in the weeks after the birth suggests a more complex picture.
It is not so much moral outrage at the murder of her baby that inspires
Lynn's escape, but her consciousness of the nearness of her own death. This
in no way undermines the symbolic importance attached to Melanie, or
her role in Lynn's sense of herself as a mother. It is more that clues about
different versions are visible in the account. There are two meaning systems
present in Lynn's report. The meaning of Melanie's birth and death are
partially understood through contemporary discourses of motherhood and

bereavement, but they are also acknowledged to have been highly meaningful ritual events within the cult. Lynn weaves her personally significant account between these, even though the 'normal' discourse clearly dominates. The survivors I interviewed did not much emphasize that the deaths of their infants had occurred within a meaning system they had rejected. Lynn did say a little about this, but the distancing devices she uses, and the lack of detail, contrast sharply with the vivid accounts of her own experience. In the context of describing an earlier infant's death, she reports:

> The ceremony was actually . . . it was about the three stages of giving your body . . . you know, giving your body, somebody else's body and then your soul. So it's like the three stages, so giving Melanie apparently was giving my soul. Have to say it probably felt like my soul at that age.
>   But this was much more about giving your body, somebody else's body, feeling much more incriminated, like you'd deliberately done this. You'd had this child that wasn't . . . you'd only carried it for whoever the deity was, and they were claiming it back. So bizarre some of the things that they say.
>
> (Lynn)

From sentence to sentence the shifts between meaning systems are apparent in this account. In written form, the ironic tone is lost but the distancing comments – 'Have to say it probably felt like my soul at that age' and 'So bizarre some of the things that they say' – are evident. In this account, the apparently meaningless cruelty of encouraging Lynn to love her baby is connected to the significance of the ritual as 'giving one's soul'. These other partially hidden (occult) meanings are present nonetheless.

If Lynn saw Melanie's death as a 'last straw' experience, Sinead describes the death of her baby as an epiphany:

> When I decided I didn't want to do this any more it was I suppose for selfish reasons . . . which was when they killed Bethany. I decided I didn't want anything to do with this any more . . . You know. . . . I didn't want this child, and then when I had this child, I couldn't have this child. I didn't want it, I was made to have it. Then when I had it, I wanted it and it was taken away. That was it. I'd had enough and I was going to wait my opportunity and I was going to get away from them. From that point on I could hear the cries of other kids. I could hear the fear and I knew what I was doing was wrong . . .

So it was Bethany that let you hear other kids?

It was hearing her while they were gutting her alive which made me realize 'No, you've done it now. You've over-stepped the mark here'.

How old were you?

Eleven . . . I had about five weeks to go when she was born.[2] I suppose in a way I was lucky that they didn't let her live . . . But I think what hurt most was that they didn't just kill her outright, they gutted her

first while she was alive. It took ten minutes for her to die. And I had
to hold her while they done it, and I was still bleeding and confused
and hurting from the birth. Just watching her. She had masses and
masses of jet-black hair, she was just perfect, not a mark on her. A lot
of people think when a baby's born it can't see. Well they can, it can't
see very well, but their eyes are open immediately. I remember her
being born on this slab floor and picking her up. She was huddled up
really tightly. My mum just got the cord and halved it, cut it with a
knife and tied it in a knot and that was it. I held her . . . And my mum
looking and saying: 'She's beautiful, perfect. My first grandchild'. And
that was it. Next thing she just grabbed it by the neck and hauled her
off me and held her up and everybody's looking. Then she started
howling, wailing and shivering. And she was dropped on to the slab
and they started.
I just thought: 'No' . . .

I was an awkward bitch though, from that day. I would not
cooperate, I would not do my training, I would not listen. And that
was what decided me to get out, I'd had enough. I ran away a number
of times then, after her birth. Every opportunity I run . . . got found
and brought back . . .

There . . . were times even up to a couple of months ago when
I'd quite often think about it and get upset, but I resolved that by
thinking that she was better off where she is. I mean I wouldn't be
out if she'd be alive anyway, I'm sure I wouldn't. I wouldn't have left
and they wouldn't have let her go.

They tried to use her four years ago by telling me she was still alive
and it was a trick, her death. If she was alive she'd be 8 now. The trick
is not to believe it . . . And I did, I actually believed it for a time, until
I thought logically about it and thought: 'I did watch her die. I know
I watched her die'.

(Sinead)

Sinead makes a direct connection between her experience of giving birth and
seeing her baby killed, and her moral development. Again the connection is
made through the body: her ears are opened to the cries of other kids with
whom she has no direct connection. Again the baby's natural, undamaged
state is emphasized: 'not a mark on her'.

Sinead believes herself 'saved' by her baby's death in a different way from
Lynn. A living child would have been a tie that she might not have been
able to break. There is also an awareness in other ways of how ambiguous
was her relation to motherhood: 'I didn't want it, they made me have it,
then when I had it and wanted it, they took it off me'. Sinead was 19 at the
time of her interview; Lynn was 43 and the mother of two grown-up children. Their relations to dominant discourses of maternity were therefore
different in terms of both generation and their stage in the life course.

Sinead is my, now adult, foster daughter, and when I interviewed her as
part of my research I was hearing a full account of Bethany's birth and death
for the third time. The first was a waking nightmare of relived contractions,

terror and vomit. The second, a couple of years later, was what I rather unkindly called the *Home and Away* version. By then Sinead was 17, and a woman she worked with had a stillborn baby. This woman provided a possible role model for Sinead's memories and, combining sentiments drawn from TV soaps, she tried to rework her account accordingly. Of course it fitted neither her age, her 'streetwise' persona, nor the circumstances, and was dropped accordingly. However, Sinead's rather unsophisticated attempt to make her experience fit the available discourse was echoed in less extreme form in various interviews. One example is the slippage between 'it' and 'her' with reference to a named baby: 'it' is all the personhood the baby concerned was ever accorded but the attribution of gender posthumously changes this. Stories of forced pregnancy and child sacrifice do not easily 'clean up' into versions of cot death in suburbia. In escaping their abuse, survivors reject the meanings attached to their experiences by their abusers. Such meanings then become hidden, or 'occult', in their accounts.

Not everyone I interviewed felt able to talk about experiences surrounding the death of a baby. For example Gene, at 18, began her interview by telling me: 'I had a baby and it died . . . you know . . . and I don't want to talk about what happened'. My feeling is that it was still important for Gene to tell me that this had occurred even though she could say no more about it. Kathleen, who found talking about the ritual aspects of her experience almost impossible – she 'drifted off', or dissociated, whenever she got close to discussing such things – was still able to tell me how she had made the death of her baby the basis of a highly symbolic action:

I'm really quite together till we get to this bit and then I lose it.

Do you remember a lot more than you're able to talk about?

Well I know how they killed her. But when I go to talk about it all
I can see is her. It's because I was standing in front of her and I
couldn't do anything about it, and she was alive one minute and then
she was dead. I saw her alive and I couldn't stop her becoming dead.
There just wasn't anything I could do . . . And they disembowelled her.
I suppose that's the way it's put. And I had to eat that [*unclear*].
   You know, my sister got married a couple of years ago and my
parents put a family notice in the newspaper, and Mum put
everybody's degrees in and stuff. And I knew everyone in the family
would get a copy of it, so I put an 'In Memoriam' in the same day
for my daughter. And I thought they won't know it, but everyone
who keeps that is going to have the truth.

(Kathleen)

Kathleen, who could not stop her baby 'becoming dead', attaches great significance to her memory and the truth of her abuse which it embodies. Another survivor I interviewed had arranged a memorial service for her baby. Such borrowings from the 'normal' world of death serve as both bridges to, and claims of, a different morality.

Debbie's memories of more than one late abortion or induced birth were mostly drug hazed and confused. The following account is therefore clearly important to her because she 'owns' the baby concerned both at the time and as a memory:

> On other occasions after I . . . the first time I asked to live with Mum I was pregnant at the Christmas this was when I was 12 . . . just 13 I think [*pause*]. She said 'no', to go back and ask the family. So I went back and in this time I went back to Mum's in the summer and I stayed there, that's when I left. But in between that time my Gran had done the tube again and nothing had really come away. And I knew I was roughly about 26 weeks, 25, 26 weeks gone, 'cos Gran had put this girdle on me as well. And I went to school that day and I was in my maths class . . . I felt really ill, hot and cold and not knowing if I was going to be sick . . . I went to the toilet and I felt something moving but er . . . can't be anything . . . an er, there was this baby about as big as my hand. It was almost . . . you could see everything, it was almost like the skin was transparent. But you could see it was a little girl, fully formed but just so small . . . And they sent me to the medical room. I didn't tell anybody 'cos I thought people would take the baby away from me and I wanted . . . every other baby had been destroyed . . . and I wanted this for myself.

So what did you do with her?

> Well I had a wooden pencil case, and I emptied all my pencils out and I put tissue in and I laid her in there. Almost made a bed for her . . . Then I went home and I kept her in the back of a teddy that I had. The zip, the head, you could unzip the head, it unfolded and there was a little compartment and I put it in there, put her in there. Still got the teddy now in fact. And then it started to smell a bit. So I took her out, put her in the box, put a rose in with her 'cos she was smelling, thought it might stop the smell and I put a photograph in of me . . . and I think my mum was on it and my brother I think. An er, we used to have a chute for the rubbish bins, so I went up and I put her down the chute. And I thought that at least my Gran hasn't got her. I wish she had lived. I know it wasn't the right age for someone to have a baby. I'm not ready now for a baby and I'm 21. But I wish she had of lived.

Did you give her a name?

> Um, it's Charlotte. [*Pause*] There's a little girl that I had, that I thought I had anyway, that was very small once again. And I think they tricked me into believing this grown-up child was mine. Alex, I named her. And she looked like me. But when I was going to leave they said that this is your child. And I know they took one away and I never saw it. But of course I don't know what's real, I don't know if they're lying.

(Debbie)

Not every woman I interviewed made such an experience central. For some a different encounter with death was pivotal; for others it was the constant repetition of pregnancy and abortion that was emphasized. As one survivor expressed it: 'Sometimes there was something, and other times it was just mush'. However, the one survivor who, because she lived first with non-abusing parents and later in a convent, never remained pregnant for very long for fear of discovery, repeatedly told me how fortunate she felt that this had been the case, for it had meant she never had to face the death of her own babies.

Ritual deaths

The three categories of incidental, personal and ritual deaths, which I am using in this chapter, are not exclusive. As is evident in the above discussion of the deaths of infants, these most frequently occurred in a ritual context. However, the ritual element was faded out in these accounts, at the same time as the personal meaning was foregrounded. The ritual deaths I now turn to were discussed less frequently in interviews. In each, the interviewee was directly involved in the killing and the victim was an older child or adult. In two of the accounts examined here there was no relationship between interviewee and victim; in the third they were father and daughter. It is clear in each that the ritual context is important to survivors struggling with issues of personal responsibility. These are the deaths which it seems were most difficult to translate 'between worlds' being already over-interpreted, their meanings given by the rituals within which they had occurred. It is interesting that although religious and ritual aspects of their abuse were generally minimized in survivors' life-histories, references to symbols, deities and 'theological' explanations were spoken of in this context. Each of these deaths was a human sacrifice, by definition something that can make no sense in profane terms. In addition, they represented individual 'rites of passage', a stage in the initiation of the speaker themselves. Inside such a framework individual moral responsibility is irrelevant, outside that framework it is everything. The fact that these are such 'strange deaths', without parallels in the surrounding society, also renders them less porous to alternative meanings. These facts need to be placed alongside two others: the 'full personhood' of the victim, represented by their age, and contrasted with the 'potential personhood' of babies and foetuses; and the survivors' direct participation in the ritual death. It is these factors taken together that seemed to make these deaths the most difficult for survivors to discuss, and thereby incorporate within their life-stories.

Such deaths appear to question one aspect of Bauman's (1989) analysis that the Holocaust can be understood only in terms of the forces of modernity. He describes how technical and bureaucratic systems were used to suppress morality and responsibility:

Under the conditions of bureaucratic division of labour, 'the other' inside the circle of proximity where moral responsibility rules supreme is a workmate, whose successful coping with his own task depends on the actor's application to his part of the job; the immediate superior, whose occupational standing depends on the co-operation of his subordinates; and a person immediately down the hierarchy line who expects his tasks to be clearly defined and made feasible . . . In the form of organizational loyalty, the actors' moral drives may be deployed for morally abject purposes.

(Bauman 1989: 195)

Bauman argues that 'science provides the fullest epitome of dissociation between ends and means' (Bauman 1989: 159). Ritual abuse survivors' accounts suggest that in relation to human sacrifice ritual structure and occult rationale fulfil the same role. The 'religious' division of labour incorporates both hierarchy and interdependency and group membership frees the individual from personal moral responsibility while clearly designating who is 'Tu' and who the Other.

> The first time was like my initiation, but they actually had a little girl there as well. I'd never seen this girl before and she had black hair and blue eyes. And . . . basically . . . they killed her and I took her place . . . she had this most brilliant white gown and that's what I had as well. I had a brilliant white gown on, if you were going to compare it to anything it was like a sodding shroud . . . my father was a Master, you know, and he had like this black gown on, and there were some people in black, some people in red and some of the women were in white as well. But um . . . my initiation as well . . . he came over, he killed this girl. She didn't move you know, she didn't move, all you could see were just her eyes flicker, but it was like she was completely paralysed. And I was tied diagonally, so my feet were next to hers. And they had the altar there, they had everything there, the altar, the cross, the goblets. They even had a black skull, do you know that? . . . a black skull. And again it's like a crematorium cloth.
> . . . And because this was special, I hate that word 'special', was a special occasion for them . . . there were more people there. There was like two indoctrinations [*sic*] you know . . . the killing of this girl, which he put his hands around my hands around the sword that went right the way through her . . . you know. And beforehand was the mixing of the bloods. [*Long pause*] And then that gets put in the book . . . your blood gets put in the book as well . . . written in blood.
> (Sophie)

As an interviewee, Lynn was the most able and willing to talk about the ritual aspects of her experience. However, I think the following description illustrates the particular difficulties in relation to meaning and responsibility around a ritual death in which she was forced to participate.

> This one's really difficult . . . I still to this day find it really hard to think that I held the knife. And I mean I've always found that

extremely . . . I have to say the reason is that I'm talking about an
11-year-old person, an 11-year-old boy. There were two kids there and
I was told I had to choose which one I was going to marry. I didn't
want to choose, and of course I was made to, and of course he dies.
I was made to feel I had done that. I was one of them. I'd killed for
Lucifer, which I'd done before but not an older person. But the thing
is when it actually came to the ceremony, we'd had the marriage
ceremony and all that: I was married to the boy who became Lucifer
because he'd died. That was the whole point. Lucifer consumed his
body 'cos he died. He was taking the role of Lucifer, they never told
me he was going to die, and as Lucifer could take on any shape or
form, or that's what we were told anyway. So we were married and
all the rest and he was placed on an upside down cross. Lots of other
things happened [*voice trails away*]. And he was directly in front of
me and er, my mother put the knife in my hand and said: 'You know
what to do'. I stood there and there was a lot of noise, I raised my
arm and then just as I was about to pull away her arm came down
on mine and pushed it in. I then, although I had my hand on it as
it entered, I then pulled back and let go. I think it was because
he in some way reacted, and she finished it. I've always found that
extremely difficult . . . very . . . Like I didn't know this boy, he'd never
done me any harm . . . I'd seen him, but he was from another group in
the same town, he'd been at our meetings sometimes. Very beautiful
child too . . . And I was made to take parts of his remains [*mumble*]
and they were brought back at another ceremony a week or ten days
later absolutely riddled with maggots and then we were made to eat
them. Part of that is when the heart and the brain, parts like that,
are riddled with maggots, that means that Lucifer is consuming them,
then we eat it to show [*voice trails away*]. Stupid, stupid stuff. It's sort
of like horoscopes in the newspaper, you can make them fit anything.
Like Freud this stuff, you can make it fit anything, they've always got
an answer, it's so all consuming . . . Like God, there's always a reason
even if we don't understand it.

(Lynn)

Through these ritual meanings, which Lynn can describe now only as this
'stupid, stupid stuff' (and which for the uninitiated she compares to Freud,
God and horoscopes), the process of becoming 'one of them' is intended
to take place. As 'one of them' such events are meaningful; as 'not one of
them' they are appallingly senseless. It is interesting that in Lynn's account
the locus of resistance is the body. Her incomplete absorption into the world
of ritual meaning is demonstrated by the parental hand which forced the
knife.

Sinead's description of her father's death as a 'voluntary sacrifice' is distinctive because of the relationship between them. The contrast between her
father's 'faith' and her own disbelief is probably the clearest statement, in
any interview, of the serious commitment to a different universe of meaning
which ritual abuse may sometimes involve:

Then my dad took ill in the September – just after my birthday. He had a bad heart and he'd had it from birth and he'd had several operations on this. And in the October he took quite ill and had a heart attack and went into hospital. He gradually picked up a bit but they said he would have to have a heart transplant. He would probably die anyway, he had a short life span owing to it.

The thing is . . . I think it's every 17 years within a cult group they can have a voluntary sacrifice which gives them a lot of power, a lot more power than enforced or chosen sacrifices.

It was set for this date in November . . . He was dressed in a white robe – which was often what was used for a sacrifice. But he wasn't like . . . Normally when somebody is being sacrificed they are drugged and spaced out, he wasn't. He was himself, he'd refused drugs . . . which was going to mean he was going to scream . . . y'know . . . He got to the altar and was lifted on it. And the robe was removed. And he had the marks on – they're painted on – it's the mark where . . . where you put the knife . . . where it's been decided it will go.

. . . The athame and that was brought in, and it was his. But . . . and I thought: 'There it goes, that's it'. But it was taken away and mine was brought. And I knew then that he'd actually decided he wanted mine . . . he wanted my knife to be the one to have his blood on, and not his.

. . . I could see that he didn't want to die. Once it had been done. And there was bugger all I could do about that. And at that point I didn't want him to die . . . Whatever the sod had done, once it had happened I didn't want him to die – I didn't want him to have died that way anyway.

(Sinead)

Within the universe of ritual meanings such a voluntary sacrifice makes sense (even though I do not expect there would have been a superfluity of applicants for this seventeenth year privilege). I think Sinead's account clearly displays the tension between the 'ritual meanings' with which survivors are brought up, and the 'abuse meanings' through which they reinterpret their experiences. I do not mean to suggest that this is an entirely *post-hoc* reinterpretation, for the two meaning systems at least begin alongside each other in survivors' lives.

Ritual deaths seem to me to be the half-hidden heart of ritual abuse. Throughout questionnaires and interviews survivors refer to them, but within the discourses available to survivors to describe, categorize and make sense of their lives, these deaths are hard to place. If a culture of sexual and financial greed, incorporating a criminal lack of respect for the value of certain human lives, can 'explain' what I have termed incidental deaths, then enforced pregnancy and abortion can be seen as continuous with physical and sexual abuse – as something done to the body of the survivor – while the death of a baby can be felt as a personal maternal loss and a key to future freedom. However, the available discourses around the abuse of women and children based on an analysis of power and the pleasures of power (frequently through its sexualization) cannot fully incorporate these accounts of ritual death which stubbornly refuse to translate into late modern terms.

In discussing a series of ritual killings in Peru and Bolivia in the 1980s, Patrick Tierney (1989) has described the synchretic mix of deities and beliefs drawn from ancient Andean civilizations with the Satan of Christian derivation. In explaining the involvement of drug traffickers and mine-owners commissioning such killings and the shamans performing the rites, he argues that:

> Although the perpetrators of these sacrifices are sincere in their faith that human sacrifice is the ultimate magic, the resulting violence is conducive to their illegal and immoral purposes. It continues because it works.
>
> (Tierney 1989: 324)

It may be that in relation to the ritual killings described in this chapter this remains the most 'modern' explanation we can find: they bring power to those who control them – they continue because they work.

Conclusion

In this chapter, I have discussed three 'types' of death as they were told to me as significant experiences in survivors' lives: incidental, personal and ritual deaths. In relation to each, survivors tended to have a different orientation. In relation to incidental deaths, the survivor rendering the account tended to be a witness or observer. In relation to the personal deaths, the primary orientation tends to be as the victim of the experience, as in the loss of a baby or significant other. In the ritual deaths, the focus is on the survivor as participant.

These orientations are not absolute. They tend to blur at the edges, and in different individuals' experiences the factors above blend in different ways. However, some aspects of ritual abuse may be articulated more readily than others: in this case, specifically those deaths which can be rendered meaningful to survivors telling their life-stories as 'survivors', and utilizing the available discourses about child abuse, motherhood and so on to do so.

At the beginning of the chapter, I suggested that experiences of death might in and of themselves be significant to survivors, because of the 'window' in the taken-for-granted immutability of the social order which they may provide. When Peter Berger writes of death as the spectre that opens the window through which ontological insecurity whistles, it is the inhabitants of Smalltown, USA, whom I picture contemplating the human constructedness of their social world. Survivors of ritual abuse have the kind of intimate knowledge of death which in Smalltown today would be reserved for medics and funeral directors. Like occupants of those professions, they must select from many such contacts with death those which are of personal significance.

I am reminded again of my mother, who was a fever nurse in an isolation hospital in the 1930s. She nursed dozens of children who died of diphtheria, scarlet and rheumatic fevers and whooping cough, but the story she returns to regularly is that of a little boy who died on Christmas Eve, having refused to have his presents early because he did not want Santa to have to make a special trip. This death was the occasion of one of my mother's, not infrequent, fallings out with God, but it also stands for all the other deaths she witnessed as a young woman. Through this story she expresses her own helplessness and rage at the pre-antibiotics and immunization world, a world of dirt, disease and poverty I have never known. The survivors who shared their life-stories with me were also trying to find stories that might enable me to glimpse the alien world they had inhabited. My understanding is that experiences of death are both openings for ontological insecurity, and are understood to be such, so that survivors' choices of accounts of death are also attempts to make connections, and generate an understanding through our shared knowledge that 'death changes everything'.

In a similar way, the idea of 'physiological connection', through the experience or potential of pregnancy and childbirth, is both a universal aspect of femaleness, and is seen to be so. Survivors' accounts of their dead babies draw on both elements – locating the 'truth of their bodies' outside the ritual abuse culture they inhabited, and claiming connection and common cause with other women. (See Chapter 5 for a discussion of male interviewees' accounts of identification with non-abusive men.)

These are two of the ways in which ritual abuse survivors struggle to create meaningful accounts 'between worlds'. I have shown how the deaths that 'translate' most easily are those 'incidental' deaths which lacked significance at the time. Such deaths fit with a common notion of violence as random, senseless and therefore socially inexplicable. In its strongest expression in cases of murder, it is often characterized as 'evil'.

The extracts from interviews included in this chapter suggest that in these 'incidental' deaths, the association is with chaos and meaninglessness. These are 'bad' deaths which open the door wide to ontological insecurity. My feeling is that it may be these impromptu backstage deaths that set the scenery wobbling around the 'big production' ritual performances. For ritually abused children, it is these deaths that have their closest parallels in the wider social world. The deaths caused by hit and run drivers or murderous psychopaths are already moralized. Their experiences of ritual deaths are far more secret, their meanings and rationalizations far less open to contradiction.

I have argued that ritual deaths always are already 'meaning-full'. In particular, those described by survivors tended to have been experienced as part of an official occult biography, involving a series of ceremonies of initiation or rites of passage. Zygmunt Bauman suggests that bureaucracy and technology were instrumental in the mass killings of the Holocaust by removing and diffusing personal responsibility. It seems that ritual abuse killings draw on an older tradition in which ritual and religion provide the mechanisms for rendering certain people morally invisible, while the ritual structure diffuses responsibility and directs moral obligation to the group.

I believe that this legitimation of ritual abuse failed for the survivors I interviewed for a number of reasons: because they inhabited a wider, contradictory, moral community through school and the media; because in the case of personal deaths their own exploitation and suffering were so closely tied to the deaths of others; because under conditions of sexual slavery, they lived with the constant threat that their own deaths might not be far away; and finally, because they witnessed the casual treatment of 'incidental deaths' and other behaviours among their abusers which suggested hypocrisy, cynicism or half-belief.

Notes

1 The 'twin solution' has a long history in relation to the paradox of child sacrifice, Romulus and Remus being the best known example (see Maccoby 1982: 75).
2 Both Lynn and Sinead expressed some confusion over their age. Sinead, whose birth had gone unregistered by her parents, thought she was probably a couple of years older than she was led to believe and had started school late. In her twenties, Lynn had been shocked by the evidence of her eldest sister that she had been born two years earlier than her 'official' date of birth. Such might account for the early onset of menstruation claimed by some interviewees.

7 | Composing the self

The issue of the facticity or otherwise of accounts of ritual abuse has been frequently entangled with the controversy over the real or invented existence of Multiple Personality Disorder (MPD), a condition (re)discovered in the 1980s in the context of providing therapy for adult survivors of child sexual abuse. When Florence Schreiber (1973) published her account of therapy with 'Sybil' in 1973, she was contributing to a literature on dissociation and 'split', 'double' or 'multiple' personality which had increased by an annual average of only one book or paper a year since the end of the eighteenth century. Between 1971 and 1980 this increased to around nine publications a year, becoming an average sixty items each year from 1981 to 1990 (Goettman *et al.* 1991). The controversial psychological and social phenomena involved have contributed to the publishing explosion:

> Sceptics argue that multiple personality is the invention of over-zealous therapists, or a product of modern times, or a dramatic but essentially false presentation of self; while those who challenge this view see it as a complex defence: a psychological survival mechanism, usually a response to extreme childhood abuse.
>
> (Walker 1999: 1)

The link between multiple personality and ritual abuse has been of little assistance to those seeking recognition for either issue: that 'multiple' patients should claim such 'unbelievable' childhood experiences gains as little credibility for the disorder, as ritual abuse accounts gain by being told in dissociated voices by survivors with a dubious diagnosis. Sociological responses to the discovery of 'multiple persons' have been sceptical. They have focused on the emergence of a new psychiatric discourse without reference to why some people rather than others have become inscribed with dissociative identities, and therefore without exploring the possibility that there may be some kind of auto/biographical 'fit' between discourse and patient. My intention in this chapter is to point to the existence of an alternative approach that accounts for the development of dissociative capacities within the social world of abusive experience and relationships, which in turn might facilitate the recruitment of particular individuals into a 'multiple' understanding of their own subjectivities. This approach will be developed in relation to the ideas about self and identity expressed by my interviewees as they attempted to describe the 'assaults on the self' which their abusers had perpetrated and to account for their own moral and psychological survival.

There is a long history of debate between social causationists and social constructivists in relation to providing alternatives to the biomedical model of 'mental illness'. What is fairly new in relation to multiple personality is that the 'accusation' of social construction is levelled specifically at a diagnosis which, like that of post-traumatic stress disorder, is based on social causes. I shall suggest that it is most helpful to think in terms of both/and rather than either/or and to consider both causes and constructions of 'multiplicity' (see Busfield 1988).

A science of multiplicity

The identification of 'multiple personality' is dependent on the existence of a psychiatric categorization. That is to say, both the designation of a category of persons and what is known about their nature has been framed largely by psychiatric discourse.[1] Broadly speaking, there are two main approaches to making sense of psychiatric classification. The first sees its categories and their refinements as products of advances in a scientific discipline, leading to ever better, more accurate descriptions and more appropriate treatments. This is the official belief of both psychiatry and common sense, and the basis on which society endorses the practice of psychiatry and its variants. The alternative approach is exemplified by the work of Thomas Szasz (1962) and Michel Foucault (1971), who regard psychiatric classifications not as identifying pre-existing sicknesses, but essentially as producing them. On the wider canvas of modern social thought, structuralism and post-structuralism have been centrally engaged in deconstructing the humanist notion of the individual, showing them to be a product of the very discourses that purports to describe 'them'. Considering psychoanalysis for example, Foucault argues that it has no privileged access to the secrets of subjectivity. Rather, the unconscious is constructed, along with other aspects of the self, within psychoanalytic discourse (Foucault 1979, 1982).

However, Foucault's work is not entirely without contradictions. There are times when he appears to believe in an already existing individual on whom power works. As a Nietzschean, he understands that power needs a recalcitrant object on which to operate. However, if this idea of individuality is necessary, it must also be indescribable – for to attempt a description would be to create a new object for power, and already the threshold of description has been lowered:

> For a long time ordinary individuality – the everyday individuality of everybody – remained below the threshold of description. To be looked at, observed, described in detail, followed from day to day by an uninterrupted writing was a privilege . . . The disciplinary methods reversed this relation, lowering the threshold of describable individuality and made this description a means of control and a method of domination.
>
> (Foucault [1977] 1981: 191)

Because what remains 'below the threshold' is untheorizable – despite being constantly visible as one party to the 'agonal' struggle between power and the objects of power – Foucault fails to develop any dialectical theory of social action and identity such as that found in the work of G.H. Mead (1934). As Turner (1984) says, Foucault shows how individuals are the subjects of discourse but not how they create discourses.

The **emergence** of **multiple personality**

Between the mid 1980s and the mid 1990s the contemporary conception of multiple personality emerged, grew a movement and fought a backlash. There are tendencies in the movement, and an apparently widening division between the senior clinicians active in the International Society for the Study of Dissociation (ISSD), and a groundswell of self-help groups and survivor newsletters. Multiple Personality Disorder has had an official change of name: it is now called Dissociative Identity Disorder (DID). The new name is important; it emphasizes the psychological process of 'dissociation' rather than the 'personalities' encountered in therapy. However, the diagnostic criteria provided in the most recent American *Diagnostic and Statistical Manual (DSM) IV* are as follows:

A. The presence of two or more distinct identities or personalities or personality states (each with its own relatively enduring pattern of perceiving, relating to and thinking about the environment and self).
B. At least two of these identities or personality states recurrently take control of the person's behaviour.
C. Inability to recall important personal information that is too extensive to be explained by ordinary forgetfulness.
D. The disturbance is not due to the direct physiological effects of a substance (e.g., blackouts or chaotic behaviour during Alcohol Intoxication) or a general medical condition (e.g., complex partial seizures). *Note*: In children the symptoms are not attributable to imaginary playmates or other fantasy play.

(American Psychiatric Association 1994: 487)

A **kind** of **person**

Such official criteria are only part of the discursive production of multiple personality. There are a number of questionnaires which purport to measure 'dissociative experience' on a scale from 'normal daydreaming' to 'failing to recognize friends or family members' or 'having no memory of your wedding' (Carlson and Putnam 1993; Steinberg 1993). It is often assumed that MPD/DID is simply a description of the disorder that exists in extremely dissociative individuals. In addition there is a popular, clinical and folklore knowledge of a 'kind of person' who is a multiple. A contradictory image emerges from originals such as Sybil (Schreiber 1973) and Eve (Thigpen and Cleckley 1954). Quiet, depressive women turn out to have aggressive and promiscuous 'alters' (alternate personalities). The prototype multiple dresses differently according to which 'alter' gets up in the morning, she carries her body differently according to who is 'in' the body. The portrait is often unflattering: 'borderline' characteristics such as 'histrionic', 'manipulative' and 'attention seeking' are frequently referred to. (It is no surprise then that diagnosed multiples are overwhelmingly female.)

A former president of the ISSD, Colin Ross, insists that: 'The diagnosis and treatment of MPD is analogous to the diagnosis and treatment of streptococcal pneumonia' (Ross 1995: 82). He understands 'multiple personality' as one outcome of a child who is severely abused learning to 'dissociate' and simultaneously experiencing 'depersonalization' and 'derealization'. If abuse is frequent he believes they may begin to carve up their lives and 'selves' into different strands: one Lizzie is the girl that goes to school, another Lizzie gets beaten and raped at night. Only the second Lizzie remembers the abuse. Each develops a personal style. The more severe and multifaceted the abuse, the more 'fragmented' a child's consciousness may become in order to survive without being overwhelmed. 'Switching' between personalities becomes automatic or habitual in the face of particular stressors.

The adult multiple to whom such a history is attributed is said to have spent a large part of her adult life denying the existence of her 'alters'. She will have ignored the voices inside her head, covered up for lost time, and only in the company of a therapist, familiar with or open to considering multiple personality, will the 'alters' begin to declare their existence. Gradually, a whole inner world of children and protectors, persecutors and helpers, animals and even angels, may emerge. Many will 'hold' traumatic memories which need to be 'processed' before personalities can integrate with the 'host' (see Putnam 1989; Ross 1989).

Sceptical responses

An early critical engagement with the resurgence of 'multiple personality' as a diagnostic classification came from anthropologist Michael Kenny (1986). Kenny opens his book with a story of meeting a man in Africa who claimed he had two souls, an account he accepted on the man's terms. Drawing on the nineteenth-century American cases of William James and colleagues,

Kenny argues that multiple personality was a construction of the newly emergent psychological sciences into which patients were socialized. Although at the same time, he suggests that patients producing multiple personalities can be seen to be responding to the social tensions of the period: the oppressive limitations of women's role and the extreme dualism of puritanical Christianity. However, in relation to the re-emergence of multiple personalities in the 1980s, he is implacably hostile to the possibility of multiplicity as a phenomenological reality. His explanation is simple: fraud, contagion and deliberate self-deception in more or less equal measures.

Kenny's nineteenth-century case studies suggest that multiple personality might have been a new label for states that had previously been seen as, or socialized into, spiritualism or other forms of possession. He himself suggests that the medicalization of what had previously been seen as a spiritual experience was central to the development of a secular science of mind. However, at the same time he claims that the contemporary performance of multiple personality is entirely disingenuous and iatrogenic, a combination of therapists' impositions and patients' posturings.

A more subtle and more thoroughly Foucauldian account is provided by Ian Hacking (1995). In *The History of Sexuality*, Foucault ([1977] 1981) describes the emergence of a biopolitics of populations and an anatomo-politics of the human body. To these, Hacking (1995), in *Rewriting the Soul: Multiple Personality and the Sciences of Memory*, adds a discourse of memoro-politics; a discourse of the 'self', the human mind, or as he prefers, the soul. Hacking's case is that in the late-nineteenth-century work of Janet and Freud, knowledge about memory became a surrogate for spiritual understanding of the soul:

> the spiritual travail of the soul, which so long served a previous onto-logy, could now become hidden psychological pain, not the result of sin that seduces us within, but caused by the sinner outside who seduced us.
>
> (Hacking 1995: 197)

Hacking's general case is an elaboration of the often made suggestion that the analyst's couch has provided a twentieth-century replacement for the confessional. However, his particular interest is in the specific emergence of contemporary discourses of multiple personality. *Rewriting the Soul* begins with a chapter entitled 'Is it real?' It is a question that Hacking then attempts to displace in favour of concerns about the way in which the historically specific configuration of multiple personality, and its relationship to childhood trauma came into being, and how it 'has made and moulded our life, our customs, our science' (Hacking 1995: 16). As in Foucault, there is an uncertainty in Hacking of what sense to make of the individual 'inscribed by the discourses of multiplicity'. Writing in 1986, Hacking contrasted their situation to that of homosexuals who had broken away from the illness inscribing discourses of psychiatry to develop a non-pathological identity. His argument was that by contrast 'multiples' were not imaginable independent from their therapeutic puppet-masters (Hacking 1986b). However, returning to the subject in 1995 he commented: 'I may yet come to eat those words'.

As Hacking makes clear, MPD/DID discourse assumes mental processes to be pre-givens requiring only correct classification. In fact, the term 'dissociation' can readily refer to a whole collection of activities: selective attention, motivated forgetting, or more colloquially 'pushing away' or 'warding off'. Freud may have made repression the 'Queen of the defences', but in much of his work he used terms like 'repression', 'suppression', 'dissociation' and 'inhibition' fairly interchangeably. Each is, of course, a word with its own particular flavour, and the operation of each involves an imaginative leap into metaphor.[2]

To Ross, multiple personality is as independently and diagnosably present within afflicted patients as pneumonia. To Hacking, multiple personality is simply a discursive 'parasite in need of a host'. The latter links the development of 'alternate' personalities with a therapist-supported process of recalling repressed memories as an adult; the former believes they result from a psychological splitting during childhood abuse. I suggest below that these polarized positions are not the only options and that sociological and psychological accounts exist which may explain the 'fit' between certain aspects of childhood experience for some child abuse survivors and the metaphor of multiplicity. For ritual abuse survivors in particular it may latch into previous experience, fantasy and self-understanding, in a way that is experienced as comforting and illuminating.

Between the poles

The identification and description of MPD/DID as a disorder of identity is the result of a complex set of processes within psychiatry and within society, as well as within individuals. Most psychiatric accounts have a tendency to leap from an abused child's ability to deny, disavow and 'trance out' from their experience, to the full-blown disorder of the adult patient:

> MPD is a little girl imagining that the abuse is happening to someone else . . . The imagining is so intense, subjectively compelling, and adaptive, that the abused child experiences dissociated aspects of herself as other people.
>
> (Ross 1989: 55)

MPD/DID is not merely 'a little girl imagining', for we continue imagining and reimagining ourselves in interactions throughout our lives. It may be that when adults begin to ask questions about their pasts, both memories and the 'selves' who experienced them are brought to mind. The lie of 'not I' becomes an alternative to the lie of 'it never happened'; multiple personalities may provide multiple defences against overwhelming distress. Of course therapists such as Colin Ross and Phil Mollon would agree that MPD is a 'pretence based disorder' like Munchausen's Syndrome (Mollon 1996). Where we part company is over the idea that *it has been present since childhood and personalities imagined into being at the time of the abuse have led an unacknowledged existence until emerging fully fledged into the therapist's consulting room.*

In the vast majority of the MPD/DID literature, the story of origins is one of overwhelming trauma; treatment is focused on the recovery and integration of traumatic memories into a unified self. DID is therefore regarded as a post-traumatic stress disorder, a way of defending against the intrusion of painful memories (Ross 1989). While it may well serve just such a function, there is a tendency to concretize descriptions that are actually metaphors, a tendency which a number of therapists from various traditions have been increasingly concerned to correct:

> Events signified by such metaphors as 'ego-state', 'amnestic barrier', 'traumatic memory' or 'abreacted affect' are often misunderstood as possessing 'thing-hood', but they would be better understood as processes occurring within an interaction between a listener and a speaker, and within a specific functional context.
>
> (Segall 1996: 154)

> It's quite impossible to keep Hollywood out of 'multiple personalities'. It's an excellent metaphor but I fear too many people – clients and practitioners – fail to understand the limits of the metaphor and they concretise it, take it too literally, act as if nothing that we know about ordinary people and everyday psychological processes can be true. It makes me furious. So you get these puerile, pseudo-scientific taxonomies of alters or bizarre statements like 'all of the personalities will be dedicated to the survival of the person'. They're like the maps that medieval priests drew of Africa – pure imagination.
>
> (Brenda Roberts 1996, personal communication)

While some therapists have focused on the tendency in diagnosing and treating DID to 'reify the figurative' and have suggested that other traditions – such as transactional analysis – provide more fluid models for understanding the internally divided self (Kowszun 1999), others have suggested that the causal 'trauma-leads-to-split' model of DID development is far too simplistic. It has been suggested that incoherence of attachment may be just as important as trauma itself in the lack of coherent identity development (Richardson 2000). Winnicott's (1953, 1965) idea of the 'false self' developing in interaction with 'the mother' has been re-explored by psychoanalysts seeking to ground the development of DID in a more complex relational view of identity formation (Barach 1991; Liotti 1992; Sands 1994).

A **sociological starting point**

G.H. Mead developed an understanding of 'mind' and 'self' being formed within the 'social, communicative activity of the group'. He argued that personality, intelligence and self-awareness arise only in society, through a constant process of 'adjustments' – actions and reactions through language and action – between people. Through this process, self-consciousness emerges as people constitute themselves as objects to their own gaze.

Consciousness is dramaturgical in Mead's description – 'the self' is composed initially through both real and imaginary dialogue with a child's significant others. Mead considered that abstract thought developed from this early dramaturgical self-consciousness, later:

> The features and intonations of the dramatis personae fade out and the emphasis falls upon the meaning of the inner speech, the imagery becomes merely the barely necessary cues. But the mechanism remains social, and at any moment the process may become personal.
>
> (Mead 1913: 146–7)

Working with similar dramaturgical metaphors in their work on sexuality, Gagnon and Simon (1973) developed a metaphor of multilevel social 'scripts' ranging from cultural scripts – 'instructional guides that exist at the level of collective life' – through interpersonal scripts to the intrapsychic scripting of rehearsal and fantasy.

In much sociological work Mead's 'I' or Gagnon and Simon's intrapsychic scripts have become residual categories – a sort of psychological junk room in which the dust-sheets are left undisturbed. However, from Erving Goffman ([1959] 1969) onwards, the understanding of social actors as multiple role-players has been fundamental to sociology. The possible relationship and distinction between 'pathological' and 'normal' multiplicity was one explored by Peter Berger:

> The actual difference [between multiple personality and 'normal' multiplicity] . . . is that for 'normal people' (that is, those so recognized by their society) there are strong pressures towards consistency in the various roles they play and the identities that go with these roles . . .
>
> There are also internal pressures towards consistency, possibly based on a very profound psychological need to perceive oneself as a totality . . . To avoid such anxieties people commonly segregate their consciousness as well as their conduct. By this we do not mean that they 'repress' their discrepant identities into some 'unconscious', for within our model we have every reason to be suspicious of such concepts. We rather mean that they focus their attention only on that particular identity that, so to speak, they require at the moment. Other identities are forgotten for the duration of this particular act . . . The Nazi concentration camp commander who writes sentimental letters to his children is but an extreme case of something that occurs in society all the time.
>
> (Berger 1963: 125–7)

What Berger's view suggests is that the social push is *generally* towards consistency, and that this may be backed up by some psychological drive in the same direction. However, some social situations encourage inconsistent and divergent selves, awareness of which are kept situationally separate. Drawing on Mead, Berger suggests that to a child, 'self' and 'society' are two sides of the same coin. If this is so, then one could reasonably seek an inconsistent and contradictory environment as the necessary accompaniment to a split sense of self. One 'multiple' survivor has described precisely this:

> The way I see it, we develop a definition of ourselves only in relation to our environment, and often use cues about how we interact with others to define ourselves. It's a dynamic relationship. As a child begins the process of self-definition, an environment which contains inherent conflicts and contradictions will create conflict and contradiction in the child's identity.
>
> (McClure 1991: 122)

Anthony Giddens (1991) has drawn on Winnicott's (1965) account of the importance of infant confidence in the reliability of caretakers in providing an inoculation against existential anxieties, and as a condition of the development of a coherent self-identity:

> The feelings of unreality which may haunt the lives of individuals in whose early childhood basic trust was poorly developed may take many forms. They may feel that the object-world, or other people, have only a shadowy existence, or be unable to maintain a clear sense of continuity of self-identity.
>
> (Giddens 1991: 43)

In addition to these tendencies to derealization and depersonalization, time may be experienced as discontinuous such that no coherent biographical narrative can be sustained.

What the approaches of Berger and Giddens provide is a sociological way of thinking about fragmented selves which is independent of their particular construction within an MPD/DID framework. In these, 'the self' has its origins in the social relationships of early childhood where the opportunities for establishing coherence and continuity may be more or less available. However, this 'self' does not stand still, but continues to produce and reproduce itself in social relationships throughout life.

For Giddens, self-identity is not a collection of traits possessed by the individual:

> [Self-identity] is the self as reflexively understood by the person in terms of her or his biography . . . The capacity to use 'I' in shifting contexts, characteristic of every known culture, is the most elemental feature of reflexive conceptions of personhood.
>
> (Giddens 1991: 53)

What this contrasts with in many, if not all, cultures is fractured or multiple identities that may be culturally tolerated or even venerated, but which are always deviant from the normative way to be a person (Walker 1972; Crapanzano 1973). Such identities are universally associated with dissociative abilities (going into trance, heightened toleration of pain and so on) which are often seen as spiritual gifts that the recipient must be trained to control and use.

The clinical and popular discourses of multiplicity in the late twentieth century suggest that divided selves cannot be tolerated in late modernity. Far from the increasing acceptance of multifaceted identities suggested by some postmodern theorists, it seems that the particular discursive form in which divided selves have been lifted over the threshold of description is one that ensures they will simultaneously be drawn into the self-reflexive project. Unlike their nineteenth-century cousin, whose involuntary, hysterical symptoms were emphasized, the modern multiple must be reflexive upon their own condition in order to effect self-control and cure. This is not simply because the process of self-reflexivity is expected to create a contented self, that is not a self in pain (after all, dissociation aims to produce the same outcome through avoidance and denial rather than self-knowledge), but because coherence and integration of the whole self are highly valued goals. By contrast, the absorption of other identities into a single 'I' is not a requirement of other discourses of 'not-I-ness'. Possession and mediumship are usually treated by encouraging peaceful cohabitation with one's spirits or by their ejection through exorcism.

The late-modern version of the individual as described by Giddens – with its insistence on embodiedness as part of an integrated whole self; the high value placed upon authenticity – involving the disentangling of true and false selves; and the presumption of autobiographical narratives – appears to have inspired a therapeutic and self-help industry committed to producing such selves for/with those who find them most difficult to achieve.

What it means to be, have and behave *as* a self in late modernity may render divided, false and disembodied selves problematic in particular ways: because they represent barriers to reflexivity. Such selves must be socialized in such a way that they can be converted to reflexivity, authenticity and a coherent narrative form. In 'fragmented' form multiple selves appear to be denying autobiographical coherence, yet in the moment of speaking their existence they commence a therapeutic narrative productive of a unitary subject.[3] Giddens' understanding of the self-reflexive late-modern subject is at fundamental odds with Foucauldian descriptions of subjects as entirely discursive products. The importance of a discourse of self-reflexivity (with its legal and medical dimensions, and panoply of advice manuals and television shows) is not denied. Rather it is regarded as one dimension of a dialectical relationship in which people create discourses which then act back upon them. What this makes space for are the negotiations and resistances of individuals in relation to the discursively produced subject positions available.

Encountering 'multiplicity'

In order to explain my particular standpoint on multiple personality I need to tell a story about my own first encounter with 'multiplicity'. It is a story I have told a number of times. For a little while, I told it as 'the diagnostic story' in terms of Sinead's MPD/DID. Seven years on I tell it more as a cautionary tale, and an account of my own changing perspective. Sinead was 14 when we first met. A few months before her sixteenth birthday, after a period of living rough on the streets of London and Manchester, she sought sanctuary with my partner and myself as she did not feel that she could finally break away from her abusers completely without help. She was afraid of being found, and afraid that she might return to the group of her own accord for reasons she could not really explain. Her sixteenth birthday was to involve her in a ceremony that she described as a 'final' stage of becoming 'one of them'; she was terrified. We decided that the whole business would be easier to cope with if we all went away to London for the weekend and had some distraction.

Two days before her birthday, Sinead spent twelve hours with her mother and other abusers. When she returned to us she appeared to be in shock. Apparently unaware of who we were and unable to hear anything we said, she sat and rocked, wild eyed and staring. We thought she had been drugged, we were sure she had been abused, and she appeared to be in pain. It seemed unlikely we were going to be able to get her to London. Emotionally, it felt as if she had turned up just to say 'goodbye', perhaps to show us how profoundly 'other' she was, maybe even to frighten us into letting her go without a fight.

However, we did make it to London for the weekend. Throughout the rail journey she seemed torn in two. Most of the time she sat meek and anxious holding tight to my hand, then as the train pulled into a station, she would dash towards the door as if her life depended on it. The next couple of days continued in similar vein. I was exhausted and confused, and I told her so on a London Underground journey:

Me: I just don't understand. One minute you're clinging to my apron strings for dear life – the next you're bolting for the door with no idea where you're going apart from 'back to them'.

Sinead: [*screaming above the noise of the train*] But you don't understand: there isn't only me!

Later that afternoon, after much coaxing, she told me that there were two 'entities' inside her. One was evil, violent and angry and we would never meet her if she, Sinead, could prevent us from doing so. The other was terrified, useless, and did exactly what she was told. She believed that these 'entities' had been 'put inside her' by those who had abused her; they 'belonged to' the cult and obeyed her 'Master' in all things. 'She' feared that she could never escape completely because 'they' could 'take over her body'.

A fortnight before this journey, I had been to my first RAINS (Ritual Abuse Information Network and Support) meeting, and I had heard a psychologist talk about a client who had MPD. I had returned home feeling profoundly uncomfortable with 'all the psychobabble', but anxious enough to ask my partner whether she thought Sinead's strange behaviour could possibly be because she had 'multiple personalities'. After all she slipped into a trance in the blink of an eye, and frequently seemed to forget where she was or who we were. My partner dismissed the idea out of hand. After Sinead's declaration of her 'entities' just two weeks later, I wondered whether she was telepathic rather than 'multiple' and had somehow extracted the idea from my head!

The idea of 'multiple personality' was alien and unnerving, but marginally more palatable than demon possession. I contacted the woman who had spoken at the meeting and began to read the rapidly expanding therapeutic literature. What I found was a framework for making sense of Sinead's practice of going in and out of trance (frequently facilitated by staring at light-bulbs) and the extremely contradictory impulses and emotions she displayed. She was eager to understand what was meant by dissociation, terrified of hypnosis and proud of her ability to 'switch off' pain or hunger. The advice in the books was to educate 'the client' about multiple personality, so we did. We loathed the idea of 'satanic alters' and never mentioned them;[4] we refrained from telling her about some of the wilder doings of American 'multiples', but we gave her a framework within which she could convert her 'entities' into secular personalities which she had created, and over whom she could therefore exercise control.

In certain respects, Sinead followed the textbooks – introducing us to a whole variety of characters who populated her imagination. The two original 'entities' turned into 5 year olds – although one said nothing apart from 'Fuck off, bitch!' for the first few months of our acquaintance. Sinead never manifested an 'internal self-helper' (ISH), a figure that loomed large in the early literature we came across (Allison 1980) but which we thought likely to be therapist wish-fulfilment. We watched, part fascinated, part horrified, at the 'many headed Hydra' we had apparently unleashed. For the first few months, a dozen characters a day sometimes careered their way through our lives, each with different tactics for avoiding straightforward discussion. Anger and terror, and the need to control, rebel, be cared for, remember, forget, self-harm, test out and take risks were acted out through 'the personalities'. Remembering often took the form of an imaginary struggle or game until gradually 'they' began to tell Sinead about forgotten experiences of abuse and terror, and bit by bit she accepted these as her own. Although we interacted with the personalities presented to us, joked with them and reassured them – often just grateful that *somebody* would eat or sleep – they never felt like 'real' or separate 'people'. Except in the emotions they expressed on Sinead's behalf, they were cardboard cut-outs, pantomime witches, vamps and macho men – a child's cast of characters. Symbolically they made good sense: touch on a painful topic and a defence mechanism, in the shape of a tough male alter called Jimmy, might well 'manifest before one's eyes'. The difference was that one normally talks to people *about* their defences, rather than conversing with the defences themselves.

Despite the distress and terror, lack of sleep and difficulties eating, Sinead held down a full-time job from the age of 16; her pain and chaos were reserved for weekends. But it was not until she was 18, at the end of a year of conflict over coping strategies that had exhausted my partner and myself beyond endurance, that Sinead really began to 'get her act together'. When she started college and gradually accepted both the real horror of her childhood and the fact that it was over, her 'multiple' behaviour declined rapidly.

I do not know how things would have been if 'multiple personality' had not been available as an account of Sinead's dissociative behaviour. Perhaps it allowed her to have a taste of the childhood she never had. It certainly allowed her to adopt her 'demons' as playmates rather than casting them out. It provided a powerful metaphor for the importance of accepting ambivalent feelings and of making peace with oneself. It provided a way of discussing the way her abusers had got inside her head, and the ways in which psychological manoeuvring can underpin survival. However, I also think that the support of a supervisor who focused on the relationships between the three of us, as Sinead negotiated her way from child to adult, rather than on the esoteric aspects of multiple personality, combined well with both our scepticism about much of what we read and Sinead's desire to achieve an 'ordinary' life.

The **research**

Multiple personality was not a primary focus of this research. I decided at the outset not to raise it as an interview topic in case my niggling doubts about the helpfulness of thinking about oneself 'like that' created a barrier with interviewees who might identify themselves as 'multiple'. I was particularly concerned not to throw any spanners into supportive or therapeutic relationships upon which survivors relied.

In the event, my fears were unfounded. The three survivors (including Sinead) who defined themselves as multiple talked freely about their concept of themselves and their descriptions allowed me to develop my own thinking about the possible relationships between abuse, dissociation and identity. In analysing the interviews, it became clear that there was little difference between the underlying concepts of 'self', or the impacts that those who abused them had had upon these, held by survivors who identified as 'multiple' and those who did not. This seemed to me important in terms of whether one should conceive of MPD/DID as an extant condition waiting to be diagnosed, as an identity into which individuals with dissociative abilities could be inducted or as a contagious fraud. In the end, I have declared for an understanding of multiple personality as a powerful metaphor for making retrospective sense of extremely inconsistent and painful experiences, and of a deeply divided sense of self who is both 'I' and 'not I'. At the same time, I suggest that it may well be an elaboration or a translation of other versions of divided selves which also provide imaginary distance from knowledge and experience which cannot be tolerated.

The accounts of interviewees who defined themselves as having 'other selves' provide an important challenge to the view of multiple personality as purely a mapping of discourse on to individuals (Kenny 1986; Hacking 1995). They rather suggest that the condition needs to be understood as arising from a collision between an individual with highly developed dissociative abilities and a historically and culturally specific psychiatric categorization.

Sources of self

Interviewees' accounts of themselves as 'selves': as persons with feelings, characteristics and self-awareness, described an understanding that emerged in and through interaction with others. They described the negative versions of who they were 'given out' in the words and actions of those around them and the divided sense of self they developed in response to these.

Retrospectively, this first self was seen as having been imposed from outside and to have always been in conflict with an 'inside', authentic self which, nourished by only the rarest shreds of recognition and validation, had managed to survive. This is the heroine of the story: the child self in whom the capacity to love was indestructible, the teenager who rebelled as best she could against the life her abusers had in mind for her, and growing up into the self-of-the-moment reflecting on healing and the future.

The **reflected self**

The most obvious way in which the self can be seen as a social product is in understandings of the self based on the assessments or statements of others. As a child my mother often told me that I had always been cheerful and confident, in contrast to my sister, who as a small girl was supposed to have been anxious, serious and shy. Our reported differences in character were connected to our physical resemblances to our parents: I had red cheeks and brown eyes and the supposedly placid sociability of my father; my sister was pale and blue eyed, delicate and sensitive, as my mother remembered her younger self to have been. In a similar vein, interviewees unpicked the reflections of self that had been provided for them as children.

With the violence and suffering in their lives ignored or covered up by their families, interviewees described how they were reflected back to themselves as troublesome, odd and amusing. Debbie lived with her paternal grandparents and her father was not physically involved in her abuse. When she was 8, he moved in with a new girlfriend:

> I would like smash her best ornaments and pooh on her best carpet, she had this big rug . . . I'd just . . . I don't know why I did it, I did it for something bad to get into. But they never asked that. And as I got older, they then got married and bought their place together, I used to just sit looking at a blank TV screen and I'd even talk sometimes to it, like there was someone there. And they would just laugh at me. She'd have friends round, or her sister and her brothers round, and er . . . I can remember even my dad laughing at me actually. It was like come round, have lunch, and laugh at Debs. But no one ever asked: 'Why are you looking at a blank TV screen?' All they used to say was: 'Do you want the TV on?'
>
> (Debbie)

In Gillean's family, the fact that she screamed blue murder at Laurel and Hardy movies was part of family folklore. It was part of her family portrayal as 'odd', 'a peculiar child'. Laurel and Hardy beat each other up wearing bowler hats, an item of costume worn by her extremely violent father. Elizabeth, on the other hand, was 'the child that cries':

And all the time they would say: 'Elizabeth cries, here she goes again'
. . . So I came to believe that crying was just something that I did.
That this was a normal thing. That I was born with this ability, or
inability not to cry. That the water lay near the surface and it would
just always come out of my eyes whether I wanted it to or not, and
it was nothing to do with my feelings. I never connected it to sadness
or unhappiness. But of course now, looking back I know what I was
actually saying was: 'There's something terrible going on in my life,
please will you listen to me, I want to tell you'. And they used to
laugh.

(Elizabeth)

This interactional invisibility or misinterpretation is described in most interviews. Often it is discussed alongside the direct statements of abusers to the
effect that a child was inherently evil, selfish, unlovable and unwanted. The
implication is that these versions of self were largely accepted in childhood,
and firmly rejected only from the perspective of the adult survivor.

The **self** by **contrast**

Three survivors described their status in their families as that of servants, and
contrasted this with the different treatment of siblings:

I feel some of the dynamics in their family were repeated in mine.
Where the oldest child of the generation, which in this case was Mary,
and in my case was me, was the scapegoat. And the youngest child is
bonny and blithe, good and gay. And in my father's generation that
was him, and in my generation it was my sister who was treated like a
pet, little doll who could do no wrong and I could do no right. And
all my growing up days I was thumped and hit and so forth by my
father, and I was made to blame for everything that was wrong in the
family, and she was the perfect child and everything about her was
wonderful.

(Gillean)

The idea that all children in a family should be treated equally has become
axiomatic to western child-rearing. However, it is a concept of relatively
recent origin related to changing patterns of inheritance and women's changing roles. The very different view that an eldest son should automatically be
preferred in decisions over distribution of family resources (the paying of an
indenture or of school fees for example), while an elder daughter should
automatically assume responsibility for younger siblings or the care of an
ageing parent, was common in all social classes up until the last few decades.
When Lynn began a segment of her interview with the words, 'My life was
planned before I was born', I felt chilled by the statement, but I am aware
that my spine tingled with a very late-twentieth-century horror.

Differences of roles and expectations, whether between siblings or 'other'
children, may be 'justified' by attributions of character that support them. A

number of survivors described some kind of 'original sin' that was used to explain their mistreatment. In three cases this was a story of a twin sibling for whose stillbirth or infant death they were held responsible:

And what did you observe about how your sister was treated by your parents?

Very differently. As the years went by it was more and more obvious. She would get Christmas presents, I wouldn't. Sure it was a grudge for me. My dad never lost his temper when she was around. If she wanted something he would help her. If she and I wanted to watch television and we wanted to watch different channels, he would always say: 'Watch Jane's channel'. She never had to help with the housework, or do the housework unless she felt like doing it. She could have friends over, I couldn't. It was very split . . .

Did you have any sense of why you were treated so differently . . . or told?

Because . . . I had an underlying feeling that . . . or it had been suggested that because my twin had died and I had killed him (quite how I don't know) . . . and also because I was just made to feel intrinsically bad. Everything I did was wrong. I couldn't lay the table properly. I couldn't do anything correctly and I needed to be punished for that, whereas Jane was as good as gold. Whereas in reality she wasn't, she was just as naughty, but it was just overlooked.

(Kate)

Kathleen remembered her education being badly disrupted by her abuse. As a child she was prostituted, and as a young woman suffered a number of pregnancies and forced abortions. By contrast, her sister was encouraged to become a doctor. (While still at medical school she stitched Kathleen's wounds after she had suffered a particularly brutal assault.) Her sister was encouraged to despise and mistreat Kathleen, and distinctions were made between them at every level:

It's a bit pathetic but she used to be read bedtime stories for instance and if I wanted to hear them I'd need to sit outside the door and just not be noticed. It was always like that.

(Kathleen)

Interviewees described the ways in which the apparently contrasting treatment of a sibling, and their assignment of a 'bad' character, increased both their isolation and their sense of dependency on their abusers:

But the message was very much you were . . . the message was always about how much she loved me, but the subtext was . . . and she even told me explicitly: 'you are a very selfish person, you are . . .' The subtext was always that I was unlovable, but she was my mother and she loved me. Only a mother could love you, she even told me that I shouldn't have children because I was too selfish.

(Gillean)

Other mirrors of self

The importance of the concept of 'reflection' to a sociological account of selfhood is illustrated by Berger in his discussion of anti-Semitism:

> As an individual is forced to gaze at himself in a mirror so constructed as to let him see a leering monster, he must frantically search for other men with other mirrors, unless he is to forget that he ever had another face. To put this a little differently, human dignity is a matter of social permission.
>
> (Berger 1963: 121)

Certainly, a number of interviewees highlighted the importance of rare altern-ative 'reflections' to those provided by their abusers. Debbie describes an important counter-reflection when as a little girl she met her mother for the first time (Debbie was brought up by her paternal grandparents):

> And she took me to the toilet and I said how beautiful I thought she was. And she said to me that a lot of people think that I look like her, and that I'm beautiful too, and I was just like . . . 'cos no one had ever told me how beautiful I was or anything like that . . . and I don't have a very good self-esteem anyway, never have had, and it was brilliant.
>
> (Debbie)

A rather less positive report of her physical appearance was also important to Lynn as she began to develop a post-abuse self under the protection of her future mother-in-law:

> She could see that I was scared and she said that I looked ill. Which I probably did, I can't honestly remember what I looked like. But then we never had many mirrors in our house at home and I wouldn't have dreamt of looking in a mirror at one time . . . I'd probably looked that way most of my life. But she says I looked ill, really ill, and my eyes were black. She told me that the only person she'd seen before with eyes as black as that was her cousin who'd died of leukaemia as a child.
>
> (Lynn)

Mirrors appear again later in Lynn's account. Here the self she is seeking, directly in the mirror, is contradicted by the image of her as 'used goods', reflected back to her by her husband when she first told him that she had been sexually abused:

> On my twenty-seventh birthday I just spent the evening looking in a mirror. That was also the night I told Rob about me being abused and him walking out. He was really angry I wasn't a virgin. And the worst of it was, I actually agreed with him [*laughs*] O Gawd. Shows you how blinkered you become in your head.
>
> (Lynn)

It was some years after this that Lynn first spoke about her family's involvement in ritual abuse at a professional seminar. She believed that she was strong 'in herself', and well able to cope with the likelihood of being labelled a liar and a mad woman. However, her new identity as a survivor was more fragile than she believed and the public attack was difficult to bear:

> It was the first time anyone in this country had spoken publicly. It killed me nearly. It was horrendous, absolutely horrendous. Apart from two people afterwards phoned me up to check I was OK. It was horrendous. The papers slaughtered me. Which I didn't have a problem with, I expected to be slaughtered. It's when you don't expect it makes it difficult. *Girl talks of killing her own children and eating them*, that sort of thing and claiming I needed medical help.
>
> (Lynn)

The terms 'killed me nearly' and 'the papers slaughtered me' are powerful reminders of how 'the self' not only may be constructed in reflection but also can be virtually destroyed. The self which someone believes to be their own 'authentic' self has to struggle with the reflection from others. Sophie describes an experience common to most interviewees, of having to watch herself engaged in activities that were antithetical to her preferred 'inner' version of herself:

> You were actually shown the pornography that we were actually in, and shown it . . . because you get drugged, whether you get injections, whether you get a drink beforehand . . . you know if you're told to smile you do it. It makes you look . . . and because it's . . . because of what happens to your body it makes you feel as though you're enjoying it. You've got this double bind, you know inside that you're not enjoying it, but then you see on the film that makes you look as though you are enjoying it, which makes it like ten times worse.
>
> (Sophie)

Throughout their life-histories, survivors described their consciousness of self developing in relation to others, in relation to their perceived difference from others, and as something that developed over time. What Sophie's account also refers to is the struggle between two contradictory versions of herself, and her attempts to deconstruct the pornographic version as an imposed version which had yet been physically inscribed upon her body. In Sophie's account of having to watch herself in a pornographic video, there is a clear sense of a tension between the observed body 'enjoying itself' and the 'real' self watching. Sexual and physical abuse is experienced through the body and survivors of sexual abuse often describe a disconnection or dissociation such that the 'true' self can observe incidents of abuse from a physical and emotional distance. The child's trick of believing 'this isn't happening to *me*' may go on to develop into a profound alienation from the life of the body. (Sanford 1991; Ainscough and Toon 1993). However, as I pointed out in Chapter 4, this is not inevitably the case, for the body's role is not fixed and its meaning may be as a site of rebellion, a source of moral knowledge or a potential unifier of self.

Splitting the other

Each interviewee spoke of the need they believed they had as a child to love and be loved, and how difficult that was to achieve. A number of interviewees identified one person as 'the beloved person' in their childhood. Four women selected a grandparent to fill this role. Three as adults had revised their belief that this grandparent was kind and loving. One wrote on her returned interview transcript that she now accepted the fact that her grandfather was involved in her abuse, an idea that she had rejected in interview. A few interviewees described how the need to love someone had led them to 'split' a particular person in their heads – dividing the evidence of their experience so that 'Granny' was two different people. Awareness of the abusing or duplicitous side of someone was pushed away in favour of preserving a fantasy of closeness and mutual affection.

Such splitting of an attachment figure is strongly reminiscent of the Kleinian insight that infants experience the giving and withholding mother as two separate people (the developmental task being to accept her unity and learn to tolerate their ambivalent feelings towards her). It may be that where this is impossible – because the behaviour of the carer is so inconsistent or so atrocious – a split model of personhood makes relating to 'part-objects' (Klein 1948) necessary to coping with everyday life. It may also be that such carers provide a multiple model of identity and of the compartmentalization of emotional responses for their charges.

Some survivors told me about their childhood capacity to love by describing their feelings for animals, their sensitivity towards them, and in the case of three household dogs, their identification with them. There is a persistent awareness in these interviews of the double-sidedness of love and attachment. It is described as enabling survival, but at the same time as something that was used to manipulate and control them. Some attachments are described as having been deliberately fostered by abusers, and there is a tension between the positive retrospective evaluation by these survivors of their capacity to love, and their anger at being deliberately misled. Sinead describes this in relation to her father:

> It was just all in my mind. I convinced myself for fifteen years that he loved me. You know, all the times that he saved me and . . . it was all false. It was all part of the game of control, and I didn't realize until that day that it was . . .
>
> Erm, yeah . . . it was more horrific than I thought at the time. You know, when I done the work on this, and finally laid this torch I had lit, albeit very dimly, for my dad, to rest about six month ago. It was like, you know: the bastard hated me!
>
> (Sinead)

Rebellious selves

Some interviewees portrayed their 'true' self as an instinctive rebel or they described a rebellious self being inadvertently called into being by the extremity of their abuse. Lynn claimed that she was always sceptical about magic and her abusers' assertions of their supernatural powers; Sinead that she was never able to take meditation seriously and used to disrupt things by laughing. Others located a turning point when they began to 'get awkward', which they explained as a response to their increased awareness of the future. Two had noticed that they seemed less valuable to their abusers as their bodies matured, and assumed that their 'price' dropped in relation to prostitution. They referred to their growing realization of and distaste for the role they were increasingly expected to fulfil in relation to younger children, and their fear of growing up and becoming 'a full member of the group'. It is at such points that interviewees located the emergence of the self of today: the one that got away.

The **contemporary self**

Interviewees emphasized their sense of continuity between past and present selves. No one referred to themselves in 'conversion' terms as being 'born again' or as being 'a different person'. This is not to say that they minimized the differences between their experiences of past and present, but that they appeared to regard themselves as being the same person throughout. Beth's interview ended quite typically in that she went into a discussion of the impact of ritual abuse on her life in the here and now:

> At one point after the hysterectomy it was like 'children'. And the difficulty is I don't want children. Even if I hadn't had the hysterectomy. But then there's part of me that's saying there is an 'if only' or a 'because of'. And when people say stuff about not having had children there's part of me that wants to say: 'Yes, but I did'. But knowing that bit you can't really share with people. That's part of the grieving thing as well. You want to let go of this stuff because why the hell would you want to carry it around with you; but if you let go of it what the hell is there going to be in its place? . . . I remember Jane saying to me: 'There will come a time when you won't be thinking about this stuff all the time'. I remember thinking 'Stupid. What does she think she's talking about'. And now it feels like it's true.
>
> (Beth)

Beth was one of the women I interviewed who described herself as 'having multiple personalities'. However, along with everyone else, she also gave a simultaneously 'singular' account of herself as 'a person'.

I . . . Not I

I want now to turn to the various accounts of a plural self as they emerged in interviews and to explore the role they played within people's life-stories. The inconsistencies and contradictions in their lived experience were repeatedly emphasized by interviewees; these included a fissure between life at school and life at home. At home, life might be further split between time that involved keeping up appearances (Sinead's parents employed domestic help, for example) and 'abuse time'. In some families, cult activities and beliefs were never discussed at home; even visible injuries would not be mentioned, and small children would be told they had dreamed or imagined any abuse they referred to.

Kate, who did not describe herself as multiple, was sent to boarding school from the age of 11, and had a difficult year adjusting to a strict Christian school. However, at a second school she quickly learned to shut out everything about her home and her abuse during term time:

> I'd turned 11, when I was sent to . . . a boarding school that could
> be easily classified as a prison camp as far as I'm concerned. It was
> very hard, rules and regulations and bibles always pushed down your
> throats. I succeeded in running away from there three times 'cos I
> couldn't . . . I suppose I couldn't in my mind apply God and Satan to
> the same things, 'cos they were two such extremes to me. And how if
> God existed why was he letting me be involved with Satan? . . .
>
> But once we [my sister and myself] moved to the next school things
> changed . . . It was paradise compared with the last boarding school.
> And I think in some ways the last boarding school in some ways
> helped me split into two basically. The person who was abused and
> the person who was at school. 'Cos when I went to the next boarding
> school I was two people. Must have done a mental click when I was
> on the aeroplane flying out home, you know. Yeah.
>
> (Kate)

Kate's account illustrates a strong relationship between the inconsistencies in her lived experience – symbolized here as God and Satan – and her divided sense of self. In addition, parents and other abusers often switched from perpetrators to rescuers, in response to which it seems some children might imagine themselves in two, rather than acknowledge the 'split' in someone on whom they were dependent.[5] Beth, who did describe herself as multiple, provides an account of dividing herself in response to relational inconsistency rather than as a direct response to trauma:

> I often used to think, when I saw other kids holding their mum's
> hands or other people's hands as they went up the street, is that the
> only person who did that for me was Uncle John. So it was like he
> gave me stuff that I wanted, but that I didn't want . . . I didn't like
> what he was doing, but if I told him to stop doing that, then was he
> going to stop doing everything, so then I wouldn't have any hugs and

I wouldn't have any cuddles, and I wouldn't have anybody who I
could be close to . . .

Could you hold those two things together at the same time?

I'm not sure what you mean. I'm not sure I can hold them together
in my mind now, actually [*laughs*]. I suppose I was aware of . . . at
that point, I was aware often of looking down from the ceiling and
watching it happen to me, but it wasn't happening to me. So I could
deal . . . I suppose by holding it together in my mind, I suppose I
could say, yes, the bit that I liked I was in touch with, and the bit
that I didn't like I used to watch it happening. And the more it
happened the easier it was to watch it. So that I suppose if someone
had actually said to me, 'Is Uncle John doing anything you don't
like?', I think I would probably have said 'No'. Because . . . after a
while he wasn't. As far as I was concerned what I wanted was the hugs
and the ice-cream cones and the time together and that's what he was
doing. That's what I was really aware of, and the things I didn't like I
could just get up on the ceiling and watch it all happen.

(Beth)

Lynn recalled her mother being called by different names by her father and
being herself given other names associated with different roles that she was
expected to perform:

some of the [cue] words were also names, like this was a name, this
was Morgana. I became Morgana, or I supposedly became Morgana.
And I suppose this is where in my mind multiple personality fits in
much more easily. I wasn't multiple and I didn't have a personality
called Morgana, but I had to act like Morgana when I was called to,
and Morgana was an abusive personality.

*So if you weren't multiple what happened when you heard yourself called
Morgana, did fear come up?*

yes on one level it is fear, but it's more like an automatic response of:
'I will do this because of', and then you don't think any more. And I
think this thing about not thinking is that if you thought too much
you couldn't survive. You learn how to switch off in order to survive.
And I mean a lot of the things I did to other children, I mean I admit
I did, were automatic, were without thinking, because I'd done them
repetitively time and time again and I didn't have to think about
them, I just did it. And if I'd have thought about it and I hadn't of
done it I wouldn't be here now speaking to you.

(Lynn)

Lynn described been given the name 'Morgana' after a prolonged period of
abuse which exhausted and disorientated her. She believed that the intention was to fix certain behaviours in relation to a cue so that she would
respond quickly and obediently in a ritual context. (This is a kind of 'mind

control' used in other torture contexts.) I asked Lynn why she thought she had never come to see herself as 'multiple'. Her reply was that she suspected 'she hadn't met the right therapist'. She explained that she had dealt with her memories of abuse on her own during the 1970s (fearing she might lose her children and her freedom if she sought professional help) and that the various ingredients in her experience that might have led her to see herself as multiple were never reinforced. When she came across the idea of multiple personality in the mid-1980s, she did not identify strongly with it herself, although she wondered if it might be an appropriate description to apply to her mother.

Kathleen was another interviewee who did not describe herself as multiple, and said that she 'didn't like labels'. However, like Lynn, she did describe the experience of being 'cued' by an abuser:

> I think . . . when my mother's . . . I don't really understand how she does it, but I know that she can. She can trigger bits of me that I would rather she wasn't able to.

What does that mean?

> Um, well, um . . . I don't quite know how to describe it to you. Um . . . actually I suppose there's a part of me that's very self-destructive and there's also bits of me that are young, younger . . . [*long pause*] So she can do that, and I think that's what happened.

So if 'a part of you' got affected by something your mother said, what would happen in practice?

> Urm . . . I could . . . kind of like . . . [my counsellor] and I now call dissociated. Urm . . . sometimes I would cut myself. More often I would just feel self-destructive and be able to not allow myself to act on it . . .

So when you say you were 'dissociated' do you mean you weren't aware of what was happening when it was happening or that you felt you had no control over it?

> I think there's always a bit of me that knows, just can't always stop it happening. You know I don't think I go off and do things and don't know about it. [*Very long pause*] And I do have a degree of control over what other bits of me do, you know there's a consultation process [*laughs*].

(Kathleen)

This is clearly a self-description that draws on some of the language of dissociation and multiplicity. However, there are other therapeutic practices which to various degrees personify aspects of self or 'ego states', and the language of the 'inner child', the 'internalized parent', or of internal conflict between conscience and desire (see Kowszun 1999). Even more closely related, as Mollon (1996) has pointed out, may be the various pretence-based 'personality disorders' such as Munchausen's Syndrome. Such ideas of psychic life, whether they are seen as metaphors for a healthy mind or 'disorders', are widely available in the everyday world.[6]

If we think of the self as described by Berger (1963), as a set of social performances of which continuity and consistency are demanded, and place this self within a life course, then we are likely to consider the importance of infant–carer interaction in the early experience of a more-or-less single self across a variety of states of consciousness and behaviour (Winnicott 1965). If the 'solo self' is a complex product of social interaction, then lack of such interaction, or its contradictory nature, are liable to lead to disturbances in one's version of self. Carers who severely and repeatedly traumatize a young child, fail to comfort it, behave towards it with great inconsistency, or deprive it of stimulation for long periods of time, as is the case with each of my interviewees, might be expected to cause just such disturbance.

However, most interviewees went further and described how dissociation and disconnection from experience had been actively encouraged by their abusers. They described the use of hypnosis from an early age, and episodes of torture during which certain behaviours would be 'suggested' and associated with a name or other 'cue'. They spoke of the control that parents or other abusers had over them, through their ability to 'suggest' behaviour and evoke states of mind associated with trauma. They recalled stories and experiences that had convinced them they were possessed by demons or inhabited by the souls of dead children.[7] Interviewees who described long periods of isolation in their preschool years included Gene, Sinead, Sophie, Debbie and Kathleen. Sinead described how out of her loneliness came an imaginary friend which her parents 'used' to expand her dissociative abilities; she goes on to describe her childhood understanding of these issues:

> The group didn't call it multiple personality. I mean, my mum is a multiple, but it wasn't the same thing. I knew about her. I knew that she changed. That sometimes she was nice and sometimes she was horrible. But what these were is these were entities again . . . I'd been brought up to believe that these were demons that lived inside her. What they were is slaves of Satan, that only entered the bodies of privileged people. So if you were a good satanist you would have entities enter into you during a ceremony. So you would have a ceremony – you might not necessarily remember that ceremony, but at some point in your early years you would have a ceremony where they would put Satan's slaves inside you, which meant you would be able to do Satan's work a lot better, because they would hold information for you. Your body would be used but it wouldn't be you.

> *And were you aware that you too could 'change'?*

> No! I had no idea! I had no idea what was happening. As far as I knew I was blanking out, or I was fainting, or I was falling asleep . . . because they were boring bastards, and they bored the arse off me and I fell asleep. Because my mum was always . . . she always knew what was going on therefore it didn't seem like the same situation at all. 'Cos I

never knew what the hell had gone on when I had lost time and my mum did, seemed to anyway.

(Sinead)

There are both similarities and contradictions between this account and further explanation of her own multiplicity, given later in the same interview:

if I was switching within the group – OK – which I didn't know I was doing at the time but I know now ... it's a part of my mind that I open up that's never been opened before, therefore it doesn't know anything about life. I would open that part of my mind and I would explain what was about to happen. I would fast forward what was going to happen and the fact that this person had to stand there, had to take a knife, had to cut, had to gut and how to do it. I would then completely switch myself off and let this part of my mind take over ... But it has to be built up, you cannot just switch to a ready-made personality ... That's how I see it anyway, that's how mine worked.

(Sinead)

What the contradictions in these accounts raise is the question of who is the 'I'? Who is the self who knew nothing of her other selves and their doings? Can she be the same self as the one who 'opened a part of her mind' and began to imagine a new personality into existence? The answer is 'yes' but only on the basis of 'trance logic' in which mutually exclusive or contradictory truths can be believed as equally self-evident.

Only in one interview did I address this directly. From the outset, Gillean's interview was different from any of the others, and different from any interaction I have ever had. Gillean's voice changed frequently throughout our time together, sometimes sentence by sentence, as if different selves were taking turns at telling the story. The different voices rarely acknowledged the change, so that once transcribed the account reads as a tale told in a single voice. Towards the end of our day together I asked Gillean about the nature of her 'I':

We've all got different characteristics like we've all got different eyesight. Gill doesn't need glasses, Gillean does ... During the course of a day I can feel myself kind of going up a gear and all of a sudden I've kicked into Ellen and I'm coping with a particular conversation with the general manager or whatever. And later ... I'll have a bit of a crumble and turn into Gillean and hide ...

Who is that 'I'? The 'I' that can feel the 'kick into Ellen' and down into Gillean?

That's a good question. I think when you were talking there that was Gillean, she's the people person. Ellen you see I'm not a people person [*voice changes*]. And the question's very, very peopley.
[*Break to answer telephone.*]

Yeah, I have a bit of an identity crisis sometimes, I try not to think about it. I mean who the hell am I?

(Gillean)

Conclusion

What struck me powerfully in the course of my interviews was the eminent reasonableness of a multiple sense of self for survivors of ritual abuse. It fitted with their childhood experiences of extreme terror and contradiction, and with their lack of 'rights' to be an individual with autonomy. A combination of the following factors seemed to have led to developing a split sense of self:

- The need to function in different and strongly contrasted social worlds, and to deny one reality in relation to another.
- Contradictory and incoherent behaviour in a carer on whom a child was dependent.
- Active encouragement to take on more than one identity, as in socialization to possession.
- The need to deny and distance oneself from actions and experiences.

All the women I interviewed talked about a divided self in response to some or all of these factors. All described the strategies of 'trancing out', 'warding off' and 'pretending away' which they had employed to survive overwhelming abuse, but only three declared themselves to have multiple personalities.[8]

I have argued in this chapter for the intensely social nature of the self as a product *both* of socially and historically located discourses and of social interaction. With John Gagnon I take 'the self' to be:

the sum of an individual's changing internal conversations, the fore-castings, the recollections, and the wishes, the voices that make up our intrapsychic life. The extent, divisions, hierarchies, components, structures, permeability, openness and closedness, the opposition or submission to 'others' take their origins in socially acquired modes of talking that become the ways in which we experience our selves.

(Gagnon 1992: 239)

I have examined the sources of selfhood described by interviewees, both those that appear to have been deliberately imposed by their abusers and the alternative sources referred to. I have also described the senses of a self within a life course that interviewees gave me: the self as someone with a history. These sources of self were present in all accounts: that is to say 'multiples' also had 'singular' selves, or a clear sense of 'I-ness' alongside their multiple identity. I have emphasized the continuities between the accounts of self in interviews with survivors who described themselves as multiple and those who did not, and the 'fit' between lived experiences and self-concept.

What is absent in social constructionist accounts, such as that of Ian Hacking (1995), is lived time. For Hacking, the discourse of MPD *is* multiple

selves and he fails to consider the individual's contribution to the organization of their own experience. In addition particular 'socially acquired modes
of talking' are privileged such that those who speak of themselves as 'multiple' are seen as having their identities entirely produced within therapeutic
discourse. My argument is that ritual abuse survivors' lives provide other
social conditions and interactional experience likely to encourage a dissociated and divided self, but that these may take a variety of shapes and forms.
These are the selves which in the context of an abusive cult may be trained
to manifest possession by demons. Equally, in therapeutic encounters they
have the potential to become 'textbook multiples'. To paraphrase Hacking:
these are hosts that may readily embrace parasitic discourses of possession or
multiple personality.

For 'the multiple', self-consciousness apparently remains, or re-emerges, in
dramatic form and 'selves' continue, in Mead's terms, to be composed through
both real and imaginary dialogue. Mead is less able to help make sense of
how individual social actors develop relatively stable, continuous versions of
themselves over time. If, as I believe, this is achieved through narrative, then
the lack of 'family stories', accounts and acknowledgement of experience
would go some way to explaining the fragmented selves described by interviewees. As social actors, we all compose ourselves through narratives in
interaction with other people's narratives, which include versions of oneself.
Different versions of a divided self are available in every culture, and are
accounted for in culturally appropriate ways. Currently available in Britain
and North America are mediumship, channelling, speaking in tongues, possession and multiple personality. All may draw on similar wellsprings of
pain. Certainly the anthropological literature suggests that Shamanism and
possession are strongly associated with trauma and pain in many cultures
(Walker 1972; Crapanzano 1973; Boddy 1989). Dissociative abilities appear
to be socialized into a variety of forms in different social contexts.[9]

Ultimately, dissociation is a fancy word for lying to oneself with passionate conviction – 'I wasn't there and it wasn't me'. One may lie as a child
imagining herself to be Pippi Longstocking (who lived without parents!), or
as possessed by spirits, or as a multiple with many alters. In each case, both
the 'splitness' and the nature of the dramatis personae will be social and
interactional products.

The diagnosis and treatment of Dissociative Identity Disorder in the course
of therapy may be an appropriate and humane accompaniment to the early
disclosure of horrendous memories of mistreatment. 'Multiplicity' may be
a medicinal metaphor. However, I think what may often be required is a
more social and relational model, which takes seriously the ongoing social
relationship of therapy and questions rather than fixes the discourses of self-
making such interactions provide.

Margo Rivera (1996) has suggested that professional rejection of multiplicity
is rooted in a defensive attachment to the idea of a unified, cohesive subject:

and a need to defend against the performance of highly dissociative
people, whose self-presentation not only speaks to their own perceptual
distortions but also to the reality of a de-centred self. This de-centred self

is more similar to the way most of us experience the world than we are comfortable seeing.

(Rivera 1996: 58)

I would suggest that the concretization/reification of the metaphor of multiplicity discussed in this chapter shares the same source, in both its rigid demarcation between unitary and fragmented selves and its definition of the therapeutic task as transforming 'them' into 'us'.

Throughout this chapter, I have been discussing the accounts given to me by women interviewees, and I am aware that the diagnosis of MPD/DID is applied to a largely female population. As a feminist, I fear that therapeutic interventions often fail to challenge the production of formulaic selves to stereotyped scripts – 'personalities' named Princess, Slag or He-man are not unusual (see Rivera 1989). In addition, I find myself perturbed that there is an international society for the study of dissociation, but no such society for research on child torture and ritual abuse. It concerns me that some of those working with survivors of ritual abuse have become more interested in the symptoms than in their cause – asking not 'what has happened to this person?' but 'what is wrong with this person?'

Louise Armstrong (1996b) has accused the therapeutic 'incest industry' of infantilizing and pathologizing women survivors of child abuse. She points specifically to the 'parading' of women displaying different personalities, clutching teddy bears and speaking in high-pitched voices on TV talk shows and at professional conferences. Armstrong believes that it is crucial that incest and sadism are spoken of with appropriate anger and dignity, not lisped over in an approximation of a 5 year old. However, I wonder if such performances protect those listening as much as those speaking. Perhaps it is necessary, for those of us who were not present, first to believe that one person can suffer so much, before we will be certain not to construct a 'cult of multiplicity' to contain the unbearable accounts of sadistic and ritual abuse.

Adult survivors of ritual abuse remembering and talking about their abuse, in the way my interviewees did, can be seen as engaging in a process of bringing information about one reality into another. This wider society largely refuses to acknowledge or accept the truth of their experience. A multiple self appears to allow the incommensurability of the two realities to continue to be tolerated in the face of denial and disbelief. For some survivors, it may seem that a DID diagnosis is the only evidence of their abuse to be recognized and that it therefore provides a vital affirmation of their lives.

Notes

1 In this chapter I use the term 'psychiatric' in the broadest sense to cover the 'psy' disciplines and associated professions concerned with knowledge and treatment of the 'mentally ill'.
2 Freud's *Studies in Hysteria* ([1893–5] 1962) include no fewer than 23 different metaphors for mental life (counted by McKellar 1979) including electric light systems, multi-storey buildings, buried cities and games of chess.

3 The tension between fragmented and unitary views of self were apparent in interview accounts such as the following:

> A lot of this I'm talking and I'm thinking: I feel like I'm saying it, but it's like
> 'cos I didn't actually do that drawing . . . Well yes, I did the drawing, but I
> didn't do the drawing [*laughs*]. So it's like I'm talking about this and I don't
> know where this is coming from as I'm saying it to you, because it's not
> actually something that I can say I remember, 'cos I don't.

Because you entirely dissociated from it?

> . . . Because so much of it feels like it wasn't me . . . If you spend your time
> telling yourself it didn't actually happen to you . . . and then when you listen
> to what other people [personalities] are saying and think well that person's
> me, and that person's me as well, it did happen to me.
>
> (Beth)

4 'A satanic alter is also commonly referred to as an enforcer, evil introject, or satanic
introject . . . These alters are given specific tasks. One alter, for example, may be
designated to bring a person back to the cult later in life . . . Another may be designated to commit suicide if the system starts to get close to memories' (Ryder 1992:
153).
5 There is some suggestion of the transgenerational 'transmission' of MPD/DID,
although little on the mechanics of this (Braun 1985). It has been suggested that
MPD can be seen as a 'disorder of attachment', in which a child's internal working
model of self and attachment figure which is multiple and incoherent will lead to
'detachment' and the predisposition to dissociation in the face of later trauma (Liotti
1992).
6 By way of example I offer the comments of a mother speaking to her 4 year old,
overheard on a bus: 'I don't think I know this naughty little girl. My little girl is a
good girl and I don't know where she's gone to today.'
7 Sinead told me of an occasion when she was tortured with electro-shock, but the
cables were apparently attached to the head of another unconscious girl. She was
told that a transfer of souls was taking place. Five years after the experience she
continued to half-believe that she was inhabited by the soul of this other child.
8 Some, of course, may have simply chosen not to tell me.
9 Janice Boddy (1989) provides a brilliant description of women who had undergone
genital mutilation in northern Sudan, who appeared to dissociate from the pain of
sex, childbirth and infibulation, being socialized into a possession cult. The spirits
that 'descended' at ritual parties smoked, danced, drank alcohol and dressed in
men's clothes – all activities forbidden to the women whose bodies they temporarily
inhabited.

Conclusion

In 1993, three men and a woman from west London were imprisoned for periods of between eighteen months and 'life' for committing acts of rape, indecent assault and cruelty towards seven children over a period of eleven years. There was insufficient evidence to bring charges against three more adults believed by the police to have also been involved, or charges concerning the abuse of another twelve children. Evidence was given by the children of sexual abuse that had begun in infancy, of being forced to watch pornography, of being kept hungry, and of being brutally beaten. The officer in charge of the investigation described the children as having been 'bred for abuse'. For a year prior to the trial, the children were allowed no contact with each other in case they 'contaminated' each other's evidence. Among the twenty-eight specimen charges brought against the accused was one concerning a sexual assault during a Hallowe'en ritual at a local church:

> The court was told that on one Hallowe'en a girl was tied naked to a chair in St Mary's church at Northolt, west London, threatened with knives and sexually abused by adults in black hoods and cloaks. The girl, who said that she was driven there by her father, uncle and grandfather, described it as the 'devil church'.
>
> (*The Times*, 8 June 1993)

The charge was rejected by the jury because the child's description of the church where these events occurred did not tally with the church named and because she had seen a video which 'centred on a church at Hallowe'en and portrayed people dressed in cloaks' (*The Times*, June 1993). In the lived experience of the children and young people, this was no isolated incident where the experience of abuse had been confused with the contents of a horror film. Ritual abuse was one strand of their lives and was interwoven with more commonplace forms of cruelty and violence. For the purposes of prosecuting their abusers, a case was constructed that allowed the accusation of ritual abuse to be jettisoned without jeopardizing the case as a whole. In the climate of the early 1990s, the strategy was sensible but several years on, it would be a far more hazardous course to take. With ritual abuse erased from official child protection guidelines in Britain, any mention of churches, cloaks or candles is liable to undermine an abuse case entirely.

However, a good deal still rests on the quality of the investigation and of the evidence. Complex, multigenerational child abuse cases can still be prosecuted. There is very little difference between the accounts of family sadism heard at Plymouth Crown Court in 1998 (for which nine people were jailed for crimes against children over a period of thirty-five years) and the accounts of childhood discussed between these covers. The boys in the family were taught to abuse their sisters from an early age; their mother kept a record of their menstrual cycles; the children were prostituted to men outside the family, and when pregnancy resulted their father performed the abortion; the children often went hungry; they never discussed the abuse with each other; abuse was often photographed by their cousin's husband; and in the middle of the night they were sometimes driven to the woods and tied over a smouldering fire before being multiply raped. Throughout the three interlinked trials in this case, the prosecution insisted that the court should not be fixated on precise dates and particular events but concerned rather with a pattern of behaviour, with abuse repeated again and again until in the victims' memories one occasion was little different from another. As Nick Davies pointed out:

> The story has echoes of the discredited cases of alleged ritual abuse in the 1980s. Those cases collapsed in procedural chaos and cries of incredulity; the accused were cleared; the accusers and their allegations were all rejected.
>
> To this day, the official line within which police and social workers are expected to work is that there is no such thing as ritual abuse; they say they are discouraged from pursuing cases of inter-generational family sadism because it is presumed that juries will instinctively reject them. There is, however, one stunning difference with this account: it could be proved.
>
> (Davies 1998)

What made the difference? The diligence of a particular police officer was supported by a fully cooperative investigation with social services. Nearly 300 witnesses were interviewed across the UK, 30-year-old files were carefully examined and the evidence methodically cross-referenced. There was a confession by one sibling that she had facilitated the abuse of her own child;

there was the corroboration of a cousin who had visited the household for one childhood 'holiday' and never returned, and there were traces of semen on a screwdriver used in a recent episode of abuse. However, the crucial difference between this case and those 'discredited' ritual abuse cases that Davies refers to was the testimony of adult survivors and the central role it played in the presentation of the case. After twelve years of therapy, one woman had gone to the police to try to prevent her parents abusing another generation of children; much later her adult siblings corroborated and expanded upon her account of the childhood they had endured. Those concerned to protect children and seek justice were painstaking in their efforts, but they had a great deal to go on: the life-stories of adult survivors, their coherence, their verisimilitude. These stories provided the evidence of the general pattern of abuse, within which the few instances for which specific corroboration or forensic evidence was available made sense. The prosecution refused the 'specimen charge' model which disaggregates and disembeds child abuse into 'incidents' as if a series of burglaries had occurred. Crimes against women and children are rarely isolated events: perpetrators are usually known to if not related to their victims; women and children live 'inside' the cruelty and violence of ongoing relationships. The amputations that are performed to transform such ongoing abuse into 'a legal case' frequently produce something weak and oddly truncated. Stories must continue to be allowed to speak to arguments if victims are to become witnesses and find justice.

At the same time as I am convinced of the absolute centrality of survivors' stories to understanding all forms of child abuse, I am also aware of their limitations. What we are able to know and choose to know will be greatly confined and shaped by the circumstances and the standpoint of 'she who tells'. For example, a number of the survivors I interviewed believed that their families had been involved in ritual abuse for many generations, and eight out of thirteen interviewees had personal experience of grandparental abuse on at least one side of the family. They described how the ideology of ritual abuse being 'in their blood', a part of their inheritance or destiny, was one aspect of an ideology that denied the possibility of escape or the viability of living a different life. Survivors 'knew' only what they had been told; their direct experience was limited to three generations and therefore questions about generational continuity remain unanswerable. In addition, their concern as children and teenagers had been with matters directly concerned with their own survival – if their abusers had secrets they were often as unwilling as they were unable to penetrate them. As one survivor said when I asked whether she had ever tried to find out the truth about some aspect of family history/mythology: 'Why on earth would I have wanted to know about that?' Taking survivors' accounts seriously is essential but it does not suggest they have some God's-eye view of the places they have inhabited.

From our earliest years, we embark on a lifelong story-telling by which we make tolerable sense of intolerably muddled experience and draft and redraft the histories of our lives. When we tell these stories only to ourselves, they go unchallenged but, once they are told to another or committed to paper, we have committed an autobiographical act and 'autobiography drapes itself across the space between history and fiction, head and hands on one side, feet precariously hooked on the other' (Clendinnen 2000). Those who have survived atrocities must construct their narratives as we all must – drawing on the available discourses, adopting the language and forms which the culture and times make available. Life-stories are always made not found, and verisimilitude not empirical proof is the 'truth' they deal in. However, the telling of certain kinds of stories is an essential precursor to seeking corroborative and forensic evidence in particular instances. They also provide a framework within which individual evidential items become meaningful. (Without the accounts of Holocaust survivors, the bricks, 'showers' and gas pipes of Auschwitz and Bergen-Belsen would make no sense.) Any particular story may be true or false, misunderstood or unproven, but collectively ritual abuse survivors' claims demand that we investigate 'bizarre' cases assiduously and with open minds.

In order to be able to take survivors' stories seriously, we must interrogate critically the situatedness of our responses to accounts of ritual abuse. In this book, I have explored numerous aspects of our orientation to the late-modern world, to children, religion, death and identity which may incline us towards disbelief. Underlying all of these is our sense of how much we know about our society. Dissection may be a good metaphor for the way we think about modern knowledge, for it is widely believed that every discipline has opened its particular cadaver to public view and we have all peered into the belly of the beasts. In particular, we like to think that the forward march of history has flung open the curtains allowing light to illuminate our darkest corners, so that only the smallest of domestic spaces could still hide horrors from the public gaze. Surveillance is regarded in some accounts as at the heart of modernity, whether in the form of the Panopticon (Foucault 1979) or the shopping centre security cameras which 'caught' the children who later killed the toddler James Bulger. Yet in another sense the progress of modernity has worked to increasingly separate public and private spheres, reducing the exposure and accountability of families and individuals to their communities, employers, landlords and priests, making new spaces for secrets. Georg Simmel provided a rare description of this double movement of modernity towards increased surveillance and towards greater secrecy:

> The historical development of society is in many respects characterized by the fact that what at an earlier time was manifest, enters the protection of secrecy; and that conversely, what once was secret, no longer needs such protection but reveals itself.
>
> (Simmel in Wolff 1950: 331)

One popular image of the late-modern family is of something fractured and residual, that has shrunk to fit the suburban semi it now inhabits. The family no longer has fortifications: professional health visitors, social workers and educational welfare officers tramp across its threshold delivering admonishment and advice. At the same time it has lost its connections – the face-to-face networks of kin and community, and its durability in the face of changes of heart or mind. Blood has thinned to the consistency of water, sons no longer follow in their fathers' footsteps. This image allows us to accept that dyadic relationships and nuclear families can sometimes hide perversion, misery and even murder, but not that networks of extended family, neighbours and colleagues might do the same. Our late-modern anxieties tend to be at the levels of the intimate and the global – as policy and policing agendum bear witness. The extended family is an institutional form no longer seen as active in forming lives and influencing destinies down the generations.

At the same time, the features that render it difficult for us see and believe in sadistic, organized networks of abuse built around three or more generations of the same family (whether or not it takes a ritual form) may also be powerful aides to the rebellion of this generation's children against accepting their 'destiny'. The ritual abuse survivors I have talked to had all spent their childhoods in dual social worlds. Unlike those brought up in some other cults, they had attended mainstream schools; a few had even attended church services on a regular basis. However, friendships and extracurricular activities were circumscribed, and in some households access to television, books and even music was strictly controlled. Their knowledge of other ways of life was often distorted, and they had considerable fear about being able to survive 'in the world out there' that they had been taught to despise. None the less, survivors had been aware from an early age that ritual abuse was not everyone's reason for living. The same self-reflexive, secularized world of feminism and divorce that makes multigenerational ritual abuse seem so unlikely also made it possible for them to question, reject and ultimately escape the networks of abuse in which they had been raised.

Throughout this book I have sought to understand how my interviewees had successfully resisted becoming the people their abusers intended them to be, and how they had begun to forge oppositional identities within the very belly of the beast. I began this research with an understanding of power based on many years of work around issues of sexual violence. I knew that even in the most extreme situations, where power appears at its most absolute – as it does in the torture chamber and the death camp – power still calls forth resistance, and resistance will extract an answer from the oppressor, so that only death can end the dialogue.

Acquiescence and co-option are common enough responses to regimes of extreme abuse and control, but stories of these belong to the mothers, uncles and siblings who, maintaining a lifelong involvement in ritual abuse, were unavailable for comment. The mystery that has concerned me here is that, despite the aridity of their circumstances, the survivors I interviewed had developed compassion and attachment to others. For women, the powerful discourses of maternity and femininity appeared to have provided the necessary materials for an alternative construction of self. While the tensions between socially constructed womanhood and ritually constructed abuser-hood aided women in their rejection of cult life, hegemonic masculinity offered far less of an alternative model for male survivors. This is one of a number of issues raised by this research which is worthy of further investigation.

The themes of belief, death, gender and identity explored in earlier chapters each have implications for deliberations about other forms of domestic and organized abuse of children. Feminists have always suggested that patriarchal mythology provides an ideology which partially legitimizes the sexual abuse of children. However, the significance of the particular belief systems of ritual abusers and their imposition of these upon their victims suggests that more detailed attention might be fruitfully paid to such matters in relation to other forms of abuse. Similarly, exploration of issues concerning identity construction by abused children and the interaction of these with contemporary discourses about what it means to be, or have a self, may be useful in examining how victims of abuse come to be either co-opted as abusers or successfully develop oppositional identities.

I have considered here how the dominant cultural frames – the discourse of disbelief in the case of ritual abuse, or psychiatric discourse in relation to multiple versions of self – shape the content and presentation of survivors' accounts. Research on child sexual abuse has suffered at times from the assumption that it simply uncovers 'raw facts' in the data it collects. I have tried throughout this book to remain aware that I was not the first to 'theorize' the life-stories of survivors, they had already done that for themselves, and they had done so in conversation with friends and counsellors, TV programmes and books, just as I had done. Allegations about contamination and the implantation of 'false memories' must not prevent research on sexual abuse reflecting on the discourses that impact on the life accounts of respondents.

In the hope that my alternative reading of ritual abuse accounts to that conjured by the discourse of disbelief is plausible, illuminating and reasonable, I have aimed to honour the suffering and the survival of those who entrusted their life-stories to my care, and to enable their accounts to speak directly to the arguments which have sought to disparage and ignore them. I believe that in doing so I have unsealed the closure of debate on ritual abuse and made possible both further understanding and future interventions.

Appendix

Methodology

The research on which this book is based began in 1994 and the PhD for which it was undertaken was awarded by the University of Manchester in 1997. Self-defined survivors of ritual abuse were contacted through the distribution of ninety questionnaires to UK organizations providing support/counselling to adult survivors of sexual abuse (Broadcasting Support Services 1994) and to individual members of RAINS (Ritual Abuse Information Network and Support), who included clinical psychologists, psychotherapists, psychiatrists, counsellors and social workers. Questionnaires were returned by thirty-six survivors, twelve of whom were approached as potential interviewees and life-history interviews were ultimately conducted with nine of these. Difficulty in making contact with male survivors in the UK led to three interviews being conducted with men in the USA. One male interviewee identified himself as mixed race, all other interviewees were white.

The questionnaire

The primary objective of the questionnaire was to establish contact with potential interviewees rather than to collect data about respondents' experiences of ritual abuse. To this end it contained sixteen open-ended questions concerning current life situation and childhood experiences. Respondents were aged from 19 to 60 years with the majority (twenty-two) aged between 30 and 50. Three respondents were male.

Respondents worked variously as nurses, teachers, students, factory and office workers; ten were not in paid employment or full-time education at the time of completing the questionnaire. Eleven identified themselves as married or in long-term partnerships; fourteen had children of their own.

Thirty-four respondents declared that members of their immediate family had been involved in ritual abuse; in twenty-one cases this included one or both natural parents. Parental death or separation had led to some five respondents being adopted – in three cases by grandparents involved in ritual abuse. In a number of cases, the nature of family relationships was complex as respondents believed that they were the result of incest, that is their grandfather was also their father.

Paternal occupations ranged from labourers to lawyers, and included doctors, small business men, civil servants and members of the armed forces. Maternal occupations conformed to stereotypical 'female' jobs ranging from secretaries to midwives; eleven mothers were referred to as housewives.

Asked 'What did ritual abuse involve in your childhood?'

The following items were most frequently mentioned in responses:

Rape/sexual abuse by adults   *35*
Murder   *34* (also referred to as killing or human sacrifice)
Ceremonies/rituals   *29*
Consumption of noxious substances   *27* (substances mentioned included urine, blood, faeces, semen, rotten flesh)
Torture   *25* (experiences described included hanging, drowning, branding, burning and electro-shock)
Killing/sacrifice of animals   *23*
Confinement in a box/cage/coffin/cupboard   *19*
Being drugged   *16*
Experiencing forced childbirth/abortion   *16*
Deprivation of sleep/food   *13*
Being used in pornography   *13*
Forced sex with animals   *12*

The majority of respondents had escaped their abusers by their early twenties. Older respondents tended to describe early marriage as their 'way out'; two of the youngest women had been taken into care; others had left home and entered prostitution, the armed forces, a religious community or nursing. All recorded that they had tried to run away, and some had made partial disclosures of the abuse to the police or to teachers in their pre-pubescent years.

Asked 'Has there ever been a time when you didn't remember being abused?'

Sixteen said 'yes' for periods ranging from two to thirty years. Eighteen said 'no' but added that they had not known the extent of the abuse, or had tried very hard to block out their memories until they had felt that they were safe enough to think about the past. As one woman put it: 'I could always remember the abuse but I chose not to think about it. For years if a memory emerged I would deny it to myself'.

Asked what their abusers had believed/claimed to believe/convinced them to believe

Five respondents identified a specific non-satanic belief system: Mormonism, Roman Catholicism, Fundamentalist Christian, Masonic, neo-Nazi and Wicca (one claimed to have been abused independently in different groups). Twenty respondents referred to belief in/worship of Satan/Lucifer/'the devil' (some to other deities as well). The other eleven were split between 'don't knows' and those who said that they were unwilling or afraid to answer the question.

Asked about what they felt was most important for other people to know about ritual abuse, or whether there was any experience that had particular significance for them personally

Thirteen wrote about a forced abortion or the killing of a baby born to them, a further eight referred to another death they had witnessed. At this point on the questionnaire a number wrote that they were 'too tired' or 'couldn't cope' with writing any more.

All respondents indicated that they would be willing to consider being interviewed.

Asked in conclusion what they would like to see come out of the research

The following answers were typical:

- A comprehensive book that validates survivors' realities and demystifies ritual abuse.
- Something accessible to those who have not yet spoken of their experience for fear of disbelief.
- A representation of survivors as ordinary and various.
- A piece of research that could stand up to scrutiny and even to bigotry – that might open a few minds and lead to careful, professional investigation.
- Just find a way to make it matter that we all survived.

The **interviews**

In addition to the questionnaires, a number of respondents wrote letters and sent copies of poems, journal entries and other written material they thought I might find useful. In the course of selecting interviewees, I talked on the telephone and had email contact with around twenty survivors. I met and conducted initial interviews with three survivors with whom a full life-history interview was not feasible for reasons of health, preference or limited recall. None of these 'informal' materials, interviews or discussions has been quoted from in this book – although naturally they made an invaluable contribution to developing my own understanding of ritual abuse.

There were a number of issues involved in selecting interviewees. I had no reason to think that those survivors who had returned questionnaires were in any way 'representative' of the total survivor population; however, I did seek to replicate their diversity in my subgroup of interviewees. The ten UK women selected for interview, therefore, ranged in age from 19 to 55 although their overall age distribution was younger than that of questionnaire respondents. Of the five younger interviewees (aged 19–25), two came from decidedly wealthy backgrounds, had been privately educated and had travelled to many parts of the world; two came from impoverished inner-city estates where family members were in unskilled work or unemployed. The fifth was difficult to locate in 'class' terms. Of the five older women (aged 30–55), three came from lower-middle-class backgrounds and two from the professional middle class.

The sample was deliberately chosen to limit the likelihood of any interviewees knowing each other (as children or adults). Their security was the foremost consideration as there was some concern about being identifiable to others who might have been victims or perpetrators in the same network. In addition, it has been suggested that 'contamination' through survivors' groups (or through sharing therapists) is a source of confabulated accounts and it therefore seemed a sensible precaution to interview people who had no contact with each other. The ten UK women had grown up in diverse corners of the British Isles, lived in the same (or different) diverse areas as adults and had no identifiable networks in common. The exceptions to this pattern are Sinead and Lynn, who met through me when in the course of my work on ritual abuse Lynn became a personal friend.

The most crucial factors in selecting interviewees were that their choice to give an interview was well considered, that they seemed reasonably emotionally robust and that they were adequately supported by friends, partners and former or current therapists. Interviewees were planning to talk to me in detail about some of their most painful and disturbing experiences and I needed to ensure that each would have someone to turn to for support when it was over.

I had far less choice in my selection of male interviewees. The men who returned questionnaires had each completed them in the scantiest way. On follow-up with two of them, it seemed clear that a life-history interview would be impossible: each had extremely fragmented memories, admitted to suffering from chronic depression and did not seem to have access to appropriate supportive relationships. Through various networks, I made contact with psychotherapists working with male survivors in Britain, the Netherlands and Germany, but in no instance did they consider their client likely to be able to cope with the demands of being interviewed. I made contact with the three men I eventually interviewed through a US survivors' network.

Confidentiality

All interviews were transcribed verbatim by myself. Interviewees retained editorial control until they had read the transcripts and made any edits or alterations they deemed necessary to protect their anonymity. Names and place-names were fictionalized or removed and guarantees were given that materials would be kept under secure conditions and original tapes returned to interviewees or destroyed as they preferred.

Interview format

All the life-history interviews took place in 1995. The majority of interviews were conducted over two days and took place in interviewees' own homes. The shortest amount of material recorded was two and a half hours and the longest seven hours – most were between four and five hours in length. I used a standardized life-history format combined with an individualized time-line to move interviews through their narrative. The time-lines were sketched out during a preliminary discussion and provided a basic shape for the inter-view proper. The 'prompt sheet' began as follows:

Family background – knowledge of parents' childhood, meeting courtship/ marriage
Grandparents – direct knowledge, parents' accounts
Older siblings
Birth – confirmed details, any 'family stories' concerning
Earliest memories – preschool
First day at school
Learning to read/tell the time
Births of younger siblings
Transition from infant to junior schools
Weekends and holidays
Transition to secondary school
First menstruation . . .

Analysis

My analysis of the life-history interviews began by collecting together mater-ial related to themes derived from a variety of sources. My initial analysis of the data focused on those themes or issues that had been prominent in questionnaire responses: sexual abuse, death, forced pregnancy/abortion. Other themes were suggested by the concerns of sceptics: memory, multiple personality; by my own pre-existing interests: gender; or 'arose' from the data itself: the nature of belief. Once these themes were identified and coded, I explored the relationship between these and my base data variables of gender, age and class. I went on to ask more complex questions of my data, seeking confirmation and disconfirmation of a variety of hypotheses arising from the themes, such as who was identified as 'religiously motivated' and who not? Were they likely to be male/female, older/younger, more powerful/ less powerful? On what evidence did interviewees accord such motivation? Did reports vary according to the profile of the interviewee? Did reports vary in relation to my questions?

In looking for patterns and exceptions within my data, I was seeking to develop explanations at the middle range. However, my analysis is not that of pure 'grounded theory' for I was equally concerned to test out theoretical understandings, my own responses and the interpretations of interviewees themselves. Where conflicts between interpretations arose, I have discussed these directly in the text.

I developed an 'interrogatory matrix' to ensure that the impact of key variables was considered in relation to each question asked and relationship identified. This systematic approach to the analysis ensured that connections and 'hunches' could be easily assessed against the data. In order to ensure the validity of my analysis, I developed explanations which attempt to do justice to the complexity of the phenomena described and which are internally consistent (Denscombe 1998). I have retained the context of 'whole lives' in my presentation of specific data, discussed alternative explanations and related my own work to the findings of other research.

Bibliography

Ainscough, C. and Toon, K. (1993) *Breaking Free: Help for Survivors of Child Sexual Abuse*. London: Sheldon.

Alderson, K. (1994) Ritual child sex abuse 'is widespread', *The Times*, 18 June.

Alderson, L. (1993) The failure of the sensible agenda, *Trouble and Strife*, 27(Winter): 45–8.

Allen, C. (1991) *Women and Men Who Sexually Abuse Children: A Comparative Analysis*. Orwell, VT: Safer Society Press.

Allison, R.B. with Schwarz, T. (1980) *Minds in Many Pieces*. New York: Rawson-Wade.

American Psychiatric Association (1994) *Diagnostic and Statistical Manual of Mental Disorders*, 4th edn (*DSM-IV*). Washington, DC: American Psychiatric Association.

Andrews, B., Brewin, C.R., Ochera, J. *et al.* (2000) The timing, triggers and qualities of recovered memories in therapy, *British Journal of Clinical Psychology*, 39: 11–26.

Ariès, P. (1972) *Centuries of Childhood*. London: Cape.

Ariès, P. (1981) *The Hour of Our Death*. London: Allen Lane.

Armstrong, L. (1978) *Kiss Daddy Goodnight*. New York: Hawthorn.

Armstrong, L. (1996a) The great incest hijack, in D. Bell and R. Klein (eds) *Radically Speaking: Feminism Reclaimed*. London: Zed Books.

Armstrong, L. (1996b) *Rocking the Cradle of Sexual Politics*. London: The Women's Press.

Attmore, C. (1995) Towards rethinking moral panic: child sexual abuse conflicts and social constructionist responses. Unpublished paper, Department of Sociology, Monash University, Australia.

Bagley, C. (1997*) Children, Sex and Social Policy*. Aldershot: Avebury.

Baker, A. and Duncan, S. (1985) Child sexual abuse: a study of prevalence in Great Britain, *Child Abuse and Neglect*, 9: 457–67.

Barach, P. (1991) Multiple personality disorder as an attachment disorder, *Dissociation*, 4(3): 117–23.

Barker, E. (ed.) (1983) *Of Gods and Men: New Religious Movements in the West*. Macon, GA: Mercer University Press.

Barker, E. (1984) *The Making of a Moonie: Brainwashing or Choice?* Oxford: Blackwell.

Barker, E. (1989) *New Religious Movements*. London: HMSO.

Barrat, A., Trepper, T. and Fish, L. (1990) Feminist informed family therapy for the treatment of intra-familial child sexual abuse, *Journal of Family Psychology*, 4: 151–66.

Barry, K. (1979) *Female Sexual Slavery*. New York: New York University Press.

Bass, E. and Davies, L. (1988) *The Courage to Heal: A Guide for Women Survivors of Child Sexual Abuse*. New York: Harper and Row.

Bauman, Z. (1989) *Modernity and the Holocaust*. Cambridge: Polity.

Bauman, Z. (1992) *Mortality, Immortality and Other Life Strategies*. Cambridge: Polity.

Becker, H.S. (1963) *The Outsiders: Studies in the Sociology of Deviance*. Glencoe, IL: The Free Press.

Becker, H.S. (1970) *Sociological Work*. Chicago: Aldine.

Becker, H.S. (1986a) Telling about Society, in his *Doing Things Together: Selected Papers*. Evanston, IL: Northwestern University Press.

Becker, H.S. (1986b) *Writing for Social Scientists*. Chicago: University of Chicago Press.

Becker, H.S. ([1967] 1990) Whose side are we on?, in W.J. Filstead (ed.) *Qualitative Methodology*. Chicago: Markham.

Beckford, J. (1985) *Cult Controversies: The Societal Response to the New Religious Movements*. London: Tavistock.

Behringer, W. (1997) *Witchcraft Persecutions in Bavaria*, trans. J.C. Grayson and D. Lederer. Cambridge: Cambridge University Press.

Behringer, W. (1998) *Shaman of Oberstdorf: Chonrad Stoeckhlin and the Phantoms of the Night*, trans. H.C. Erik Midelfort. Charlottesville, VA: University Press of Virginia.

Beitchman, J., Zucker, K., Hood, J. *et al.* (1992) A review of the long-term effects of child sexual abuse, *Child Abuse and Neglect*, 16: 101–18.

Bell, V. (1993) *Interrogating Incest: Feminism, Foucault and the Law*. London: Routledge.

Ben-Tovim, A., Elton, A., Hildebrand, J., Tranter, M. and Vizard, E. (eds) (1988) *Child Sexual Abuse within the Family: Assessment and Treatment – The Work of the Great Ormond Street Team*. London: Wright.

Berger, P. (1963) *Invitation to Sociology*. New York: Doubleday.

Berger, P. ([1967] 1990) *The Sacred Canopy: Elements of a Sociological Theory of Religion*. New York: Anchor.

Berger, P. and Kellner, H. (1981) *Sociology Reinterpreted*. Garden City, NY: Doubleday.

Berliner, L. and Briere, J. (1999) Trauma, memory and clinical practice, in L.M. Williams and V.L. Banyard (eds) *Trauma and Memory*. Thousand Oaks, CA: Sage.

Berliner, L. and Conte, E.J. (1990) The process of victimization: the victim's perspective, *Child Abuse and Neglect*, 14(1): 29–40.

Berliner, L. and Stevens, D. (1982) Clinical issues in child sexual abuse, in J. Conte and D. Shore (eds) *Social Work and Child Sexual Abuse*. New York: Haworth.

Bernheimer, C. and Kahane, C. (1985) *In Dora's Case: Freud – Hysteria – Feminism*. New York: Columbia University Press.

Best, J. (1989) *Images of Issues: Typifying Contemporary Social Problems*. New York: Aldine de Gruyter.

Best, J. (1990) *Threatened Children: Rhetoric and Concern about Child-Victims*. Chicago and London: University of Chicago Press.

Best, J. (1994) Troubling children: children and social problems, in J. Best (ed.) *Troubling Children: Studies of Children and Social Problems*. New York: Aldine de Gruyter.

Bibby, P. (1994) Definition of organized abuse, *Child Abuse Review*, 3(3): 163–4.
Bloch, M. (1992) *Prey into Hunter: The Politics of Religious Experience*. Cambridge: Cambridge University Press.
Bibby, P. (ed.) (1996) *Organized Abuse: The Current Debate*. Aldershot: Arena.
Blumer, H. (1939) *Critiques of Research in the Social Sciences: 1. An Appraisal of Thomas and Znaniecki's 'The Polish Peasant in Europe and America'*. London: Social Science Research Council.
Boddy, J. (1989) *Wombs and Alien Spirits: Women, Men and the Zar Cult in Northern Sudan*. Madison, WI: University of Wisconsin Press.
Bowman, C.G. and Meertz, E. (1996) Legal intervention in sexual abuse survivor therapy, *Harvard Law Review*, 109(3): 551–639.
Braun, B. (1985) The transgenerational incidence of dissociation and MPD: a preliminary report, in R. Kluft (ed.) *Childhood Antecedents of Multiple Personality*. Washington, DC: American Psychiatric Press.
Braun, B. (1986) *Treatment of Multiple Personality Disorder*. Washington, DC: American Psychiatric Press.
Bromley, D. (1991) Satanism: the new cult scare, in J. Richardson, J. Best and D. Bromley, *The Satanism Scare*. New York: Aldine de Gruyter.
Bromley, D. and Richardson, J.T. (eds) (1983) *The Brainwashing/Deprogramming Controversy: Sociological, Psychological, Legal and Historical Perspectives*. New York: Edwin Mellen.
Broadcasting Support Services (1994) *Survivors' Directory*. Manchester: Broadcasting Support Services.
Brown, L.S. (1996) Politics of memory, politics of incest: doing therapy and politics that really matter, *Women and Therapy*, 19(1): 5–18.
Brownmiller, S. (1976) *Against Our Will: Men, Women and Rape*. New York: Simon and Schuster.
Bruce, S. (1995) *Religion in Modern Britain*. Oxford: Oxford University Press.
Bruner, J. (1986) *Actual Minds: Possible Worlds*. Cambridge, MA: Harvard University Press.
Burkert, W. (1983) *Homo Necans: The Anthropology of Ancient Greek Sacrificial Ritual and Myth*. Berkeley: University of California Press.
Burgess, A. with M. Clark (eds) (1984) *Child Pornography and Sex Rings*. Lexington, MA: Lexington Books.
Burgess, A., Groth, N. and McCausland, M. (1981) Child sex initiation rings, *American Journal of Orthopsychiatry*, 51: 110–18.
Burkitt, I. (1991) *Social Selves*. London: Sage.
Busfield, J. (1988) Mental illness as a social product or social construct: a contradiction in feminists' arguments?, *Sociology of Health and Illness*, 10: 521–42.
Butler, K. (1995) Did Daddy really do it?, *Los Angeles Times Book Review*, 5 February: 1.
Cameron, D. and Frazer, E. (1994) Cultural difference and the lust to kill, in P. Harvey and P. Gow (eds) *Sex and Violence: Issues in Representation and Experience*. London: Routledge.
Campagna, D.S. and Poffenberger, D.L. (1988) *The Sexual Trafficking of Children: An Investigation of the Child Sex Trade*. Dover, MA: Auburn House.
Campbell, B. (1988) *Unofficial Secrets: Child Sexual Abuse – the Cleveland Case*. London: Virago.
Campbell, C. (1995) Half-belief and the paradox of ritual instrumental activism: a theory of modern superstition, *British Journal of Sociology*, 46(4): 151–66.
Carlson, E.B. and Putnam, F. (1993) An update on the Dissociative Experiences Scale, *Dissociation*, 6: 16–27.
Carrithers, M. (1985) An alternative social history of the self, in M. Carrithers, S. Collins and S. Lukes (eds) *The Category of the Person: Anthropology, Philosophy, History*. Cambridge: Cambridge University Press.

Carrithers, M., Collins, S. and Lukes, S. (1985) *The Category of the Person: Anthropology, Philosophy, History*. Cambridge: Cambridge University Press.
Child Abuse and Neglect (1991) vol. 15(3). Denver: Pergamon.
Child Abuse Review (1993) vol. 2(4). Chichester: Wiley.
Clark, A. (1987) *Women's Silence, Men's Violence: Sexual Assault in England 1770–1845*. London: Pandora.
Clark, D. (1993) *The Sociology of Death*. Oxford: Backwell.
Cleaver, H. and Freeman, P. (1996) Child abuse which involves wider kin and family friends, in P. Bibby (ed.) *Organized Abuse: The Current Debate*. Aldershot: Arena.
Clendinnen, I. (2000) Homo Narrator, *London Review of Books*, 16 March: 9–10.
Clifford, J. and Marcus, G. (eds) (1986) *Writing Culture: The Poetics and Politics of Ethnography*. Berkeley, CA: University of California Press.
Cohen, S. (1972) *Folk Devils and Moral Panics*. New York: MacGibbon and Kee.
Cohn, N. (1970) The myth of Satan and his human servants, in M. Douglas (ed.) *Witchcraft Confessions and Accusations*. New York: Tavistock.
Cohn, N. (1975) *Europe's Inner Demons*. New York: Basic Books.
Coleman, J. (1994) Satanic cult practices, in V. Sinason (ed.) *Treating Survivors of Satanist Abuse*. London: Routledge.
Coleman, L. (1992) Creating 'memories' of sexual abuse, *Issues in Child Abuse Accusations*, 4(4): 166–76.
Collins, P.H. (1990) *Black Feminist Thought*. London: HarperCollins.
Conte, J. (1999) Memory, research and the law: future directions, in L.M. Williams and V.L. Banyard (eds) *Trauma and Memory*. Thousand Oaks, CA: Sage.
Conte, J., Wolf, S. and Smith, T. (1989) What sexual offenders tell us about prevention strategies, *Child Abuse and Neglect*, 13(2): 293–302.
Cooey, P. (ed.) (1992) *After Patriarchy: Feminist Transformations of the World Religions*. New York: Orbis.
Corby, B. (1993) *Child Abuse: Towards a Knowledge Base*. Buckingham: Open University Press.
Crapanzano, V. (1973) *The Hamadsha: A Study in Moroccan Ethnopsychiatry*. San Francisco, CA: University of California Press.
Crouch, B. and Damphouse, K. (1991) Law enforcement and the Satanic crime connection: a survey of 'cult cops', in J. Richardson, J. Best and D. Bromley (eds) *The Satanism Scare*. New York: Aldine de Gruyter.
Daniel, G. and Thompson, P. (1995) Stepchildren's memories of love and loss: men's and women's narratives. Paper given at Auto/biography Study Day, University of Manchester, January.
Davies, M. (1993) Healing Sylvia: accounting for the textual 'discovery' of unconscious knowledge, *Sociology*, 27(1): 110–20.
Davies, N. (1998) Lives that were beyond belief, *Guardian*, 1 August.
de Mause, L. (ed.) (1976) *The History of Childhood*. London: Souvenir Press.
de Sade, Marquis ([1789] 1992) *120 Days of Sodom*. London: Arrow.
Delphy, C. (1984) *Close to Home: A Materialist Analysis of Women's Oppression*. London: Hutchinson.
Delphy, C. (1992) Mother's union?, *Trouble and Strife*, 24: 12–19.
Dennett, D.C. (1991) *Consciousness Explained*. London: Allen Lane.
Denscombe, M. (1998) *The Good Research Guide*. Buckingham: Open University Press.
Denzin, N.K. (1989) *Interpretive Biography*. Newbury Park, CA: Sage.
Department of Health (1991) *Working Together under the Children Act 1989: A Guide to Arrangements for Inter-Agency Co-operation for the Protection of Children from Abuse*. London: HMSO.
Department of Health (1998) *Working Together under the Children Act: Consultation Paper*. London: HMSO.

Dimsdale, J.E. (ed.) (1980) *Survivors, Victims and Perpetrators: Essays on the Nazi Holocaust*. New York: Hemisphere.

Dingwall, R., Eekelaar, J. and Murray, T. (1983) *The Protection of Children: State Intervention and Family Life*. Oxford: Blackwell.

Dutton, D. and Painter, S.L. (1981) Traumatic bonding: the development of emotional attachments in battered women and other relationships of intermittent abuse, *Victimology*, 6: 139–55.

Eakin, P.J. (1992) *Touching the World: Reference in Autobiography*. Princeton, NJ: Princeton University Press.

Elias, N. (1978) *The History of Manners: The Civilizing Process Volume 1*, trans. E. Jephcott. Oxford: Blackwell.

Elliott, M. (1993) *Female Sexual Abuse of Children: The Ultimate Taboo*. London: Longman.

Ellis, H. (1913) *Studies in the Psychology of Sex, Vols 1–6*. Philadelphia, PA: F.A. Davis.

Ennew, J. (1986) *The Sexual Exploitation of Children*. Cambridge: Polity.

Evans-Pritchard, E.E. (1937) *Witchcraft among the Azande*. Oxford: Oxford University Press.

Evans-Pritchard, E.E. (1965) *Theories of Primitive Religion*. Oxford: Clarendon.

Faller, K.C. (1987) Women who sexually abuse children, *Violence and Victims*, 12(4): 236–76.

Faller, K.C. (1991) Poly-incestuous families: an exploratory study, *Journal of Interpersonal Violence*, 6(3): 310–22.

Faller, K.C. (1994) Ritual abuse: a review of research, *The Advisor*, 7(1): 19–27.

Faludi, S. (1991) *Backlash: The Undeclared War against American Women*. New York: Crown.

Finch, J. (1984) Community care: developing non-sexist alternatives, *Critical Social Policy*, 9: 6–18.

Finkelhor, D. (1984) *Child Sexual Abuse: New Theory and Research*. New York: The Free Press.

Finkelhor, D. (1986) *A Sourcebook on Child Sexual Abuse*. Beverly Hills, CA: Sage.

Finkelhor, D., Meyer Williams, L. and Burns, N. (1988) *Nursery Crimes: Sexual Abuse in Day Care*. Newbury Park, CA: Sage.

Firestone, S. (1979) *The Dialectic of Sex*. London: The Women's Press.

Foucault, M. (1971) *Madness and Civilization: A History of Insanity in the Age of Reason*. London: Tavistock.

Foucault, M. (1979) *Discipline and Punish: The Birth of the Prison*. Harmondsworth: Peregrine.

Foucault, M. ([1977] 1981) *The History of Sexuality, vol. 1*. Harmondsworth: Penguin.

Foucault, M. (1982) *I, Pierre Riviere, Having Slaughtered My Mother, My Sister and My Brother*. Lincoln, NB: University of Nebraska.

Foucault, M. (1984) *The Foucault Reader*, edited by P. Rabinow. New York: Pantheon.

Freud, S. ([1896] 1962) The aetiology of hysteria, in *Standard Edition of the Complete Works of Sigmund Freud, Volume 3* (trans. J. Strachey). London: Hogarth Press.

Freud, S. and Breuer, J. ([1893–5] 1962) Studies in hysteria, in *Standard Edition of the Complete Works of Sigmund Freud, Volume 2* (trans. J. Strachey). London: Hogarth.

Furniss, T. (1984) Organizing a therapeutic approach to intrafamilial child sexual abuse, *Journal of Adolescence*, 7(4): 309–17.

Gagnon, J. (1965) Female child victims of sex offences, *Social Problems*, 13: 176–92.

Gagnon, J.H. (1992) The self, its voices and their discord, in C. Ellis and M.G. Flaherty (eds) *Investigating Subjectivity: Research on Lived Experience*. Newbury Park, CA: Sage.

Gagnon, J.H. and Simon, W. (1973) *Sexual Conduct: The Social Sources of Human Sexuality*. London: Hutchinson.

Gallagher, B., Hughes, B. and Parker, H. (1996) The nature and extent of known cases of organised child sexual abuse in England and Wales, in P. Bibby (ed.) *Organised Abuse: The Current Debate*. Aldershot: Arena/Ashgate.

Ganaway, G.K. (1990) A psychodynamic look at alternative explanations for satanic ritual abuse memories in MPD patients. Paper presented at the Seventh International Conference on Multiple Personality and Dissociation, Chicago, November.

Ganaway, G.K. (1991) Alternative hypotheses regarding satanic ritual abuse memories. Paper presented at the Annual Convention of the American Psychological Association, San Francisco, CA, August.

Ganaway, G.K. (1993) Dissociative disorders and psychodynamic theory: trauma vs conflict and deficit. Paper presented at the False Memory Syndrome Foundation Symposium, Valley Forge, PA.

Gardner, R. (1992) Belated realization of child sex abuse by an adult, *Issues in Child Abuse Accusations*, 4(4): 177–95.

Garrett, T.B. and Wright, R. (1975) Wives of rapists and incest offenders, *Journal of Sex Research*, 11(2): 275–89.

Gebharb, P.H., Gagnon, J.H., Pomeroy, W.B. and Christenson, C.V. (1965) *Sex Offenders: An Analysis of Types*. New York: Harper and Row.

Geertz, C. (1966) Religion as a cultural system, in M. Banton (ed.) *Anthropological Approaches to the Study of Religion*. London: Tavistock.

Geertz, C. (1983) *Local Knowledge: Further Essays in Interpretive Anthropology*. New York: Basic Books.

Gellner, E. (1985) *The Psychoanalytic Movement*. London: Fontana.

Gerrie, A. (1993) The accused, *Options*, 20 June.

Gibbens, T.C. (1963) *Child Victims of Sex Offences*. London: Institute for Study and Treatment of Delinquency.

Gibbens, T.C. (1984) Incest and sexual abuse of children, in J. Hopkins (ed.) *Perspectives on Rape and Sexual Assault*. London: Harper and Row.

Gibson, J.T. and Haritos-Fatouros, N. (1986) The education of a torturer, *Psychology Today*, November: 50–8.

Giddens, A. (1984) *The Constitution of Society*. Cambridge: Polity.

Giddens, A. (1990) *The Consequences of Modernity*. Cambridge: Polity.

Giddens, A. (1991) *Modernity and Self-Identity: Self and Society in the Late Modern Age*. Cambridge: Polity.

Gillespie, T. (1994) Under pressure: rape crisis centres, multi-agency work and strategies for survival, in C. Lupton and T. Gillespie (eds) *Working with Violence*. London: Macmillan.

Ginzburg, C. (1990) *Ecstasies: Deciphering the Witches' Sabbath*, trans. R. Rosenthal. London: Hutchinson Radius.

Girard, R. (1977) *Violence and the Sacred*. Baltimore: John Hopkins University Press.

Glaser, S. and Frosh, S. (1988) *Child Sexual Abuse*. London: Macmillan Education.

Goettman, C., Greaves, P. and Coons, P. (1991) *Multiple Personality and Dissociation, 1791–1990: A Complete Bibliography*. Atlanta, GA: George Greaves.

Goffman, E. (1961) *Asylums: Essays on the Social Situation of Mental Patients and Other Inmates*. New York: Doubleday.

Goffman, E. ([1959] 1969) *The Presentation of Self in Everyday Life*. Harmondsworth: Penguin.

Golston, J.C. (1992) Raising hell in psychotherapy, part two: comparative abuse – shedding light on ritual abuse through the study of torture methods in political repression, sexual sadism and genocide, *Treating Abuse Today*, 2(6): 2–16.

Goodwin, J.M. (1994) Credibility problems in sadistic abuse, *Journal of Psychohistory*, 21(4): 479–96.

Goodwin, J. and Di Vasto, P. (1979) Mother–daughter incest, *Child Abuse and Neglect*, 3: 953–57.

Goodwin, J., McCarthy, T. and Di Vasto, P. (1981) Prior incest in mothers of abused children, *Child Abuse and Neglect*, 5(2): 87–95.

Goodyear-Smith, F. (1993) *First Do No Harm: The Sexual Abuse Industry*. Auckland, NZ: Benton-Guy.

Gordon, L. (1989) *Heroes of Their Own Lives: The Politics and History of Family Violence, Boston 1880–1960*. London: Virago.

Graham, H. (1984) Surveying through stories, in C. Bell and H. Roberts (eds) *Social Researching: Politics, Problems, Practice*. London: Routledge and Kegan Paul.

Grant, L. (1993) A past imperfect?, *Guardian*, 24 May.

Greven, P. (1992) *Spare the Child: The Religious Roots of Punishment*. New York: First Vintage.

Griffin, S. (1971) Rape: the all-American crime, *Ramparts Magazine*, 10.

Griffin, S. (1981) *Pornography and Silence: Culture's Revenge Against Nature*. London: The Women's Press.

Groth, N. (1979) *Men Who Rape*. New York: Plenum.

Groth, N. (1982) The incest offender, in S. Sgroi (ed.) *Handbook of Clinical Intervention in Child Sexual Abuse*. Lexington, MA: Lexington Books.

Groth, N. and Burgess, A. (1979) Sexual trauma in the life histories of rapists and child molesters, *Victimology*, 4: 10–16.

Guze, S.B. (1993) Psychotherapy and the medical model. Paper presented at the American Psychiatric Association Annual Convention, Gainsville, FL, August.

Hacking, I. (1986a) The invention of split personalities, in A. Donagan, A.N. Perovich and M.V. Wedin (eds) *Human Nature and Natural Knowledge*. Dordrecht: D. Reidel.

Hacking, I. (1986b) Making up people, in T.C. Heller, M. Sosna and D.E. Wellberg (eds) *Reconstructing Individualism: Autonomy, Individuality and the Self in Western Thought*. Stanford, CA: Stanford University Press.

Hacking, I. (1995) *Rewriting the Soul: Multiple Personality and the Sciences of Memory*. Princeton, NJ: Princeton University Press.

Hall, L. and Lloyd, S. (1989) *Surviving Child Sexual Abuse: A Handbook for Helping Women Challenge their Past*. London: Falmer.

Hames, M. (1996) A police view of pornographic links, in P. Bibby (ed.) *Organized Abuse: The Current Debate*. Aldershot: Arena.

Hammersley, M. (1992) *What's Wrong with Ethnography? Methodological Explorations*. London: Routledge.

Hammersley, M. and Atkinson, P. (1995) *Ethnography*, 2nd edn. London: Routledge.

Hanks, H., Wynne, J. and Hobbs, C. (1989) 'Why do women do it?', letter to the editor, *Observer*, 13 August.

Hanmer, J. and Saunders, S. (1984) *Well-Founded Fear: A Community Study of Violence to Women*. London: Hutchinson.

Harding, S. (ed.) (1987) *Feminism and Methodology*. Milton Keynes: Open University Press.

Harding, S. (1991) *Whose Science? Whose Knowledge? Thinking from Women's Lives*. Buckingham: Open University Press.

Haritos-Fatouros, M. (1988) The official torturer: a learning model for obedience to the authority of violence, *Journal of Applied Social Psychology*, 18: 1107–20.

Harré, R. (1984) *Personal Being: A Theory for Individual Psychology*. Cambridge, MA: Harvard University Press.

Harris, R. (2000) *Lourdes: Body and Spirit in the Secular Age*. Harmondsworth: Penguin.

Harrison, H. (1993) Female abusers: what children and young people have told ChildLine, in M. Elliott (ed.) *Female Sexual Abuse of Children*. London: Longman.

Hassan, S. (1988) *Combatting Cult Mind Control*. New York: Park Street Press.

Hasselbach, I. (1996) *Fuhrer-Ex*. London: Chatto and Windus.

Hearn, J. (1990a) Child abuse and men's violence, in The Violence Against Children Study Group, *Taking Child Abuse Seriously*. London: Unwin Hyman.

Hearn, J. (1990b) *Men, Masculinities and Social Theory*. London: Unwin Hyman.

Hearst, P.C. and Moscow, A. (1982) *Every Secret Thing*. New York: Doubleday.

Hechler, D. (1988) *The Battle and the Backlash: The Child Sexual Abuse War*. Boston, MA: Lexington Books.

Heelas, P. (1996) *The New Age Movement*. Oxford: Blackwell.

Heelas, P. (1998) On differentiation and dedifferentiation, in P. Heelas (ed.) *Religion, Modernity and Postmodernity*. Oxford: Blackwell.

Herman, J.L. (1981) *Father–Daughter Incest*. Cambridge, MA: Harvard University Press.

Herman, J.L. (1992) *Trauma and Recovery*. New York: Basic Books.

Herman, J.L. (1993) The false memory debate: social science or social backlash? *Harvard Mental Health Newsletter*, 9(10): 4–6.

Herman, J.L. and Harvey, M.R. (1993) The false memory debate: social science or social backlash, *Harvard Mental Health Letter*, 9(10): 4–6.

Hertz, R. (1960) *Death and the Right Hand*. New York: Cohen and West.

Hicks, R.D. (1991) The police model of satanism crime, in J. Richardson, J. Best and D. Bromley (eds) *The Satanism Scare*. New York: Aldine de Gruyter.

Hilberman, E. (1980) 'The wife-beater's wife' reconsidered, *American Journal of Psychiatry*, 137: 1336–47.

Hochschild, A.R. (1983) *The Managed Heart: Commercialization of Human Feeling*. Berkeley, CA: University of California Press.

Hockey, J.L. (1990) *Experiences of Death: An Anthropological Account*. Edinburgh: Edinburgh University Press.

Hoggart, S. (1994) Tricks of memory, *Observer*, 27 March.

Hood, S. and Crowley, G. (1995) *Marquis de Sade for Beginners*. Cambridge: Icon.

Hooper, C.A. (1992) *Mothers Surviving Child Sexual Abuse*. London: Routledge.

Hubert, H. and Mauss, M. ([1899] 1964) *Sacrifice: Its Nature and Function*, trans. W.D. Halls. Chicago: University of Chicago Press.

Hudson, P. (1991) *Ritual Child Abuse: Discovery, Diagnosis, Treatment*. Saratoga, CA: R&E.

Ireland, K. (1993) *Sexual Exploitation of Children and the Connection with Tourism*. London: Save the Children.

Itzin, C. (1992) *Pornography: Women, Violence and Civil Liberties*. Oxford: Oxford University Press.

Itzin, C. (1996) Pornography and the organisation of sexual abuse, in P. Bibby (ed.) *Organized Abuse: The Current Debate*. Aldershot: Arena.

Jackson, S. and Scott, S. (1997) Gut reactions to matters of the heart, *Sociological Review*, 45(4): 551–75.

Jagger, A. (1983) *Feminist Politics and Human Nature*. Totowa, NJ: Rowman and Allanheld.

Jameson, F. (1991) *Postmodernism: The Cultural Logic of Late Capitalism*. London: Verso.

Jamieson, L. (1998) *Intimacy: Personal Relationships in Modern Societies*. Cambridge: Polity.

Jeffreys, S. (1982) The sexual abuse of children in the home, in S. Friedman and E. Sarah (eds) *On the Problem of Men*. London: The Women's Press.

Jenkins, P. (1992) *Intimate Enemies: Moral Panics in Contemporary Great Britain*. New York: Aldine de Gruyter.

Jenkins, P. and Maier-Katkin, D. (1992) Satanism: myth and reality in a contemporary moral panic, *Crime, Law and Social Change*, 17(1): 53–75.

Josselson, R. (1995) Imagining the real: empathy, narrative and the dialogic self, in R. Josselson and A. Lieblich (eds) *Interpreting Experience: The Narrative Study of Lives*. Thousand Oaks, CA: Sage.

Josselson, R. and Lieblich, A. (1995) *Interpreting Experience: The Narrative Study of Lives*. Thousand Oaks, CA: Sage.

Journal of Child and Youth Care (1990) Special issue: In the Shadow of Satan: The Ritual Abuse of Children.

Kahaner, L. (1988) *Cults that Kill*. New York: Warner.

Kelley, S.J. (1989) Stress responses of children to sexual abuse and ritualistic abuse in day care centers, *Journal of Interpersonal Violence*, 44(4): 502–13.

Kelly, L. (1988) *Surviving Sexual Violence*. Cambridge: Polity.

Kelly, L. (1991) Unspeakable acts, *Trouble and Strife*, 21(Summer): 13–21.

Kelly, L., Regan, L. and Burton, S. (1991) *An Exploratory Study of the Prevalence of Sexual Abuse in a Sample of 16–21 Year Olds*. London: Child Abuse Studies Unit, University of North London.

Kempe, C.H., Silverman, F.N., Steele, B.F., Droegemueller, W. and Silver, H.K. (1962) The battered child syndrome, *Journal of the American Medical Association*, 181: 17–24.

Kempe, R. and Kempe, C. (1978) *Child Abuse*. London: Fontana.

Kenny, M. (1986) *The Passion of Ansel Bourne: Multiple Personality in American Culture*. Washington, DC: Smithsonian Institution Press.

Kent, S.A. (1993a) Deviant scripturalism and ritual Satanic abuse part one: possible Judeo-Christian influences, *Religion*, 23: 229–41.

Kent, S.A. (1993b) Deviant scripturalism and ritual Satanic abuse part two: possible Masonic, Mormon, Magick and Pagan influences, *Religion*, 23: 355–67.

Kent, S.A. (1994) Diabolical debates: a reply to David Frankfurter and J.S. La Fontaine, *Religion*, 24: 361–78.

Kinsey, A., Pomeroy, W., Martin, C. and Gebhard, P. (1953) *Sexual Behaviour in the Human Female*. Philadelphia, PA: Saunders.

Klein, M. (1948) *Contributions to Psychoanalysis 1921–1945*. London: Hogarth Press.

Kowszun, G. (1999) Multiple personalities: a cautionary note, in M. Walker and J. Anthony-Black (eds) *Hidden Selves: An Exploration of Multiple Personality*. Buckingham: Open University Press.

Kristiansen, C., Felton, K. and Hovdestad, W. (1996) Recovered memories of child abuse: fact, fantasy or fancy?, in M.J. Gutfreund and S. Contratto (eds) *A Feminist Clinician's Guide to the Memory Debate*. New York: Haworth Press.

La Fontaine, J. (1993) Defining organized sexual abuse, *Child Abuse Review*, 2(4): 223–32.

La Fontaine, J. (1994) *The Extent and Nature of Organised and Ritual Abuse*. London: HMSO.

La Fontaine, J. (1996) Ritual abuse: research findings, in P. Bibby (ed.) *Organized Abuse: The Current Debate*. Aldershot: Arena.

La Fontaine, J. (1998) *Speak of the Devil: Tales of Contemporary England*. Cambridge: Cambridge University Press.

LaVey, A. (1969) *The Satanic Bible*. New York: Avon.

Layder, D. (1993) *New Strategies in Social Research: An Introduction and Guide*. Cambridge: Polity.

Leonard, D. (1990) Persons in their own right: children and sociology in the UK, in L. Chisholm, P. Buchner, H. Kruger and P. Brown (eds) *Childhood, Youth and Social Change: A Comparative Perspective*. London: Falmer.

Lerner, G. (1986) *The Creation of Patriarchy*. New York: Oxford University Press.

Levy, A. and Kahan, B. (1991) *The Pindown Experience and the Protection of Children: Report of the Staffordshire Child Care Inquiry 1990*. Stafford: Staffordshire County Council.

Linden, R. (1993) *Making Stories, Making Selves: Feminist Reflections on the Holocaust*. Columbus, OH: Ohio State University Press.

Liotti, G. (1992) Disorganized/disorientated attachment in the etiology of the dissociative disorders, *Dissociation*, 5(4): 196–204.

Lofland, J. (1966) *Doomsday Cult: A Study of Conversion, Proselytization and Maintenance of Faith*. Englewood Cliffs, NJ: Prentice-Hall.

Loftus, E.F. (1993) The reality of repressed memories, *American Psychologist*, 48: 518–37.

Loftus, E.F. (1994a) Memories of childhood sexual abuse: remembering and repressing, *Psychology of Women Quarterly*, 18: 67–84.

Loftus, E.F. (1994b) Deposition no. 91-2-01102-5 and verbatim court testimony for the defence in *Crook v. Murphy*, Superior Court of the State of Washington, Benton Co, 24 January and 17 February.

Loftus, E. and Ketchum, K. (1994) *The Myth of Repressed Memory*. New York: St Martin's Press.

Loftus, E. and Pickrell, J.E. (1995) The formation of false memories, *Psychiatric Annals*, 25: 720–5.

Loftus, E., Polonsky, S. and Fullilove, M. (1994) Memories of childhood sexual abuse: remembering and repressing. Unpublished manuscript, University of Washington and Columbia University School of Public Health.

Logan, K. (1988) *Paganism and the Occult*. London: Kingsway.

Longdon, C. (1993) A survivor's and therapist's viewpoint, in M. Elliott (ed.) *Female Sexual Abuse of Children*. London: Longman.

Luhrmann, T.M. (1989) *Persuasions of the Witch's Craft: Ritual Magic in Contemporary England*. Cambridge, MA: Harvard University Press.

Lupton, C. (1994) The British refuge movement: the survival of an ideal?, in C. Lupton and T. Gillespie (eds) *Working with Violence*. London: Macmillan.

Lustig, N., Dresser, J.W., Spellman, S.W. and Murray, T.B. (1966) Incest, *Archives of General Psychology*, 14: 31–40.

McClure, R. (1991) *Loving in Fear: An Anthology of Lesbian and Gay Survivors of Child Sexual Abuse*. Toronto: Queer Press.

Maccoby, H. (1982) *The Sacred Executioner: Human Sacrifice and the Legacy of Guilt*. New York: Thames and Hudson.

Macfarlane, A. (1970) *Witchcraft in Tudor and Stuart England: A Regional and Comparative Study*. London: Routledge and Kegan Paul.

McKellar, P. (1979) *Mindsplit*. Guildford: J.M. Dent.

MacKinnon, C. (1982) Feminism, Marxism, method and the state: an agenda for theory, *Signs*, 7(3): 515–44.

McRobbie, A. and Thornton, S.L. (1995) Rethinking 'moral panic' for multi-mediated social worlds, *British Journal of Sociology*, 46(4): 559–74.

Maffesoli, M. (1996) *The Time of the Tribes: The Decline of Individualism in Mass Society*. London: Sage.

Maguire, P. (1987) *Doing Participatory Research: A Feminist Approach*. Amherst, MA: Center for International Education, University of Massachusetts.

Malmquist, C.P. (1986) Children who witness parental murder: post-traumatic aspects, *Journal of the American Academy of Child Psychiatry*, 25: 320–5.

Marshall, A. (1994) Sensuous Sapphires: a study of the social construction of black female sexuality, in M. Maynard and J. Purvis (eds) *Researching Women's Lives from a Feminist Perspective*. London: Taylor & Francis.

Martin, B. (1981) *A Sociology of Contemporary Cultural Change*. Oxford: Blackwell.

Masson, J. (1984) *The Assault on Truth: Freud's Suppression of the Seduction Theory*. New York: Farrar, Straus and Giroux.

Masters, W.H. and Johnson, V.E. (1976) The aftermath of rape, *Redbook*, 147(November): 12–19.

Matthews, J.K. (1993) Working with female sexual abusers, in M. Elliott (ed.) *Female Sexual Abuse of Children: The Ultimate Taboo*. London: Longman.

Matthews, R., Matthews, J.K. and Speltz, K. (1991) Female sexual offenders: a typology, in M.Q. Patton (ed.) *Family Sexual Abuse: Frontline Research and Evaluation*. London: Sage.

Mauss, M. (1979) *Sociology and Psychology*, trans. B. Brewster. London: Routledge and Kegan Paul.

Maynard, M. (1994) Methods, practice and epistemology: the debate about feminism and research, in M. Maynard and J. Purvis (eds) *Researching Women's Lives from a Feminist Perspective*. London: Taylor and Francis.

Mead, G.H. (1913) The social self, *Journal of Philosophy*, 10: 374–80.

Mead, G.H. (1924) The genesis of the self and social control, *International Journal of Ethics*, 35: 251–77.

Mead, G.H. (1934) *Mind, Self and Society*. Chicago: University of Chicago Press.

Meiselman, K. (1978) *Incest*. San Francisco: Jossey Bass.

Mellor, P. (1993) Death in high modernity: the contemporary presence and absence of death, in D. Clark (ed.) *The Sociology of Death*. Oxford: Blackwell.

Mellor, P. and Shilling, C. (1997) *Re-forming the Body: Religion, Community and Modernity*. London: Sage.

Melton, J.G. (1989) *The Encyclopedia of American Religions*, 3rd edn. Detroit, IL: Gale.

Milgram, S. (1965) Some conditions of obedience and disobedience to authority, *Human Relations*, 18(1): 57–76.

Miller, A. (1984) *Thou Shalt Not Be Aware*. London: Pluto.

Mills, C.W. (1959) *The Sociological Imagination*. Oxford: Oxford University Press.

Mollon, P. (1996) *Multiple Selves, Multiple Voices: Working with Trauma, Violation and Dissociation*. Chichester: Wiley.

Moody, E.J. (1974) Magical therapy: an anthropological investigation of contemporary Satanism, in I. Zaretsky and M. Leone (eds) *Religious Movements in Contemporary America*. Princeton, NJ: Princeton University Press.

Moore, H. (1994) The problem of explaining violence in the social sciences, in P. Harvey and P. Gow (eds) *Sex and Violence: Issues in Representation and Experience*. London: Routledge.

Morgan, D.H.J. (1990) Review of Marilyn Monroe: The Body in the Library, *Theory, Culture and Society*, 7(1): 173–5.

Morgan, D.H.J. (1992) *Discovering Men*. London: Routledge.

Morgan, D.H.J. (1996) *Family Connections: An Introduction to Family Studies*. Cambridge: Polity.

Morgan, P. (1982) Alcohol and family violence: a review of the literature, in National Institute of Alcoholism and Alcohol Abuse, Alcohol Consumption and Related Problems, *Alcohol and Health Monograph 1*. Washington, DC: Department of Health and Human Services.

Morgan, R. (1989) *The Demon Lover: On the Sexuality of Terrorism*. London: Methuen.

Muller, F.M. (1878) *Lectures on the Origin and Growth of Religion*. London and Oxford.

Nelson, S. (1992) Deadlier than the male?, *Guardian*, 25 March.

Norwood, R. (1986) *Women Who Love Too Much*. Los Angeles: Tarcher.

O'Brien, M. (1981) *The Politics of Reproduction*. London: Routledge and Kegan Paul.

Ofshe, R. and Watters, E. (1994) *Making Monsters: False Memories, Psychotherapy and Sexual Hysteria*. New York: Charles Scribner's.

Parton, J.H. (1978) Personality differences appearing between rapists of adults, rapists of children, and non-violent sexual molesters of children, *Research Communications in Psychology, Psychiatry and Behaviour*, 3(4): 385–93.

Parton, C. (1990) Women, gender oppression and child abuse, in Violence Against Children Study Group (eds) *Taking Child Abuse Seriously*. London: Unwin Hyman.

Penrose, A., Ivan-Smith, E. and Thomson, M. (1996) *Kids for Hire*. London: Save the Children.

Peters, J.J. (1976) Children who are victims of sexual assault and the psychology of offenders, *American Journal of Psychotherapy*, 30: 395–421.

Pinchbeck, I. and Hewitt, M. (1973) *Children in English Society, Volume II: From the Eighteenth Century to the Children Act of 1948*. London: Routledge and Kegan Paul.

Plummer, K. (1983) *Documents of Life*. London: Allen & Unwin.

Plummer, K. (1995) *Telling Sexual Stories: Power, Change and Social Worlds*. London: Routledge.

Pope, K.S. (1996) Scientific research, recovered memory, and context: seven surprising findings, *Women and Therapy*, 19(1): 123–40.

Purves, L. (1994) Comment on Holly Romona case, *The Times*, 16 May.

Putnam, F. (1989) *Diagnosis and Treatment of Multiple Personality Disorder*. New York: Guilford Press.

Raschke, C.A. (1990) *Painted Black*. New York: HarperCollins.

Rich, A. (1977) *Of Woman Born: Motherhood as Experience and Institution*. London: Virago.

Rich, A. (1980) Compulsory heterosexuality and lesbian existence, *Signs*, 5(4): 631–60.

Richardson, J.T. (ed.) (1978) *Conversion Careers: In and Out of the New Religions*. Beverly Hills, CA: Sage.

Richardson, J.T., Best, J. and Bromley, D.G. (eds) (1991) *The Satanism Scare*. New York: Aldine de Gruyter.

Richardson, S. (2000) Will you sit by her side? An attachment-based approach to work with dissociative conditions, in V. Sinason (ed.) *The Shoemaker and the Elves: Working with Multiplicity*. London: Routledge.

Rivera, M. (1989) Linking the psychological and the social: feminism, poststructuralism and multiple personality, *Dissociation*, 2(1): 24–31.

Rivera, M. (1996) *More Alike than Different: Treating Severely Dissociative Trauma Survivors*. Toronto: University of Toronto Press.

Robbins, T. (1988) Cults, converts and charisma: the sociology of new religious movements. Special edition of *Current Sociology*, 36(1).

Robbins, T. and Anthony, D. (eds) (1990) *In Gods We Trust: New Patterns of Religious Pluralism in America*, 2nd edn. New Brunswick, NJ: Transaction.

Rogers, E. and Weiss, J. (1953) Study of sex crimes against children, in K. Bowman (ed.) *California Sex Deviation Research*. Sacramento, CA: Assembly of the State of California.

Roos, J.P. (1994) The true life revisited: autobiography and referentiality after the 'posts', *Auto/Biography* 3(1) and 3(2): 1–17.

Rosaldo, R. (1992) *Culture and Truth: The Remaking of Social Analysis*. Boston, MA: Beacon.

Rose, E.S. (1993) Surviving the unbelievable: a first person account of cult ritual abuse, *Ms Magazine*, January/February: 40–5.

Rose, N. (1990) *Governing the Soul: The Shaping of the Private Self*. London: Routledge.

Ross, C. (1989) *Multiple Personality Disorder: Diagnosis, Clinical Features and Treatment*. New York: Wiley.

Ross, C. (1995) *Satanic Ritual Abuse: Principles of Treatment*. Toronto: University of Toronto Press.

Ruether, R.R. (1992) *Sexism and God-Talk*. London: SCM Press.

Rush, F. (1977) The Freudian cover-up, *Chrysalis*, 1: 31–45.

Rush, F. (1980) *The Best Kept Secret*. Englewood Cliffs, NJ: Prentice-Hall.

Rush, F. (1990) The many faces of backlash, in D. Leidholdt and J. Raymond (eds) *The Sexual Liberals and the Attack on Feminism*. Oxford: Pergamon.

Russell, D. (1983a) The incidence and prevalence of intrafamilial and extrafamilial sexual abuse of female children, *Child Abuse and Neglect: The International Journal*, 7(2): 133–46.

Russell, D. (1983b) The prevalence and incidence of forcible rape and attempted rape of females, *Victimology: An International Journal*, 7: 1–4.

Russell, D. (1984) *Sexual Exploitation*. Beverly Hills, CA: Sage.

Russell, D. (1986) *The Secret Trauma: Incest in the Lives of Girls and Women*. New York: Basic Books.

Ryder, D. (1992) *Breaking the Circle of Satanic Ritual Abuse*. Minneapolis, MN: CompCare.

Salter, A.C. (1991) *Accuracy of Expert Testimony in Child Sexual Abuse Cases*. Boston, MA: New England Commissioners of Child Welfare Agencies.

Samiti, G.B. (1996) Case study of project with commercial sex workers in Jaipur, India. Used in compiling *Effective HIV/AIDS Activities: NGO Work in Developing Countries*. London: UK NGO/AIDS Consortium.

Sanday, P.R. (1981) The socio-cultural context of rape: a cross cultural study, *Journal of Social Issues*, 37: 5–27.

Sanders, J.O. (1975) *Satan is No Myth*. Chicago: Moody Press.

Sands, S. (1994) What is dissociated?, *Dissociation*, 7(3): 145–52.

Sanford, L. (1991) *Strong at the Broken Places: Overcoming the Trauma of Childhood Abuse*. London: Virago.

Saradjian, J. (1996) *Women who Sexually Abuse Children: From Research to Clinical Practice*. Chichester: John Wiley and Sons.

Scarry, E. (1985) *The Body in Pain*. Oxford: Oxford University Press.

Schecter, M.D. and Roberge, L. (1976) Sexual exploitation, in R.E. Helfer and C.H. Kempe (eds) *Child Abuse and Neglect*. Cambridge, MA: Ballinger.

Schreiber, F. (1973) *Sybil*. Chicago: Regnery.

Scott Peck, M. (1988) *People of the Lie*. London: Arrow.

Scott, S. and Dickens, A. (1982) *Tick, Hock and Tally: Women, Money and Managing in Salford, 1920–1935*. Salford: Ordsall Community Arts.

Scott, S. and Kelly, L. (1989) With our own hands, *Trouble and Strife*, 16(Summer): 26–8.

Scott, S. and Kelly, L. (1991) Demons, Devils and Denial: towards a feminist understanding of ritual abuse, *Trouble and Strife*, 22: 33–6.

Scott, S. (1993) Beyond belief: beyond help? *Child Abuse Review*, 2(4): 243–51.

Scott, S. and Kelly, L. (1993) The current literature about the organised abuse of children, *Child Abuse Review*, 2(4): 281–7.

Scott, S. (1995) Dicing with disbelief: researching ritual abuse. Unpublished paper given at Department of Applied Community Studies, Manchester Metropolitan University, November.

Scott, S. (1997a) Feminists and false memories: a case of postmodern amnesia, *Feminism and Psychology*, 7(1): 33–8.

Scott, S. (1997b) The body's rebellion in survivors' accounts of ritual abuse and torture in childhood. Unpublished paper, given at British Sociological Association Conference, York.

Scott, S.J., Jackson, S. and Milburn, K. (1997) Swings and roundabouts: the impact of risk anxiety on the everyday worlds of children, *Sociology*, 32(4): 689–705.

Scully, D. (1990) *Understanding Sexual Violence: A Study of Convicted Rapists*. Boston, MA: Unwin Hyman.

Seale, C. (1995) Heroic death, *Sociology*, 29(4): 597–615.

Segall, S.R. (1996) Metaphors of agency and mechanism in dissociation, *Dissociation*, IX(3): 154–60.

Sennett, R. and Cobb, J. (1977) *The Hidden Injuries of Class*. Cambridge: Cambridge University Press.

Sereny, G. (1984) *The Invisible Children: Children 'On the Game' in America, West Germany and Great Britain*. London: Pan.

Sgroi, S. (1982) *Handbook of Clinical Interventions in Child Sexual Abuse*. Cambridge, MA: Lexington Books.

Shahar, S. (1990) *Childhood in the Middle Ages*. London: Routledge.

Sharansky, N. (1988) *Fear No Evil*, trans. S. Hoffman. New York: Random House.

Shilling, C. (1993) *The Body and Social Theory*. London: Sage.

Showalter, E. (1987) *The Female Malady: Women, Madness and English Culture*. London: Virago Press.

Showalter, E. (1997) *Hystories: Hysterical Epidemics and Modern Culture*. London and Basingstoke: Macmillan.

Silbert, M.H. and Pines, A.M. (1981) Sexual abuse as an antecedent to prostitution, *Child Abuse and Neglect*, 5: 407–11.

Silbert, M.H. and Pines, A.M. (1984) Pornography and sexual abuse of women, *Sex Roles*, 10: 857–69.

Sinason, V. (ed.) (1994) *Treating Survivors of Satanist Abuse*. London: Routledge.

Sinason, V. and Svensson, A. (1994) Going through the fifth window, in V. Sinason (ed.) *Treating Survivors of Satanist Abuse*. London: Routledge.

Smart, C. and Smart, B. (eds) (1978) *Women, Sexuality and Social Control*. London: Routledge and Kegan Paul.

Smith, D.E. (1990a) *The Conceptual Practices of Power: A Feminist Sociology of Knowledge*. Boston, MA: Northeastern University Press.

Smith, D.E. (1990b) K is mentally ill, in her *Texts, Facts and Femininity: Exploring the Relations of Ruling*. London: Routledge.

Smith, M. and Padzer, L. (1980) *Michelle Remembers*. New York: Pocket Books.

Solomon, T. (1990) Integrating the 'Moonie' experience: a survey of ex-members of the Unification Church, in T. Robbins and D. Anthony (eds) *In Gods We Trust: New Patterns of Religious Pluralism in America*, 2nd edn. New Brunswick, NJ: Transaction.

Spanos, N.K., Weekes, J.R. and Bertrand, L.D. (1985) Multiple personality: a social psychological perspective, *Journal of Abnormal Psychology*, 94(3): 362–76.

Speltz, K., Matthews, J.K. and Matthews, R. (1989) *Female Sexual Offenders: An Exploratory Study*. Orwell, VT: Safer Society Press.

Spender, D. (1980) *Man Made Language*. London: Routledge and Kegan Paul.

Spradley, J.P. (1979) *The Ethnographic Interview*. New York: Holt, Rinehart and Winston.

Stanko, E. (1985) *Intimate Intrusions: Women's Experience of Male Violence*. London: Routledge and Kegan Paul.

Stanley, L. and Wise, S. ([1990] 1993) *Breaking Out Again*. London: Routledge.

Steinberg, M. (1993) *Interviewer's Guide to the Structured Clinical Interview for the DSM-IV Dissociative Disorders (SCID-D):* Structured Clinical Interview. Washington, DC: American Psychiatric Press.

Strachey, J. (ed.) (1957) *The Standard Edition of the Complete Psychological Works of Sigmund Freud, vol. 14*. London: Hogarth Press.

Stratford, L. (1988) *Satan's Underground*. London: Pelican.

Strentz, T. (1982) The Stockholm Syndrome: law enforcement policy and victim behaviour, in F.M. Ochberg and D.A. Soskis (eds) *Victims of Terrorism*. Boulder, CO: Westview.

Summit, R. and Kryso, J. (1978) Sexual abuse of children: a clinical spectrum, *American Journal of Orthopsychiatry*, 48(2): 237–51.

Svedin, C.G. and Back, K. (1996) *Children Who Don't Speak Out About Children being Used in Child Pornography*. Stockholm: Radda Barnen.

Szasz, T. (1962) *The Myth of Mental Illness*. London: Secker and Warburg.

Tate, T. (1990) *Child Pornography: An Investigation*. London: Methuen.

Terry, M. (1987) *The Ultimate Evil*. New York: Bantam.

Tester, K. (1997) *Moral Culture*. London: Sage.

Thigpen, C.H. and Cleckley, H. (1954) A case of multiple personality, *Journal of Abnormal and Social Psychology*, 49: 135–51.

Thomas, K. (1971) *Religion and the Decline of Magic*. Harmondsworth: Penguin.

Thompson, W. (1990) Moral panics, pornography and social polity. Paper presented at the annual meeting of the American Society of Criminology, Baltimore, MD, November.

Tierney, P. (1989) *The Highest Altar: The Story of Human Sacrifice*. New York: Viking Penguin.

Trevor-Roper, H.R. ([1967] 1990) *The European Witch Craze of the Sixteenth and Seventeenth Centuries*. Harmondsworth: Penguin.

Turner, B.S. (1984) *The Body and Society*. Oxford: Blackwell.

Turner, B. (1991) *Religion and Social Theory*. London: Sage.

Victor, J. (1993) *Satanic Panic: The Creation of a Contemporary Legend*. Chicago: Open Court.

Virkkunen, M. (1975) Victim-precipitated pedophilia offences, *British Journal of Criminology*, 15(2): 401–5.

Waddington, P.A.J. (1986) Mugging as a moral panic: a question of proportion, *British Journal of Sociology*, 37(2): 245–59.

Wagner, C.P. and Pennoyer, F.D. (1990) *Wrestling with Dark Angels*. Houston, TX: Monarch Press.

Walby, S. (1990) *Theorizing Patriarchy*. Oxford: Blackwell.

Walker, M. (1999) A century of controversy: multiplicity or madness; memory or make-believe? in M. Walker and J. Anthony Black (eds) *Hidden Selves: An Exploration of Multiple Personality*. Buckingham: Open University Press.

Walker, S.S. (1972) *Ceremonial Spirit Possession in Africa and Afro America*. Leiden: E.J. Brill.

Wallace, T. and March, C. (eds) (1991) *Changing Perceptions*. Oxford: Oxfam UK and Ireland.

Walter, T. (1991) Modern death: taboo or not taboo?, *Sociology*, 25: 293–310.

Waterhouse, R. (1990) The satanic ritual abuse myth, parts 1–4, *Independent on Sunday*, 7 October, 14 October, 21 October, 28 October.

Waterman, J., Kelley, S.J., Oliveri, M.K. and McCord, J. (1993) *Behind the Playground Walls: Sexual Abuse in Pre-Schools*. New York: Guilford Press.

Watney, S. (1987) *Policing Desire: Pornography, AIDS and the Media*. London: Methuen.

Wax, R. (1971) *Doing Fieldwork: Warnings and Advice*. Chicago: University of Chicago Press.

Wedge, T. (1988) *The Satan Hunters*. New York: Calibre.

Weiner, I.B. (1964) Father–daughter incest: a clinical study, *Psychiatric Quarterly*, 36: 607–32.

Weir, I.K. and Wheatcroft, M.S. (1995) Allegations of children's involvement in ritual sexual abuse: clinical experience of 20 cases, *Child Abuse and Neglect*, 19(4).

West, D.J. (1984) The victim's contribution to sexual offences, in J. Hopkins (ed.) *Perspectives on Rape and Sexual Assault*. London: Harper and Row.

White, M. (1995) *Re-Authoring Lives: Interviews and Essays*. Adelaide: Dulwich Centre Publications.

White, M. and Epston, D. (1990) *Narrative Means to Therapeutic Ends*. New York: W.W. Norton.

Whitfield, C.L. (1995) *Memory and Abuse*. Deerfield Beach, FL: Health Communications.

Wild, N. (1989) Prevalence of child sex rings, *Pediatrics*, 83: 553–8.

Wild, N. and Wynne, J. (1986) Child sex rings, *British Medical Journal*, 293: 183–5.

Williams, L.M. (1994) Recovered memories of abuse in women with documented child sexual victimization histories, *Consciousness and Cognition*, 4: 1167–76.

Williams, L.M. (1994) Recall of childhood trauma: a perspective study of women's memories of child sexual abuse, *Journal of Consulting and Clinical Psychology*, 62: 1167–76.

Williams, L.M. and Banyard, V.L. (1997) Perspectives on adult memories of childhood sexual abuse: a research review, in L.J. Dickstein, M.B. Riba and J.M. Oldham (eds) *American Psychiatric Press Review of Psychiatry*. Washington, DC: American Psychiatric Press.

Wilson, B.R. (1982) *Religion in Sociological Perspective*. Oxford: Oxford University Press.

Winnicott, D. (1953) Transitional objects and transitional phenomena, *International Journal of Psycho-analysis*, 34: 89–97.

Winnicott, D. (1965) *The Maturational Processes and the Facilitating Environment.* New York: International Universities Press.

Wolff, K.H. (ed.) (1950) *The Sociology of Georg Simmel.* Glencoe, IL: The Free Press.

Women's Research Centre (1989) *Recollecting Our Lives: Women's Experience of Childhood Sexual Abuse.* Vancouver: Press Gang Publishers.

World Congress Against the Commercial Sexual Exploitation of Children (1996) Declaration. Stockholm.

Wyre, R. (1987) *Working with Sex Offenders.* Oxford: Perry.

Wyre, R. (1996) The mind of the paedophile, in P. Bibby (ed.) *Organized Abuse: The Current Debate.* Aldershot: Arena.

Wyre, R. and Tate, T. (1995) *The Murder of Childhood.* Harmondsworth: Penguin.

Zaretsky, I. and Leone, M. (eds) (1974) *Religious Movements in Contemporary America.* Princeton, NJ: Princeton University Press.

Index

An 'n' following a page number indicates an endnote; for example 60n3 refers to note 3 on page 60.

CHILD ABUSE
TOWARDS A KNOWLEDGE BASE
Second Edition

Brian Corby

Praise for the first edition of *Child Abuse*:

This is a well written, comprehensive and informative book.
Journal of Sociology and Social Welfare

The format is clear, the size compact, and the text comprehensive, making this an invaluable reference volume for teaching libraries and anyone with a specific interest in the subject.
Child Health

... a book which social work students interested in child care and family work, and students on post-qualifying child protection courses, will want to have by them for constant reference.
Issues in Social Work Education

The revised edition of this bestselling text provides a concise but comprehensive introduction to a wide range of knowledge which is of crucial importance to students and practitioners in the child protection field. It stresses the need to understand child abuse in a historical, social and political context, and critically reviews a wide range of relevant contemporary research in Britain, the USA and Europe.

While maintaining the strengths of the original book, this second edition incorporates a wealth of new material. It provides a full account of policy developments in Britain since the early 1990s, including the emerging concerns about the extent and nature of institutional abuse, and the shift towards more preventive, family supportive approaches to child protection work. New research on the consequences of child abuse and on practice initiatives in both Britain and the USA are also included.

Child Abuse: Towards a Knowledge Base is recommended reading for practitioners and students who are working, or intending to work in the child protection field.

Contents
Acknowledgements – Introduction – Childhood, child abuse and history – A history of child abuse and neglect 1870–1991 – Child protection and family support in the 1990s – Defining child abuse – The extent of child abuse – Who abuses whom – The causation of child abuse – The consequences of child abuse – The consequences of child sexual abuse – Research into child protection practice – Current issues in child protection work – Notes – Bibliography – Index.

272pp   0 335 20568 2 (Hardback)   0 335 20567 4 (Paperback)

WOMEN, VIOLENCE AND STRATEGIES FOR ACTION
FEMINIST RESEARCH, POLICY AND PRACTICE

Jill Radford, Melissa Friedberg and Lynne Harne (eds)

This collection gives important insight into the new issues and questions that have become central to understandings of women, violence and resistance. It focuses on the connections between research and the development of strategies for change by providing excellent examples of policy-relevant feminist research, rooted in both academe and activism. The emphasis throughout is on the link between research and strategies for action at the local, national and international level.

The book gathers together the many exciting ideas, discussions and developments arising from the work of the researchers and activists who are part of the British Sociological Association Violence Against Women Study Group. The contributing authors share a commitment to research that centres on the material reality of women's lives and assists the generation of strategies for action. It complements the earlier volume, *Women, Violence and Male Power*, extending the latter's coverage in important ways by addressing differences as well as commonalities between women, and the complexities of feminist analysis and activism in a changing context.

Women, Violence and Strategies for Action is of direct relevance to practitioners working in the professions of probation, social work and law, as well as students and researchers in the fields of women's studies, sociology, social policy, social work, criminology and socio-legal studies. It will also be of interest to women's organizations, including local inter-agency forums.

Contents
Introduction – Stalking and paedophilia: ironies and contradictions in the politics of naming and legal reform – Feminist strategy and tactics: influencing state provision of counselling for survivors – Virtual violence?: pornography and violence against women on the internet – Prostitution, pornography and telephone boxes – Damaged children to throwaway women: from care to prostitution – Sexual violence and the school curriculum – Shifting the margins: black feminist perspectives on discourses of mothers in child sexual abuse – Supping with the devil?: multi-agency initiatives on domestic violence – Caught in contradictions: conducting feminist action orientated research within an evaluated research programme – Domestic violence in China – Theorizing commonalities and difference: sexual violence, law and feminist activism in India and the UK – Index.

Contributors
Claudia Bernard, Melissa Friedberg, Terry Gillespie, Lynne Harne, Marianne Hester, Catherine Humphreys, Celia Jenkins, Liz Kelly, Ellen Malos, Jill Radford, Tina Skinner, Ruth Swirsky, Emma Williamson.

208pp   0 335 20370 1 (Hardback)   0 335 20369 8 (Paperback)

WOMEN, VIOLENCE AND MALE POWER
FEMINIST RESEARCH, ACTIVISM AND PRACTICE

Marianne Hester, Liz Kelly and Jill Radford (eds)

Making public the issue of sexual violence – men's violence to women and children – has been a major feminist success story of the past couple of decades. This book gives an important insight into the new issues and questions that have become central to our understanding of sexual violence and abuse, and the new directions in which research in this area has developed. It is a collection of the many exciting ideas, discussions and developments arising from the work of the researchers and activists who are part of the British Sociological Association Violence Against Women Study Group. It reflects a shared commitment to research that centres on the material reality of women's lives and assists the generation of strategies for change. The authors explore differences in women's experiences and how these relate to different ways of coping with men's violence.

Women, Violence and Male Power is of direct relevance to practitioners working with survivors of abuse, as well as students and researchers in the fields of: women's studies, criminology, sociology, social policy and social work.

Contents
Introduction – Part 1: Making sense: theory and conceptualization – 'Nothing really happened' – When does the speaking profit us? – Reading danger – Part 2: Law, protection and criminal justice – Violence against women and children – Contradictions and compromises – Unreasonable doubt – Part 3: Researching experience and supporting women – Sexual experiences and sexual abuse of women with learning disabilities – Researching prostitution and violence – Rape crisis centres and 'male rape' – Who is in control? – Close to home – Index.

Contributors
Marian Foley, Terry Gillespie, Marianne Hester, Liz Kelly, Sue Lees, Michelle McCarthy, Jo Moran-Ellis, Maggie O'Neill, Jill Radford, Lorraine Radford, Elizabeth A. Stanko.

208pp   0 335 19506 7 (Paperback)   0 335 19507 5 (Hardback)

EMOTIONAL AND PSYCHOLOGICAL ABUSE OF CHILDREN

Kieran O'Hagan

Recent public inquiries, research and new legislation have all compelled child care professionals to widen their focus beyond the narrow parameters of the physical health of the child. Emotional and psychological health are now rightly regarded as crucial. This book aims to enable practitioners to articulate precisely what is meant by the terms 'emotional' and 'psychological' abuse; to be able to identify it, and to formulate effective strategies for dealing with it. The author identifies certain categories of parent and parental circumstances which are conducive to the emotional and psychological abuse of children. He makes clear however, that parents are not the only care-givers who abuse children in this way. He explores such abuse within a historical, global and cultural context, and examines recent inquiry reports which have exposed the emotional and psychological abuse of children within the child care and child protection systems. Numerous case histories are provided, and one is explored in detail within the context of new child care legislation.

... we can certainly commend this as a knowledgeable, balanced, thoughtful and sensitive study of a harrowing subject ...

(Books Ireland)

The book makes an important contribution to this very difficult area of study ...

(Adoption and Fostering)

A useful contribution to the literature.

(Journal of the Institute of Health Education)

Contents

176pp   0 335 09884 3 (Paperback)   0 335 09889 4 (Hardback)

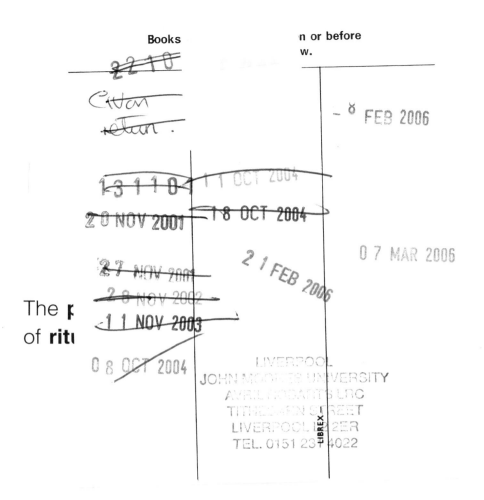

The p
of rit